Reimagining Industrial Site

The discourse around derelict, former industrial and military sites has grown in recent years. This interest is not only theoretical and landscape professionals are taking new approaches to the design and development of these sites. This book examines the varied ways in which the histories and qualities of these derelict sites are reimagined in the transformed landscape and considers how such approaches can reveal the dramatic changes that have been wrought on these places over a relatively short time scale.

It discusses these issues with reference to eleven sites from the UK, Germany, the USA, Australia and China, focusing specifically on how designers incorporate evidence of landscape change, both cultural and natural. There has been little research into how these developed landscapes are perceived by visitors and local residents. This book examines how the tangible material traces of pastness are interpreted by the visitor and the impact of the intangible elements – hidden traces, experiences and memories.

The book draws together theory in the field and implications for practice in landscape architecture and concludes with an examination of how different approaches to revealing and reimagining change can affect the future management of the site.

Catherine Heatherington was awarded her PhD (Landscape) from the University of Sheffield, UK. Her research focuses on people's responses to landscape change and continuity in developed brownfield sites with particular emphasis on the implications for practice. Catherine is a landscape designer and consultant based in the UK and is a Fellow of the Society of Garden Designers.

Routledge Research in Landscape and Environmental Design

Series editor:
Terry Clements
Associate Professor, Virginia Tech

Routledge Research in Landscape and Environmental Design is a series of academic monographs for scholars working in these disciplines and the overlaps between them. Building on Routledge's history of academic rigour and cutting-edge research, the series contributes to the rapidly expanding literature in all areas of landscape and environmental design.

The complex legacy of post-industrial and military landscapes presents ecological challenges across the world today, requiring close scrutiny and imaginative responses. Catherine Heatherington's fine-grained exploration of the successful recuperation of the former gun-ranges at Rainham Marshes near London, along with other case studies, provides essential insights into how best to approach this new landscape condition. The book provides an invaluable resource for those who now manage such derelict and neglected sites and, ultimately, for the wider public – for whom they are the new landscapes of leisure and environmental renewal.

Ken Worpole, Emeritus Professor, Cities Institute,
London Metropolitan University, UK

Reimagining Industrial Sites

Changing Histories and Landscapes

Catherine Heatherington

LONDON AND NEW YORK

First published 2018 by Routledge

2 Park Square, Milton Park, Abingdon, Oxfordshire OX14 4RN
52 Vanderbilt Avenue, New York, NY 10017

Routledge is an imprint of the Taylor & Francis Group, an informa business

First issued in paperback 2020

British Library Cataloguing-in-Publication Data
A catalogue record for this book is available from the British Library

Library of Congress Cataloging-in-Publication Data
A catalog record for this book has been requested

ISBN: 978-1-138-22820-7 (hbk)
ISBN: 978-0-367-50204-1 (pbk)

Typeset in Sabon
by Keystroke, Neville Lodge, Tettenhall, Wolverhampton

To Anna Jorgensen

Contents

List of illustrations

Photos are taken by the author unless otherwise stated.

Figures

Tables

Acknowledgements

I would like to thank Dr Anna Jorgensen and Dr Stephen Walker for their continued encouragement and inspiration. They have supported me through inevitable ups and downs and helped me grow from a practicing landscape designer to an academic researcher and author. I am very grateful for the funding I have received from the Department of Landscape at the University of Sheffield and the faith Anna showed in me in applying for this funding.

I would also like to thank all of the participants who contributed to this research: the landscape architects and designers, the staff and volunteers at the case study sites and the interviewees themselves who were prepared to walk and talk with a strange woman who accosted them whilst they were getting on with their everyday lives. Their thought-provoking contributions are the foundations of this book.

My family have grown to love the Lea Valley and the lesser-known stretches of the River Thames as it flows past Purfleet and Tilbury. Thank you to Larry for his support and his belief in me, to Beth for our discussions about our respective research processes – it is surprising the connections that can be made with research into deep-sea fish traits – and to Ellie for accompanying me on many walks and for enjoying decay and disorder.

Thank you also to Ingrid, Malcolm and Maggie and to my sister, Jenny, for their advice and encouragement. Finally, thank you to Ian who, when I was uncertain all those years ago about whether to embark on this research, encouraged me to 'go for it'.

Abbreviations

AHD	Authorised heritage discourse
AMD	Acid mine drainage
AWRE	Atomic Weapons Research Establishment
CTRL	Channel Tunnel Rail Link
DUN	Derelict, underused and neglected
IBA	International Building Exhibition
LVRPA	Lee Valley Regional Park Authority
M2W	Military to wildlife
MOD	Ministry of Defence
PDL	Previously developed land
RSPB	Royal Society for the Protection of Birds
SHFA	Sydney Harbour Foreshore Authority
SHFT	Sydney Harbour Federation Trust

Preamble

In the last few decades a fascination with post-industrial sites and derelict landscapes has become part of a growing *Zeitgeist* that has arisen as a result of the large scale decommissioning and abandonment of our industrial heritage. I was brought up in Suffolk on the east coast of Britain where fishing and shipbuilding had once thrived. By the 1960s the herring industry in Lowestoft was in decline and the fish markets and wharfs stood idle (Newcastle University, 2016). Ship and boat building lasted longer, but shipyards came and went (Wikipedia, 2016). Factories closed and were reincarnated for short periods only to close again. Much of this was hidden from view but it was possible to wander along the water's edge of Lake Lothing (an expanse of open water leading to the harbour) past boat-building sheds and the remains of industrial buildings. We always stopped at the skeletal timber frames of two sunken boats rotting on the tidal mud banks; they remain there today, still decaying, still mysterious. Remnants of World War II also cropped up in our play spaces; along the crumbling North Sea cliffs were concrete lookouts surrounded by bracken and brambles, unpleasantly abject inside.

Long before the changes wrought on my everyday landscape by industry, the area was used for sand and gravel extraction; on the rare occasions that it snowed we would take our sledges to the steep wooded slopes of what we were told was an old quarry. The more significant cultural landscape of the Norfolk Broads was merely another place to play. Until the 1950s these lakes and waterways were believed to be natural but even here evidence of a centuries-old trade has left its mark. The Broads are in fact flooded peat works; between the twelfth and fourteenth centuries peat was extracted and sold for fuel, the proceeds forming a large part of the income of individual local families and manors (The Broads Authority, 2014).

These diverse and, in some cases, ancient remnants of working landscapes were just an ordinary part of my life, however, my holidays took me to a very different and exciting place – the coalfields of Lancashire. For me this was no quotidian landscape: for a start it smelt different. As we left the flat lands of East Anglia and crossed the Peak District and the Pennines, winding tortuously uphill behind open coal lorries, the smell of coal dust became more persistent. We were going to stay with my grandfather who, after his retirement, had taken up a position as an ecologist with the University of Salford to experiment on greening the many slag and spoil heaps that had changed the topography of this landscape. Although these places were for me so far removed from the landscape of home, children and adults living in the shadow of the heaps were using them for a wide range of activities: 'as if they were living right alongside some fine unexplored adventure country: such as we could not afford to provide, even if we knew how' (Graham, 1973: 223). These cultural landscapes were seen as blighted wastelands and yet for local people they were valued open spaces and often regeneration attempts by the authorities resulted in less space for children's play. As grandfather pointed out, improvements in the visual appearance of the industrial landscape were 'based on the values of middle-class adults passing through, instead of being on the values of working-class children who live there' (Graham, 1973: 224).

My intention in this brief preamble is to draw the reader's attention to the potentialities of these messy and disordered waste spaces. They hold possibilities for reimagining the past, for play, for excitement and are often places where people can experience the natural world within an urban environment. Then, as now, perceptions and expectations of former industrial landscapes differ: for grandfather they had the potential to become informal green spaces for local people; for children they were part of their everyday lives; for others they were nothing but an eyesore. And for me these places of my childhood have a tenuous link to my interest in cultural landscapes that are more often seen as abject, as messy, as ordinary, and to a desire to dig through the layers of dirt and to reimagine the fragments of the pastness that I find there.

References

Graham, M. (1973) *A natural ecology.* Manchester: Manchester University Press.

Newcastle University (2016) *The tale of the herring: History of Lowestoft.* Available from: www.taleoftheherring.com/lowestoft/history/ [Accessed 30 November 2016].

The Broads Authority (2014) *Proposed Oulton Broad Conservation Area Public Consultation, Report by Historic Environment Manager.* The Broads Authority.

Wikipedia (2016) *Brooke Marine.* Available from: https://en.wikipedia.org/wiki/Brooke_Marine [Accessed 30 November 2016].

1 Introduction

Imagine an industrial landscape and what springs to mind? There are probably huge buildings, the ever-present whirr of machinery, trucks and lorries moving back and forth, steam, smoke, smells, grime, pollution, teams of workers, materials being extracted and transformed, things being produced. This is a landscape that revels in its materiality. Even small-scale industrial sites leave a physical mark on the landscape. Yet the nature of industry dictates that these landscapes will be temporary: part of an economic and political system that determines when they are unproductive, no longer needed, obsolete (Orange, 2015). The company moves on, is closed down, forgotten, and yet the physical presence in the landscape remains, together with the men and women who worked and still live there. These people's past lives and memories are intertwined with the now increasingly derelict landscape; 'the past is persistent, not just in memory or written histories, but also in the materiality of things literally *present*' (LeCain, 2014: 72).

Often, when writing about the relationship between people and place, material things are overlooked, or left unexamined, with discussions of place identity or place attachment taking preference. The literature in this field is extensive; see Lewicka (2011) for a summary of the discourses around place attachment and Manzo (2005), Gustafson (2001) and Twigger-Ross and Uzzell (1996) for discussions of place meaning and identity. As LeCain points out, 'the idea that matter itself … might influence the patterns of historical change and continuity as much as social and cultural factors has received little attention' (LeCain, 2014: 64). In this book I start from the material – the 'thingyness' of these places – together with a cognisance of the states of flux that these sites are subject to. However, materiality is only one aspect; people bring their own memories and histories to bear on these landscapes. It is therefore through both the tangible and the intangible that I explore the ways that designers approach the development of brownfield sites and the responses, the experiences and the memories of the people who visit them, both when they were derelict and in their new incarnations. Viewing these landscapes from this perspective calls for an exploration of a range of multi-disciplinary texts from the realm of social science, anthropology, philosophy and cultural and human geography in order to build a

conceptual framework for discussions within the field of landscape architecture. As might be expected from a book that starts from the standpoint of
the materiality of brownfield sites, my concern is with the implications my
findings have for the practice of landscape architecture.

Former industrial and military sites that have fallen into dereliction give
rise to particular challenges. First impressions are often of dirty and dangerous
places, contaminated, vandalised, forgotten and unwanted: so-called wastelands. However, this overlooks positive and distinctive aspects of these
brownfield sites where juxtapositions between cultural and natural processes:

> Occur in an extremely condensed manner, layering issues of cultural,
> social, economic and ecological construction and fragmentation in their
> interdependences, hinting to more fundamental questions of human
> existence and interrelations with the environment.
>
> (Langhorst, 2004: 6)

This book explores the layers of pastness waiting to be uncovered in brownfield sites and examines how designers work with these remnants to create
'collisions and overlaps' (Langhorst, 2004: 6) between the past and the
present.

In recent years there has been a reassessment of what constitutes landscape beauty and a discussion of the different ways in which we might value
landscapes. This in turn has influenced the development of discourse about
landscape and this volume contributes to the growing body of literature. The
European Landscape Convention defines landscape as 'an area, perceived by
people, whose character is the result of action and interaction of natural and/
or human factors' (Council of Europe, 2000: 3). This definition includes not
only the countryside but also the urban and urban fringes and everything in
between. The Convention also affirms that landscape is important to people's
sense of identity and a part of their heritage, both natural and cultural,
however, it points out that this applies to landscapes in 'degraded areas as
well as in areas of high quality, in areas recognised as being of outstanding
beauty as well as everyday areas' (Council of Europe, 2000: 2).

This concept of landscape as being about everyday places carries with it
the implication that these sorts of landscapes have particular characteristics
which are worth examining, hence the importance of researching redeveloped
derelict sites and wastelands. In what follows I focus on landscapes that
were once under industrial or military use and have then, after a period of
abandonment, been developed as green spaces. Policy makers and the public
in the UK commonly refer to these as brownfield sites and they are often
seen as a blight on their surroundings. With this label comes a set of expectations about their future; the removal of blight is usually considered essential to regeneration and there is often pressure to sweep away all evidence of
the histories of these places as part of the development strategy for the local
area. Alternatively, the derelict landscape is replaced with a commoditised

form of industrial heritage that is intended to aid the transformation process. Waterton observes that this form of heritage assumes that 'areas characterised as "post-industrial" will be lacking in identity and cohesion *without* the implementation of explicit reclamation and regeneration policies and practices that target heritage' (Waterton, 2011: 344). However, if we consider that derelict sites are also formed through a mix of natural processes and human interventions and, as the Convention says, are a valued part of people's heritage, then it is important to explore the ways in which these processes and interventions can inform the future of these landscapes and the resulting perceptions of the people who visit these places.

Chapter 2 – *The qualities of derelict, underused and neglected sites* begins with an outline of UK Government policy to brownfield sites and introduces the phrase 'derelict, underused and neglected' to define these landscapes. It counters the perceptions mentioned above, that see derelict sites only in terms of blight, with an examination of the more positive recent discourses that focus on the industrial ruin. The terms material, spatial and temporal qualities are advanced to illustrate aspects of the derelict landscape that might be incorporated into the developed site: examples include artefacts, remnants, successional vegetation and landforms together with less tangible temporal processes and rhythms of change. Diverse theoretical approaches to the past history of such landscapes are considered, whilst noting that there has been little research into the experiences and perceptions of people living near developed post-industrial sites. In Chapter 3 – *Eleven landscapes and their qualities* I introduce eleven case study landscapes from the UK, Germany, the USA, China and Australia. These were formerly industrial or military sites that have fallen into dereliction and subsequently been developed as green spaces and all can be described as derelict, underused and neglected. For each case study there follows a summary of the site, both when it was abandoned and as it has been redeveloped, in order to give the reader background information about the landscapes and to set the scene for subsequent chapters. The material, spatial and temporal qualities of the derelict site are elucidated and a typology of qualities drawn up to illustrate the uses made of them by designers of the new landscapes. These qualities are examined in more detail in Chapter 4 – *Designing to reveal change,* where I analyse the eleven case studies to reveal the underlying approaches taken by landscape architects when incorporating the qualities of the derelict industrial landscape into the new site. The chapter addresses the question of how change is revealed in these new parks and public spaces and three overarching solutions are explored. First, the use of materials and processes, either through a palette of materials that makes reference to the past use, or by incorporating qualities as metaphors or symbols. Second, I examine the ways the concept of a palimpsest landscape can be used to incorporate time layers (Lynch, 1972) and time edges (Relph, 2004) – juxtapositions between old and new, past and present. The chapter concludes with a discussion of the relationship approach (Raxworthy, 2008) to design whereby people are guided into a relationship with the layers of the site's history through the ways they access the site, the materials they come into contact with and the views out into the wider surroundings.

The next three chapters focus on an examination of the perceptions and experiences of visitors interviewed at three case study sites in the UK: the Middlesex Filter Beds in London, the RSPB reserve at Rainham Marshes in Essex and the Hidden Gardens in Glasgow. In Chapter 5 – *Perceptions of material and spatial qualities in developed sites*, I explore how the material and spatial qualities evoke a sense of indeterminacy and mystery that can contribute to the ways visitors reimagine the past history of the industrial and military sites. This chapter also discusses how visitors create frames for reading the past (Treib, 2002), drawing on official and unofficial narratives to create meaning, and considering the importance of the wider landscape in this dialogue. Chapter 6 – *Perceptions of temporal qualities in developed sites*, turns to the temporal qualities, examining how visitors understand the temporal collages, time layers and time edges first introduced in Chapter 4. I conclude with a suggestion that perceptions of the temporal qualities contribute to a sense of the passage of time and a narrative of continuity for the visitors to these sites. Completing this section of the book, Chapter 7 – *Perceptions of the qualities and their impact on memories*, discusses the entanglement of memory and history. Memories are sometimes emplaced in the material, spatial and temporal qualities and are then conjured up as stories to be told and retold, but memories also arise by chance from the embodied experiences of visitors in the landscape. In this chapter I also consider the role played by absences and forgetting in reminiscences of the past and conclude with an examination of the ways in which memories contribute to perceptions of continuity.

Alongside these three chapters I include three interludes that are more discursive in nature and explore memory, materiality and temporality from the standpoint of my personal experiences during the research and interview process.

The two concluding chapters bring together the qualitative research findings from Chapters 5, 6 and 7 together with the discussion of ways of revealing landscape change outlined in Chapter 4. Chapter 8 – *Implications for practice*, draws attention to the importance that can be attached to the qualities of brownfield sites for local people. It examines the approaches taken by landscape architects to developing these sites in the light of visitors' experiences and perceptions documented for the three UK case studies and draws conclusions about the effectiveness of different approaches. Chapter 9 – *Managing change*, looks to the future of these post-industrial sites and examines the ways the material and spatial qualities are managed and the implications of temporal qualities, such as decay and the growth of successional vegetation. The boundaries between unbridled nature, the qualities of the derelict site and the new landscape are blurred and the gradients between these three states are slippery. This leads to diverse reimaginings of the industrial landscape but also raises the question of whether ultimately all evidence of the derelict site will disappear.

The concept of reimagining runs throughout this book – seeing places anew, abandoning preconceived ideas of what is valuable in landscape, reinventing narratives about the past in the present. Perceptions of derelict sites are changing; there is a growing recognition of the potential they have for telling stories about the past and also for pointing the way to different futures. The contested histories of these brownfield sites means that many people from different backgrounds and areas of expertise have a stake in imagining their future. This book brings to light the potential these former industrial and military sites have for visitors to encounter multiple and changing temporalities leading to different imaginings, memories and stories about the past.

References

Council of Europe (2000) *European Landscape Convention*. Available from: www. coe.int/t/dg4/cultureheritage/heritage/landscape/ [Accessed 2 August 2014].

Gustafson, P. (2001) Meanings of place: Everyday experience and theoretical conceptualizations. *Journal of Environmental Psychology*, 21 (1), pp. 5–16.

Langhorst, J. (2004) *Rising from ruins: Postindustrial sites between abandonment and engagement*. Open Space: Tourist places/Theories and Strategies 2004, Edinburgh.

LeCain, T. J. (2014) Ontology of absence. In: B. Olsen & Þ. Pétursdóttir (Eds.) *Ruin memories: Materialities, aesthetics and the archaeology of the recent past*. London: Routledge, pp. 62–78.

Lewicka, M. (2011) Place attachment: How far have we come in the last 40 years? *Journal of Environmental Psychology*, 31 (3), pp. 207–230.

Lynch, K. (1972) *What time is this place?* Cambridge, MA: MIT Press.

Manzo, L. C. (2005) For better or worse: Exploring multiple dimensions of place meaning. *Journal of Environmental Psychology*, 25 (1), pp. 67–86.

Orange, H. (2015) Introduction. In: H. Orange (Ed.) *Reanimating industrial spaces: Conducting memory work in post-industrial societies*. Walnut Creek, CA: Left Coast Press, pp. 13–27.

Raxworthy, J. (2008) Sandstone and rust: Designing the qualities of Sydney Harbour. *Journal of Landscape Architecture*, 3 (2), pp. 68–83.

Relph, E. (2004) Temporality and the rhythms of sustainable landscapes. In: T. Mels (Ed.) *Reanimating places: A geography of rhythms*. Aldershot: Ashgate Publishing Limited, pp. 111–122.

Treib, M. (2002) Must landscapes mean? (1995). In: S. Swaffield (Ed.) *Theory in landscape architecture*. Philadelphia, PA: University of Pennsylvania Press, pp. 89–101.

Twigger-Ross, C. L. & Uzzell, D. L. (1996) Place and identity processes. *Journal of Environmental Psychology*, 16 (3), pp. 205–220.

Waterton, E. (2011) In the spirit of self mockery? Labour, heritage and identity in the potteries. *International Journal of Heritage Studies*, 17 (4), pp. 344–363.

2 The qualities of derelict, underused and neglected sites

In Chapter 1 I pointed out that the European Landscape Convention recognises the value to local people of everyday landscapes and suggested that these places need not be conventionally beautiful, but could easily be the derelict sites and wastelands that are found in our cities and urban fringes. Nevertheless there continues to be an understanding on the part of the media, conservation organisations and of successive governments in the UK that it is the green belt around our cities that is worth protecting and thus there has been a drive to site new developments, in particular housing, on previously developed land (Department for Communities and Local Government, 2012c).[1] Expediency and economic considerations have usually ensured that the *tabula rasa* approach is the preferred option when developing brownfield sites (English Partnerships, 2006), even when creating new green spaces. The result of these policies has been that in many cases all traces of previous use are erased and thus evidence of landscape change is lost or hidden. In drawing attention to the past, present, and possibly the futures of these landscapes I hope to demonstrate their importance and the contribution they can make to the lives of local people.

There is a range of terms in official and common usage to describe the types of sites I have selected as case studies in this research: brownfield, previously developed land, derelict, wasteland. I have elected to call these sites DUN sites, standing for derelict, underused and neglected. The category of derelict, underused and neglected land encompasses both previously developed land and brownfield sites and also addresses the concept of care, thus reflecting a common public perception of wasteland as uncared for. It is worth noting that the definition of previously developed land does not apply to cases where the buildings and structures on the site have blended into the surroundings in the course of time (Department for Communities and Local Government, 2012b). The flow chart (Figure 2.1) demonstrates how this definition is arrived at. The references are taken from the UK Labour Government's 2006 planning documents, as these were the policies in use when I commenced my research. In the new National Planning Policy Framework of 2012 (Department for Communities and Local Government, 2012a), the core concepts defining previously developed land remain as shown. However, although I use the term DUN to describe these sites,

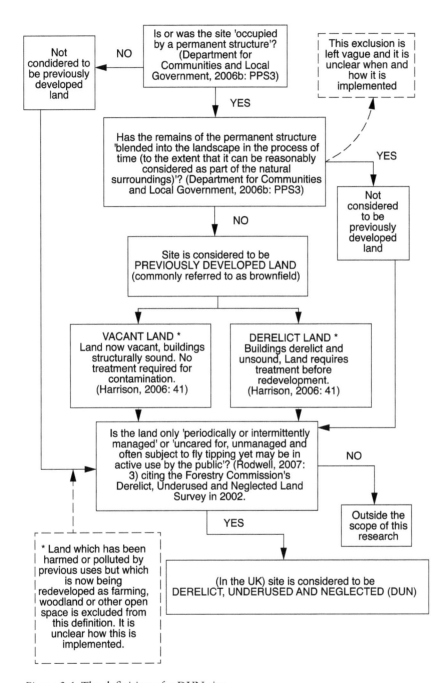

Figure 2.1 The definition of a DUN site

brownfield is commonly used to distinguish these landscapes from greenfield (or green belt) and I therefore also use this term when talking in general about these sites and wastelands.

Brownfield sites and the UK Government policy[2]

Abandoned buildings, derelict sites and wastelands often remain boarded up behind security fences until their redevelopment becomes a profitable opportunity. Mah describes these sites as 'the footprint of capitalism' (Mah, 2010: 399); they are places left behind, no longer useful, waiting for regeneration. However, derelict and vacant spaces have become increasingly identified as potential sites for the construction of new housing. In 2006 Baroness Andrews stated that 'suitable brownfield land must be a priority for any new development' (Department for Communities and Local Government, 2006a: para. 6 of 7). Throughout the 1990s the percentage of new houses built on previously developed land (PDL) was a little over 50%. This proportion quickly rose to 78% in 2008, however, since then it has fallen and the latest figure available in 2015 is 57% (Department for Communities and Local Government, 2016a). The demand for new housing, combined with the desire to preserve green belt land, led the Labour Government in 2003 to commission its National Regeneration Agency, English Partnerships, to carry out extensive consultation and research into the development of brownfield land. The resulting publication, *The Brownfield Guide* (English Partnerships, 2006), gave detailed information for practitioners, local councils and developers. The Labour Government's response, *Securing the Future* (Department for Communities and Local Government, 2008), put forward a target for at least 60% of new homes to be built on PDL (Department for Communities and Local Government, 2008: 6). Local authorities were expected to identify 'latent brownfield' land – sites with a potential that had not so far been recognised (Department for Communities and Local Government, 2008: 8). In 2016 the push to build housing on brownfield sites was again intensified and local councils were encouraged to publish brownfield registers of available land that could be utilised by house-builders (Department for Communities and Local Government, 2016b). The intention is that these registers will eventually be mandatory.

In 2012 the Coalition Government made radical changes to planning policy with the aim of reducing regulation. The National Planning Policy Framework states that:

> Planning policies and decisions should encourage the effective use of land by re-using land that has been previously developed (brownfield land), provided that it is not of high environmental value. Local planning authorities may continue to consider the case for setting a locally appropriate target for the use of brownfield land.
>
> (Department for Communities and
> Local Government, 2012a: 26)

There is no mention in the recent National Planning Policy Framework of the value that brownfield sites might have, either as habitats or indeed as resources for local people, apart from the reference above to sites that can be considered to be of high environmental value. Brownfield sites are more usually referred to as a 'blight' on local communities; Caroline Flint MP wrote 'the greening of previously developed land removes blight and brings with it important social and health benefits' (Department for Communities and Local Government, 2008: 3).[3] More recently Communities Secretary, Greg Clark MP, reiterated this edict, 'a key part of our ambition to build one million homes is to get work started on brownfield sites across the country – many of which are currently nothing more than blight on a community's landscape' (Department for Communities and Local Government, 2016b).

In 2007 the UK Biodiversity Partnership (2007: 54–55) (now known as the UK Post-2010 Biodiversity Framework) identified 'Open Mosaic Habitats on Previously Developed Land' as a habitat type for the first time (Department for Communities and Local Government, 2008: 14; Joint nature conservation committee, 2016). These habitats were defined as consisting of small areas colonised with different groups of pioneer species depending on the substrates on the site: substrates such as industrial spoil, waste slag, broken brick, railway clinker, fly ash and more. This category of habitat now appears in the Biodiversity Planning Toolkit (Association of Local Government Ecologists, 2011). As well as the unusual assemblage of vegetation found on these sites the unmanaged nature of the habitats is seen as an asset and the toolkit suggests that these, often fragile, ecological mosaics can be damaged if there are attempts to tidy up and improve their visual appearance. The Open Mosaic Habitat category is particularly applicable to those sites where the previous uses to which they were put have not blended into the landscape. It is these places that are most commonly described as blight and identified for development.

In spite of this recognition that some DUN sites support important habitats there is no indication in the 2012 Planning Policy Framework of the definition of 'high environmental value'. The charity, Wildlife and Countryside Link, an organisation that brings together 45 voluntary organisations that between them manage over 750,000 hectares of land, has attempted to bring some clarity to the question of when brownfield land can be considered to be of high environmental value (Wildlife and Countryside link, 2015).[4] They point out that two of the top five of the UK's most wildlife diverse sites are on brownfield land and for many people in urban areas these places are the only 'wild space' that they have access to (Wildlife and Countryside link, 2015: 1). However, in the Thames Gateway, where both these sites are situated and home to one of the case studies in this book, recent research carried out for the organisation Buglife (Robins *et al.*, 2013), shows that little notice is taken of the requirement to consider whether a site is of high environmental value. The research found that over a six year period within the Thames Gateway, including London, Essex and Kent, 51% of significant brownfield sites have been compromised or lost completely, leading to the conclusion that 'the planning system does not deliver safeguards for invertebrate conservation and brownfield habitats (Robins *et al.*, 2013: 16).

Perceptions of blight

Throughout the twentieth century a grand narrative of progress, in which the old is destroyed and the new takes its place, has been the driving force, see for example (Berman, 1983; Harvey, 1990). Things are 'made to be broken tomorrow, smashed or shredded or pulverized or dissolved, so they can be recycled or replaced next week' (Berman, 1983: 99). A by-product of this is the production of waste, and it is waste in the form of derelict buildings, neglected strips of ground and overgrown vegetation that is the starting point of the research that has culminated in this book. These sites, often left over when industries close, remain in a state of dereliction until it becomes profitable to redevelop them. The cultural and social value of the spaces to local people who might use them for recreation or see them as reminders of past histories of the area is not usually taken into account when their futures are considered. Instead, as I mention above, the sites are more often identified as a blight on the local area; but what constitutes blight and how is it perceived?

Bales, writing in *Human Ecology*, shows that qualitative research into blight suggests it is 'durable, visually demeaning, and somehow aesthetically depressing' (Bales, 1985: 371). More recent research in the UK into the public perception of derelict landscapes supports the official view that these sites are usually disordered and chaotic and may be seen as dangerous places where gangs of youths congregate, they may be full of litter and subject to flytipping, buildings may be dangerous and waste products are hazardous (Jorgensen and Tylecote, 2007 citing, Ward-Thompson *et al.*, 2004). The lack of any rules to prescribe behaviour in the derelict site can justify a comparison with the liminal spaces described by the sociologist Rob Shields (1992): spaces on the margins or edges where different behaviours can take place. More recently Doron describes derelict sites as being with 'no official programme or usage and as such they trigger and embody limitless choice and desires' (Doron, 2007: 17). In the derelict space spatial and temporal controls are loosened. Franck and Stevens refer to spaces characterised by an absence of specific rules of usage as 'loose space', demonstrating how they engender other possibilities: 'activities not anticipated ... activities that have no other place' (Franck and Stevens, 2007: 17). However, the qualities which open up such possibilities are the very opposite of those most valued by the public, namely, 'certainty, homogeneity and order' (Franck and Stevens, 2007: 17). Nevertheless, this perception of ruins as places where illegal or anti-social behaviour takes place is countered by an understanding that these are also places where people, excluded from the mainstream, can live, explore, play and even work (Edensor, 2005b; Franck and Stevens, 2007; Hudson, 2014; Schneekloth, 2007).

Are there other ways of looking at derelict sites? Recently the body of literature, both academic and popular, that discusses the value of such sites has grown. As early as 1967 the artist Robert Smithson (1996) made a tour of the urban fringes of his home state of New Jersey photographing the industrial relics that he reimagined as great monsters: 'prehistoric creatures trapped in the mud, or better, extinct machines – mechanical dinosaurs stripped of their skin' (Smithson, 1996: 71). The term *terrain vague* could be applied to Smithson's New Jersey wastelands; they are the 'indefinite, indeterminate and forgotten sites in the urban landscape' (de Solà-Morales Rubió, 1995: 120). However, for de Solà-Morales Rubió these are places where 'the memory of the past seems to predominate over the present' (1995: 120), whereas Smithson sees empty wastelands where industrial buildings once stood as devoid of any past and reminders of a lost future: 'Passiac seems full of "holes" … and those holes … are monumental vacancies that define, without trying, the memory-traces of an abandoned set of futures' (Smithson, 1996: 72).

Whether these wastelands are seen as reminders of the past, or as a desolate reflection on lost futures, is of little concern to planners and developers who are more likely to assess such sites' values as commercial propositions. However, this is not always the case. In 2006 the Greater London Authority published a series of essays as part of the East London Green Grid framework to promote the development of green infrastructure and green spaces in East London. Accompanying the essays is a series of photos depicting landscapes that many would rightly consider having little to do with greening the area. These images by Jason Orton (2006) show abandoned car tyres exposed on muddy river banks, pylons, a disused power station, a fireworks factory and rotting piers, together with working industrial sites and expanses of green fields and a golf course. All were to be found on the fringes of East London and many were brownfield sites at risk of redevelopment; 'developers see these "post-industrial" landscapes as blank canvasses which can be cleared or levelled flat, depriving future communities of any sense of what has gone before' (Orton, 2006: 16). The prevailing perception of wastelands in our cities as blight often overlooks the opportunities such spaces offer for bringing people closer to nature and 'wild' places. Marion Shoard (2002a) has long called for an appreciation of these urban edgelands, describing the untold value of these landscapes that many have written off. Shoard (2002b) writes of how the diverse, frequently chaotic and disordered nature of these areas can inspire when compared with the homogeneity of our towns, and even with the agricultural landscapes of the countryside, and decries the obsession for developing brownfield sites in preference to other options. This interest in the urban and semi-urban edgelands has recently been more lyrically highlighted by poets Farley and Roberts (2012) who extol the virtues of allotments, wastelands, ruins and landfill sites on the fringes of our towns and cities. Ken Worpole (2006) and landscape architect Peter Beard (2006) also address the issue of the urban fringes and the forgotten spaces and wastelands where nature has taken over. Worpole points out that although many people appreciate the inclusion of nature and wild spaces in their cities, there are others who are fearful, seeing such places as 'unruly, unmanaged and visually disruptive' (Worpole, 2006: 11). Beard (2006) describes how the contamination of a large area of land that was once the Beckton gas works has prevented housing development in the area, with the result that new habitats and wild spaces have been permitted to exist on the fringes of London. Similarly, in another area of East London, at Barking, ash heaps are home to rare orchids. Beard not only advocates protecting selected areas of landscape but, like Worpole, calls for greater education when he suggests that landscapes should be transformed to 'develop a new creative and regenerative understanding of ecology and landscape which is rooted in place, memory and local history of settlements' (Beard, 2006: 7).

The importance of these connections between nature and culture within the context of city life is recognised by writers in the field of landscape architecture, notably by Jorgensen and Tylecote (2007) who call for an understanding on the part of planners and designers of the temporal dimension of these urban wildernesses and the possibilities they hold for experiencing freedom, discovery and a sense of adventure. Jorgensen and Lička suggest that it is the lack of intervention that is significant; such places 'have not had "local identity" imposed on them, they are just themselves: the palpable result of a set of interactions and processes over a period of time' (Jorgensen and Lička, 2012: 232). Gandy calls these interstitial spaces in our towns and cities, unintentional landscapes, pointing out that when these places are discussed 'the term "empty" is often juxtaposed with "unsightly" to denote those spaces that are perceived to be threatening or lacking in any cultural or economic value' (Gandy, 2016: 436).

Discourses around brownfield sites – material, spatial and temporal qualities

Running alongside this growing appreciation of wastelands is a more specific discourse focusing on the informal activities that can thrive in the industrial ruin (see DeSilvey and Edensor, 2013; Doron, 2007; Edensor, 2005b; Garrett, 2011). It is an intermediate space between the public and private, a place of fantasy and freedom of movement that also supports habitats for opportunist wildlife. These discourses, although extensive, do not consider how ruined sites and wastelands could be approached when development becomes inevitable or desirable. If there is such a wealth of positive aspects, is it possible to bring some of these 'qualities' of the derelict site into the new landscape? I use the word qualities to describe those aspects of the DUN sites which allude to the pastness of the landscape or to the passage of time, and thus contribute to the special nature of these DUN landscapes.

Materiality and temporality

In the derelict site material and, to a lesser extent, spatial qualities are often easily identifiable. At one end of the scale there may be evidence of huge buildings, factories, machinery, chimneys, towers and tanks, and at the other end a myriad of artefacts and traces can be found scattered amongst the debris. Spatially the topography of the site may be altered by transport infrastructure or by spoil and waste heaps. Temporal qualities, such as rhythms of change and a sense of the passage of time, are less obvious but are evidenced through continuing processes of ruination. As the material buildings, machinery, structures and artefacts decay they become removed from their ordered relationships, disengaged from the surrounding infra-structure and from their original functions and purposes (Edensor, 2005c). Within this lost, contextualising structure, objects decay and disappear or are recombined with other things, and thus 'teeter on the edge of intelligibility' (DeSilvey, 2006: 336). The resulting loss of meaning and the changing juxta-positions of disparate objects and vegetation contributes to the pervasive sense of disorder and indeterminacy that is seen as a fundamental part of the attraction of the derelict site (Doron, 2007; Jorgensen and Tylecote, 2007). The possibility for sensual engagement with these decaying materials is an important experiential aspect (Edensor, 2005c), and the jumble of ruined materials can create a sense of the abject that may, for some, also be a part of the enchantment (Armstrong, 2006). The changes in the normal spatial arrangements in the landscape present possibilities for unstructured play-fulness (Armstrong, 2006) and encourage visitors to experience different ways of moving around and over the decaying buildings (Edensor, 2005c). This embodied relationship can facilitate diverse ways of relating to the site's past history; ghosts of past workers and narratives about their lives may be imagined and there are possibilities for other forms of recollection, remembering and storytelling (Edensor, 2005a; Garrett, 2011). However, the ambiguity of the material traces of these sites means that these narratives are necessarily disjointed, unfinished, devoid of chronology, and imagined. Edensor explains how material things are subject to processes that may be indecipherable and unexpected and therefore they become 'impossible to narrate in any totalising fashion' (Edensor, 2011: 250):

> Ruins foreground the value of inarticulacy … disparate fragments, juxta-positions, traces, involuntary memories, uncanny impressions and peculiar atmospheres cannot be woven into an eloquent narrative. Stories can only be contingently assembled out of a jumble of disconnected things, occurrences, and sensations.
>
> (Edensor, 2005a: 846)

However, as well as discussing the positive aspects of interaction with ruined sites, DeSilvey and Edensor (2013) also point out the danger of indulging in what has come to be termed 'ruin porn': a focus on the aesthetic qualities of the site that ignores 'the contextual economic and social devastation' (2012: 6) that is an inherent factor in its evolution. There is a growing body of photographic work that idealises the industrial ruin, no more so than in the seductive images of the ruined sections of the city of Detroit, where the wealth of images has also spawned a small tourist industry (Abbey-Lambertz, 2014). Gandy writes of an 'aesthetics of toxicity' that glorifies in oil streaked puddles and fragments of brightly coloured manufactured materials and artefacts (Gandy, 2016: 435). It is easy to admire such beautifully composed pictures that tell little of the poverty and despair of the people whose homes and lives have been destroyed by the closure of heavy industry and the loss of jobs. If these material qualities are to be incorporated into a developed landscape it is important to remember that the histories of these industrial ruins are multiple and contested.

Another aspect of the allure of the derelict site is in observing changes to the material qualities through the process of decay and the growth of successional vegetation. These processes result in material changes affording the possibility for engagement with multiple temporalities; the combinations of layers of material and visible processes create time layers that are open to a diverse range of readings and understandings (Armstrong, 2006; DeSilvey, 2006; DeSilvey and Edensor, 2013; Garrett, 2011; Swanton, 2012). Indeterminacy is increased through the temporalities that are made visible in the successional vegetation, the crumbling stone, the entanglings of nature and culture and the action of agencies on the fabric of the site (Edensor, 2005c; Jorgensen and Tylecote, 2007). The ruin can be seen as a microcosm of relationships between space and time where decay can reveal previously unseen material layers whilst at the same time obscuring or destroying others (DeSilvey, 2006).

Nature–culture

Any discussion of the temporal qualities of the derelict site must necessarily consider the links between nature and culture. Although this has traditionally been seen as a binary opposition, more recently it is accepted that the two are inextricably linked and it is increasingly pointed out that many, if not all, landscapes (especially in the UK) can be described as cultural; there are very few places that have not been affected by human activity of some kind. As Barbara Bender notes, landscapes 'make a mockery of the oppositions we create between ... nature (science) and culture (anthropology)' (Bender, 2002: S106). Cultural landscapes evolve through the relationships between people and the natural and built environment (Roe and Taylor, 2014). The nature–culture binary has also shifted in the field of landscape architecture; there is now emphasis on 'the conceptualization of landscape existing within a field of relationships, involving both nature and culture' (Swaffield, 2002: 73). This new focus on landscapes that express the interconnection of nature and culture is particularly relevant to the case studies in this book, as is Anne Whiston Spirn's concept of 'nature [as] a continuum, with wilderness at one pole and the city at the other' (2002: 174): the same processes at work in both. It is interesting to consider the 'slipperiness' of this gradient when examining my case studies, many of which were originally highly constructed landscapes in urban or urban fringe sites. Yet when abandoned, it is the agency of non-human factors that create much of their atmosphere; the action of natural processes on the built structures moves the landscapes along the gradient towards wilderness in a way that many find disturbing and unattractive, and yet for others this is part of the seduction of these places.

The concept of a gradient between nature and culture rather than an opposition, is also suggested by Treib (2005) in his paper on inflected landscapes. He describes how buildings might aspire to merge into the landscape or may be designed to be distinct from it. Landscapes of inflection lie on the gradient between these two extremes – towards the merger end – and are conceived of as 'places that retain in part the natural order of indigenous materials while articulating an arrangement distinct from the prior form of the landscape' (Treib, 2005: 46). One can conceive of the derelict landscape moving along the gradient towards merger. Whilst it was an industrial site, nature was kept at bay as much as possible, the buildings and infrastructure standing out as distinct, and then as it is abandoned the site becomes one of inflection, natural processes start to take over and gradually it moves towards merger, before disappearing completely. The state of inflection is an ambiguous one where the boundaries between the natural and the built 'seem to shift and change under differing environmental or temporal conditions' (Treib, 2005: 46). Roe (2014) also describes a gradient between a landscape where nature dominates and human impact is not always evident, and a landscape in which human activity is prevalent and the processes of nature are hard to discern. She suggests that between these extremes there is an 'intertwining of human and natural processes in some kind of harmony or symbiotic relationship' (Roe, 2014: 242). However, the way in which the derelict industrial site is always in flux, moving to and fro along the gradient, suggests a tension rather than a harmony; the processes – both natural and human – evident in the landscape, tug and pull it into different configurations that are never completely resolved.

DeSilvey (2006, 2012), Edensor (2005c), and Jorgensen and Tylecote (2007) when writing of the temporality of derelict sites and wastelands highlight the tensions created by juxtapositions of the natural and cultural, the human and the non-human. As Jorgensen points out, these sites with their interweaving of ruined buildings and opportunist vegetation cannot easily be categorised, but instead 'confound accepted boundaries between nature and culture' (Jorgensen, 2012: 5). Qviström goes further suggesting that the examination and development of industrial ruins can become a way of critiquing the 'nature–culture divide embedded in the fabric of contemporary cities' (Qviström, 2012: 256) singling out the High Line and Südgelände, sites I discuss in Chapter 4, as places where the hybridity of dereliction is highlighted. It is the potential of such places that is important, their emerging properties, and the relationships between the human and the non-human, and in this book I ask how visitors perceive these forms of relationships.

Brownfield sites – history and recollection

Heritage

In the late twentieth century the concept of travelling back in time in order to empathise with people from a bygone era led to the growth of the heritage museum as a popular way of engaging visitors with the history of an area. These sites, often in areas of high unemployment due to the closure of heavy industry, were promoted as a way of regenerating deprived local economies. Andreas Huyssen describes this as 'culture as compensation' (Huyssen, 1995: 26). He suggests that by privileging the traditional forms of cultural identity, the disturbing constant changes experienced in the modern world can be mitigated. Hewison went further when writing of the period of industrial decline when Margaret Thatcher was in office: 'the substitution of this imaginary past has become official policy, even as the same government elsewhere has allowed the present to decline' (Hewison, 1987: 99).

Over the last few decades people have begun to challenge such a heritage approach to history that leads to the development of landscapes designed to tell a particular story: one that is determined by those in power. As early as 1976, Relph, in his book *Place and Placelessness* (1976), suggests that landscapes have become expressions of an idealised past, and promise a similarly ideal future; they are seen as concrete expressions of the narrative of progress that epitomises the modern era. The archeologist Kevin Walsh (1992) also discusses how in the late twentieth century conceptualisations of heritage and conservation were selective and partial and the approach did not consider the valuable and varied heritages of a range of local people and communities. What resulted was the commodification and sanitisation of both place and history. Walsh sites open-air museums, often in former industrial sites, that 'produce representations of life-styles that are devoid of conflict and antisocial behaviour', where 'the visitor is placed in an environment of nostalgia-arousal' (Walsh, 1992: 97–98).[5] These museums often espouse a predetermined narrative, sometimes told from one point of view and at one moment in the site's history; this is 'the past *domesticated* for present purposes' (Orange, 2015: 23). Dicks also discusses this form of cultural consumerism from the sociologist's point of view, and in particular examines place-based regeneration strategies based on a premise of 'salvaging the past and presenting it as a visitable experience' (Dicks, 2003: 119), but one that is static and predetermined.[6]

More recently, academics, notably Emma Waterton and Laurajane Smith, suggest new ways of understanding heritage landscapes. They question the approach to heritage that 'emphasises the authority of expertise to act as stewards for the past' (Waterton and Smith, 2010: 12) and challenge the understanding that heritage is universal and unchanging – that it must always be preserved for future generations (Smith, 2006). This has given rise to a more nuanced understanding of the connections between heritage and place: for examples see (Corsane *et al.*, 2008; Hawke, 2010; Lien and Davison, 2010; Summerby-Murray, 2007; Swensen *et al.*, 2013).

However, this book does not examine sites that have been created with the prime purpose of displaying a particular heritage narrative. I have suggested that derelict landscapes are open to a multiplicity of meanings and narratives – in contrast with the fixed and often partial narrative of the heritage site – and I am interested in exploring whether these qualities of the derelict site can persist into the developed landscape.

Reimagining the past in the present

If derelict sites are not to be erased completely nor preserved to tell a particular story, how might they be developed in creative ways in order to challenge how we relate to our recent past? Here I introduce Ingold's (2012) discussion of how we might relate to history through landscape, as an alternative way of thinking about the past. For Ingold, when we embodily engage with the landscape through our senses we are not merely recollecting past experiences but we can be considered to be imagining the landscape (Ingold, 2012). His embodied approach to perceiving and engaging with landscape leads him to propose at least three ways of imagining the past in landscape. There is the '*materialising* mode' that treats the past in a conventional manner as heritage; artefacts become 'object[s] of memory, to be displayed and consumed'. Then there is the '*gestural*' that considers memories that are created through the act of 'redrawing the lines and pathways of ancestral activity'. Finally, he describes the '*quotidian* mode in which what remains of the past provides a basis for carrying on' (Ingold, 2012: 8). Ingold is attempting to understand the different ways in which we might engage with the past in the present, and thus offers an alternative way of thinking about sites such as wastelands and derelict landscapes, that do not display conventional representations of past histories. Jorgensen *et al* (2017) suggest that this approach to understanding the multiplicity of histories in a landscape can help to elucidate three very different narratives arising from the study of a wasteland on the urban fringes of Sheffield.

Is it possible, therefore, to interpret the different ways in which individuals engage with the ruin in the light of Ingold's three modes for imagining the past? The decrepit and decaying buildings and the material artefacts found in a ruined site are certainly 'objects of memory' (Ingold, 2012: 8) but they are very different from artefacts selected for their heritage potential. As they decay they become more and more unrecognisable and their original functions are obscured (Edensor, 2005c). These temporal processes paradoxically allow the materiality of the object to come to the fore, rather than its history, which is left to the imagination of the visitor, who may ascribe it with meanings and memories of their own. This is a more fluid version of Ingold's materialising mode: one in which the functionality and meaning of the object can change over time and is dependent on who is doing the perceiving.

The ruin can also be understood within the context of the gestural mode; Vergunst (2012) describes how the action of stepping over a threshold into a ruined building immediately brings with it certain feelings and expectations. The bodily gesture of stepping into a house is inscribed in our memories and actions; similarly the explorer in the ruin might, by following the actions and routes taken by the workers on the site, remember these past actions through their own bodies (Edensor, 2005a; Edensor, 2005b; Garrett, 2011). Again though, as the ruin disintegrates, ways of moving through the site become more random and less structured until ultimately many of the original pathways of activity are hidden or forgotten and instead the visitor might drift or wander in indeterminate ways (Armstrong, 2006) or revert to a childlike quality in their movements through the site (Edensor, 2005a).

Ingold (2012) gives as an example of the quotidian mode, the way in which local people in Lewis perceive the traditional blackhouses of their near ancestors. These houses were gradually superseded by more modern dwellings but they are still used as parts of other structures or as barns. Poller (2012) describes the matter-of-fact way the inhabitants treat these remnants of the past that have become unremarked parts of their everyday life. In the ruin this quotidian mode is evidenced in the temporary and opportunist uses to which it is put (Schneekloth, 2007): visitors build campfires out of debris; use the walls for graffiti or carry out illegal transactions, hidden from public view (Swanton, 2012). Or it can be seen in the ways young people, unobserved by adults, find a place to engage with the natural world in urban settings (Ward-Thompson, 2012).

This suggests that Ingold's modes of imagining can be used as a starting point in understanding the ways in which we relate to the past in my case study sites; however, although compelling as a theory, it is clear that these modes do not sufficiently describe the extent of the engagements that an individual might have with the qualities of the derelict site. The indeterminacy of the ruin subverts the narratives (or imaginings) both in the materialising and in the gestural modes.

Alternative histories

A traditional heritage approach to history that follows Ingold's materialising mode results in the preservation of material objects in a state of stasis. DeSilvey suggests there might be an alternative to this museum-style approach to heritage: one in which the object is seen as 'a dynamic entity that is entangled in both cultural and natural processes' (DeSilvey, 2006: 324). This way of approaching the concept of heritage can be useful when thinking about the materiality of derelict sites and the ways in which such sites can be designed and developed. DeSilvey asks: 'Might it be possible to experiment with other ways of storying landscape, framing histories around movement rather than stasis, and drawing connections between past dynamism and future process?' (DeSilvey, 2012: 31).

She advocates bringing together a combination of historical and recent data so people might understand the process of landscape change and this might then suggest alternative futures. DeSilvey calls this approach an 'anticipatory history': a history that points to possible futures. She refers to Lynch's (1972: 168) call for designers to make visible reference to historical events by means of a 'temporal collage' in which different material elements are juxtaposed in ways which give new meaning whilst still ensuring that each 'layer' is understandable (Lynch, 1972). Lynch suggests integrating the history of the site into the new landscape in such a way as to:

> Enhance the complexity and significance of the present scene ... to make visible the process of change. The achievement of the aim requires creative and skillful demolition, just as much as skillful new design. We look for a setting that, rather than simply being a facsimile of the past, seems to open outward in time.
>
> (Lynch, 1972: 57)

DeSilvey's concept of an anticipatory history, her re-evaluation of the decaying artefact and reassessment of what it might mean to preserve a historic site or a landscape, is particularly relevant to the sites in this book. The inevitable result of allowing material things to decay without intervention is that they take on new forms and indeed eventually disappear. However, DeSilvey (2006) points out that all conservation strategies make choices as to what is worth preserving and what can be lost, and she suggests that decay may encourage alternative remembrances. Later in this book I discuss the landscape at Orford Ness where the National Trust is already taking a non-interventionist approach to the management of the military structures and artefacts left behind when the Atomic Weapons Research Establishment (AWRE) abandoned the site (DeSilvey, 2014).

Perceptions of redeveloped brownfield sites

In parallel with, and in some cases predating, this growing body of scholarly literature there has also been a move on the part of landscape architects to incorporate industrial buildings and artefacts into the developed landscape.[7] The forerunner of this trend is Richard Haag's Gas Works Park in Seattle, in the USA. The city of Seattle bought the site in 1962 and the project has divided opinion ever since. In 1969, the Chair of the University of Washington's Anthropology Department writing in the *Seattle Magazine* advocated the preservation of the gas towers, describing their historic significance and their materiality in both poetic and apocalyptic prose (Read, 1969). Soon after, in 1970, Richard Haag was commissioned to draw up a master plan for the park. Pirzio-Biroli quotes Haag describing the site when he first saw it 15 years after it was abandoned: there were 'no sacred forests, but towering totems of iron; no seductive pools, but pits of tar; and no plants' (2004: 28). Nevertheless Haag was determined to save the gas towers; 'we went through this industrial revolution and it's a very important part of the world that we lived in … this is the last of an extinct species' (CCLRtv, 2009).

This was the beginning of a long process of argument and counter argument throughout which Haag battled to explain his vision to the city and even to fellow landscape architects in his own office (Hester, 1984). It was not until 1975 that the first phase of the park opened to the public and even then entrance to the gas towers themselves was soon prohibited, much to Haag's dismay (Hester, 1984). However, the public quickly responded to the new ideas this park espoused and as well as concerts, kite flying and other more traditional activities, it became a gathering place for protest and other counter-cultural events.

Perhaps one of the best known and most influential of these types of site is Duisburg Nord Landscape Park, designed more than 15 years after Gas Works Park by Peter Latz and Partners. I discuss Duisburg Nord in Chapter 4. The site has been admired around the world and much has been written about the regeneration strategy of the Ruhr Valley in Germany. However, this form of development is not well theorised in the UK and although the Latz philosophy is sometimes referred to in the initial stages of redevelopment, it still often appears to be an alien idea to some policy-makers and developers. There is also a paucity of research into the ways the people who live near these developed post-industrial landscapes experience them, and I intend to address this deficit in the discourse later in this book. However, the following three studies from Europe and the USA do consider these issues. Although the research methodologies and the sites studied are not comparable, one of the findings from all three studies was the preference on the part of significant groups of participants for prioritising green space in some form over evidence of the pastness of the landscape.

In post-industrial areas of Belgium, researchers (Ruelle *et al.*, 2013) used photos of the Duisburg Nord landscape as one of their examples of possible landscape styles and found that there was a strong relationship between preference for this style and the age of respondents. Those between the ages of 18–28 expressed the most satisfaction with this type of landscape and those over 60 expressed dislike. Of those who preferred the Duisburg-like landscape, 38.7% gave the presence of green nature and 25.8% heritage conservation as reasons for their preference. Ruelle *et al* (2013) suggest that the sight of nature recolonising such sites may be attractive to this group of people.[8] A further finding showed that respondents were less likely to appreciate such landscapes when evidence of industrial pollution was still widespread in their own local area (Ruelle *et al.*, 2013). Sociologist, Alice Mah's (2010) research into memory undertaken with residents of the Walker shipbuilding area of Newcastle also notes generational differences in responses and suggests that these may be due to the fact that, for older generations, memories of the industrial history of the area are still relatively recent and their associations with this history are deep-rooted.

A further study that examines reactions of local people to the regeneration of industrial landscapes is de Waal and de Wit's (2012) research into the development of large areas of land in Germany that had been devastated by opencast mining. One of their main findings was that people's preference was to erase the evidence of this industrial history, although they found a difference between the views of local people who wished for a return to a green, pre-industrial landscape and tourists who were interested in the layers of history that might be highlighted in an alternative form of redevelopment (de Waal and de Wit, 2012).

In the USA, since 1988, over 20 military sites have been developed as green spaces (Havlick, 2016) and later in this book I will discuss in detail a former Ministry of Defence (MOD) site now transformed into a bird reserve on the Thames Estuary. David Havlick carried out research into visitors' perceptions of two military-to-wildlife refuges (M2W), namely the Assabet River National Wildlife Refuge in Massachusetts and the Rocky Mountain Arsenal National Wildlife Refuge in Colorado. The visible history of these sites differs. At the Rocky Mountain Arsenal any legacy of the contamination from the chemical production, that once earned this area a frightening reputation, is long gone. Bison now graze on the prairie landscape and the priority for the refuge staff is conservation; Havlick (2016) quotes an official who points out that visitors come expecting to see bison and eagles rather than to learn about the history of the site. Although the prime aim of the National Wildlife Refuge System is nature conservation, the approach at Assabet is different: this was a storage site for ammunition and contamination was negligible when compared with the Rocky Mountain Arsenal. There are visible military remains including many large concrete ammunition stores, known as igloos, beside the walking trails. Havlick comments that 'to unsuspecting visitors who come across these concrete monoliths, the igloos may be the first indication of the site's layered histories' (2016: 165). Nevertheless, at both sites one of Havlick's key findings was that visitors prioritised the restoration of the site to a state that had existed prior to human disturbance over any protection of recent histories. The concept of these landscapes as 'natural' places was of prime importance.

The three studies discussed here suggest that, given a choice, many visitors would like these post-industrial and post-military landscapes to be 'returned to nature' in some form: in the case of the M2W sites the preference is to a 'pristine nature'. Discussions about whether it is preferable, or indeed possible, to return landscapes to a state before humans started to intervene are outwith the scope of this book.[9] The concept of an authentic wilderness or unadulterated nature is not necessarily useful when, as Roe (2014) points out, it is hard to see that pristine nature actually exists today. Treib also asks why there is a belief that 'reflecting a pre-existing condition creates a design more meaningful to the inhabitants' (Treib, 2002: 93). Can the term authenticity ever be applied to these derelict and regenerated landscapes? If it is understood as a return to a state prior to human interference then I would agree with Roe that such a state is impossible. Perhaps instead it is useful to consider the authenticity and integrity of the historic landscape. The Operational Guidelines for the Implementation of the World Heritage Convention define integrity as 'a measure of the wholeness and intactness of the natural and/or cultural heritage and its attributes' (UNESCO World Heritage Centre, 2015: 18). By their very nature, derelict sites cannot be assessed in terms of integrity; they can never be considered to be 'whole'. Authenticity of cultural heritage is equally problematic when such attributes as form and design, materials and substance, function and tradition are involved (UNESCO World Heritage Centre, 2015: 17): attributes that on their own appear to deny the possibility of temporal change.[10] Nevertheless, ruined historic landscapes that have been preserved for the heritage industry in a state of apparent decay are often referred to as authentic. (See DeLyser (1999) for a discussion of how this is applied to Bodie, a Californian gold-mining town.) DeLyser points out that the public expects a ghost town to be run down and decaying, 'to show signs of age and wear, and it is in large part this antiquated patina that lends a ghost town its authenticity' (1999: 614). Of course when the town was a working mining community it probably bore little resemblance to the ghost town that is carefully preserved today. It is clear that authenticity in this sense is not about how the artefacts really looked when they were in use in the late 1800s but about how we interpret the past history of the site in the present (DeLyser, 1999). This tendency to define authenticity with reference to the present context is similar to the desire to return places to pristine natural landscapes. We advocate naturalness as a way of atoning for the damage humans have inflicted on the world and we make these judgements in the light of our current concerns.

This suggests that for the post-industrial and post-military landscapes discussed here it is necessary to reinterpret authenticity; Hourdequin and Havlick suggest that it is possible to 'reconceptualize landscapes as complex and evolving socioecological systems that carry multiple forms of meaning, value and significance' (Hourdequin and Havlick, 2016: 3). Authenticity is dynamic: changing with the political, social and cultural context that lies outside the physical boundaries of the landscape (Melnick, 2014). In this book my starting point therefore is to accept that there will be multiple, and sometimes conflicting, layers of pastness in these cultural landscapes, and different interest groups may claim to be telling the definitive story of the site's history. In the following chapters I will examine landscapes with this in mind, however, it is important to acknowledge that authenticity becomes more problematic under this reconceptualisation rather than less: 'opening up a wider range of options may also make choices more difficult and open to greater contestation' (Hourdequin and Havlick, 2016: 3).

Notes

1 The 2012 National Planning Policy Framework section 9 states that: 'The Government attaches great importance to Green Belts. The fundamental aim of Green Belt policy is to prevent urban sprawl by keeping land permanently open; the essential characteristics of Green Belts are their openness and their permanence' (Department for Communities and Local Government, 2012c).

2 For a comparative discussion of European and US brownfield policy, see Erdem, M. & Nassauer, J. I., 2013.

3 In a similar vein President Clinton in his 1997 State of the Union Address advocated the clean-up of brownfield sites and wastelands and the creation of new green open spaces for local people, with the catch phrase 'parks not poison' (Kirkwood, N. 2001a: 7).

4 Wildlife and Countryside Link (2015) maintain that as a minimum requirement a site should be considered of high environmental value if: 'it contains priority habitats listed under section 41 Natural Environment and Rural Communities Act 2006' and it 'holds a nature conservation designation … or is defined as a Local Wildlife Site (or equivalent) in local planning policy' (2015: 2). They state that under these criteria only 6–8% of brownfield sites would be protected, however, they also discuss the value of protecting sites outwith these criteria that have evidence of an open mosaic habitat.

5 Walsh (1992) describes the Beamish Open Air Museum in County Durham, a former mine close to one of the case studies in this book, as an example of this approach to heritage. Staff – interpreters of the past – dress in costumes appropriate to the late nineteenth and early twentieth century, operate the machinery, take visitors on guided tours and present a particular narrative of the past. Beamish employs local people, some of whom were originally miners; however, by restricting their script to one period in the site's history, these first-person narrators are not speaking from lived experience. When I visited in 2005 the stories were upbeat – 1913, a year mentioned frequently, was a good year for miners and their families. However, 1926, the year of the general strike, or more recent years of mine closures, poverty and unemployment, were absent. This approach may be changing; Beamish has received a Heritage Lottery Fund grant to construct a 1950s town, thus including a period that will be in the living memory of some of its visitors. However, the concept of interpreting history through dressing up and re-enacting appears to remain a key part of the visitor experience. See www.beamish.org.uk for more information.

6 Dicks suggests that museums such as Beamish are an attempt to 'force meaning and value onto places' (2003: 18) and although they attempt to enhance the 'visitability' (2003: 35) of the area they also contribute to the loss of a sense of place.

7 For a discussion of the adaptive reuse of former industrial sites around the world and in particular, consideration of the remediation of these landscapes, see Niall Kirkwood's (2001b) book.

8 This research (Ruelle *et al.*, 2013) relies on photographs and photomontages to assess landscape preference and I question the value of these results. The participants were given six photos of the very diverse, lush post-industrial landscape of Duisburg Nord and two groups of photos of more open and less diverse landscapes. One of these groups showed photos with an open expanse of grass in the foreground. In another group five of the six photos showed what appears to be a road or path in the foreground. The level of complexity in the Duisburg photos was much greater than the other two examples and, if the photos were in colour as I assume, the greenery of the vegetation would predominate. The authors draw conclusions about the value of the conservationist approach to

post-industrial landscapes, however, it may be that the level of diversity and complexity in the Duisburg landscape was influencing these results.

9 The term 'rewilding' is used to describe the concept of taking the land back to a state of pristine nature. In the UK, in popular imagination, rewilding is often taken to refer to the reintroduction of wolves, or beavers, and the restriction of grazing animals, such as sheep. For a discussion of one case in the Lake District see (Olwig, K., 2016).

10 This is not to say that industrial landscapes cannot be World Heritage Sites. In fact the former mine, Zollverein in Essen, in Germany is a listed UNESCO site.

References

© Department for Communities and Local Government

All resources licensed under the Open Government Licence v3.0 except where otherwise stated. To view this licence, visit www.nationalarchives.gov.uk/doc/open -governmentlicence/version/3.

Abbey-Lambertz, K. (2014) *Detroit's abandoned ruins are captivating, but are they bad for neighborhoods?* The Huffington Post. Available from: www.huffingtonpost. com/news/detroit-ruin-porn/ [Accessed 30 November 2016].

Armstrong, H. (2006) *Time, dereliction and beauty: An argument for 'landscapes of contempt'*. The landscape architect, IFLA, Sydney.

Association of Local Government Ecologists (2011) *Biodiversity planning toolkit: Open mosaic habitats on previously developed land*. Available from: www. biodiversityplanningtoolkit.com/stylesheet.asp?file=774_open_mosaic_habitat_ on_previously_developed_land [Accessed 3 November 2014].

Bales, K. (1985) Determinants in the perceptions of visual blight. *Human Ecology*, 13 (3), pp. 371–387.

Beard, P. (2006) *East London Green Grid: Slack nature and the working wild*. London, Greater London Authority, pp. 6–7.

Bender, B. (2002) Time and landscape. *Current Anthropology*, 43 (SUPPL. 4), pp. S103–S112.

Berman, M. (1983) *All that is solid melts into air: The experience of modernity*. London: Verso.

CCLRtv (2009) *Recycling Gas Works Park, interview with Richard Haag*. CCLRtv. Available from: www.youtube.com/watch?v=hdhZq4niv44 [Accessed 12 November 2014].

Corsane, G. E., Davis, P. S., Hawke, S. K. & Stefano, M. L. (2008) *Ecomuseology: A holistic and integrated model for safeguarding 'spirit of place' in the North East of England*. 16th ICOMOS General Assembly and International Symposium: Finding the spirit of place – between the tangible and the intangible, Quebec, Canada.

de Solà-Morales Rubió, I. (1995) Terrain Vague. In: C. Davidson (Ed.) *Anyplace*. Cambridge, MA: MIT Press, pp. 118–123.

de Waal, R. & de Wit, A. (2012) The restoration of opencast coal mines. In: A. Jorgensen & R. Keenan (Eds.) *Urban wildscapes*. London: Routledge, pp. 99–109.

DeLyser, D. (1999) Authenticity on the ground: Engaging the past in a California ghost town. *Annals of the Association of American Geographers*, 89 (4), pp. 602–632.

Department for Communities and Local Government (2006a) *One million new homes could be built on brownfield land*. Available from: www.communities.gov. uk/news/corporate/onemillionnew [Accessed 9 January 2010].

Department for Communities and Local Government (2006b) *Planning Policy Statement 3 (PPS3) Housing.* Norwich: TSO.

Department for Communities and Local Government (2008) *Securing the Future Supply of Brownfield Land.* London: Communities and Local Government Publications.

Department for Communities and Local Government (2012a) *National Planning Policy Framework.* London: Department for Communities and Local Government.

Department for Communities and Local Government (2012b) *National Planning Policy Framework, Annex 2.* London, Department for Communities and Local Government. Available from: http://planningguidance.communities.gov.uk/blog/policy/achieving-sustainable-development/annex-2-glossary/ [Accessed 30 November 2016].

Department for Communities and Local Government (2012c) *National planning policy framework: 9. Protecting green belt land.* Available from: http://planningguidance. communities.gov.uk/blog/policy/achieving-sustainable-development/delivering-sustainable-development/9-protecting-green-belt-land/ [Accessed 30 November 2016].

Department for Communities and Local Government (2016a) *Live tables on land use change statistics: table P300.* Available from: www.gov.uk/government/statistical-data-sets/live-tables-on-land-use-change-statistics [Accessed 30 November 2016].

Department for Communities and Local Government (2016b) *Press release: first areas to push for faster brownfield land development.* Available from: www.gov. uk/government/news/first-areas-to-push-for-faster-brownfield-land-development [Accessed 30 November 2016].

DeSilvey, C. (2006) Observed decay: Telling stories with mutable things. *Journal of Material Culture,* 11 (3), pp. 318–338.

DeSilvey, C. (2012) Making sense of transience: An anticipatory history. *Cultural Geographies,* 19 (1), pp. 31–54.

DeSilvey, C. (2014) Palliative curation: Art and entropy on Orford Ness. In: B. Olsen & Þ. Pétursdóttir (Eds.) *Ruin memories: Materialities, aesthetics and the archaeology of the recent past.* London: Routledge, pp. 79–91.

DeSilvey, C. & Edensor, T. (2013) Reckoning with ruins. *Progress in Human Geography,* 37 (4), pp. 465–485.

Dicks, B. (2003) *Culture on display: The production of contemporary visitability.* Berkshire: OUP.

Doron, G. (2007) *Badlands, blank space* ... Available from: www.field-journal.org [Accessed 24 January 2010].

Edensor, T. (2005a) The ghosts of industrial ruins: Ordering and disordering memory in excessive space. *Environment and Planning D: Society and Space,* 23 (6), pp. 829–849.

Edensor, T. (2005b) *Industrial ruins.* Oxford: Berg.

Edensor, T. (2005c) Waste matter – The debris of industrial ruins and the disordering of the material world. *Journal of Material Culture,* 10 (3), pp. 311–332.

Edensor, T. (2011) Entangled agencies, material networks and repair in a building assemblage: The mutable stone of St Ann's Church, Manchester. *Transactions of the Institute of British Geographers,* 36 (2), pp. 238–252.

English Partnerships (2006) *The brownfield guide: A practitioner's guide to land reuse in England.* London: English Partnerships Department for Communities and Local Government.

Erdem, M. & Nassauer, J. I. (2013) Design of brownfield landscapes under different contaminant remediation policies in Europe and the United States. *Landscape Journal,* 32 (2), pp. 277–292.

Farley, P. & Roberts, M. S. (2012) *Edgelands: Journeys into England's true wilderness*. London: Vintage.

Franck, K. & Stevens, Q. (2007) Tying down loose space. In: K. A. Franck & Q. Stevens (Eds.) *Loose space*. London: Routledge, pp. 1–33.

Gandy, M. (2016) Unintentional landscapes. *Landscape Research*, 41 (4), pp. 433–440.

Garrett, B. (2011) Assaying history: Creating temporal junctions through urban exploration. *Environment and Planning D: Society and Space*, 29, pp. 1048–1067.

Harrison, A. (2006) *National Land Use Database: Land Use and Land Cover Classification Version 4.4, (App. A)*. Norwich: Office of the Deputy Prime Minister, HMSO.

Harvey, D. (1990) *The condition of postmodernity*. Oxford: Blackwell.

Havlick, D. (2016) Restoration, history and values at transitioning military sites in the United States. In: M. Hourdequin & D. Havlick (Eds.) *Restoring layered landscapes*. New York: Oxford University Press, pp. 160–180.

Hawke, S. K. (2010) Belonging: The contribution of heritage to sense of place. In: R. Amoeda, S. Lira & C. Pinheiro (Eds.) *Heritage 2010: Heritage and sustainable development, vols 1 and 2*. Barcelos, Portugal: Green Lines Institute for Sustainable Development, pp. 1331–1339.

Hester, R. (1984) Labors of love in public landscapes. *Places*, 1 (1), pp. 18–27.

Hewison, R. (1987) *The heritage industry, Britain in a climate of decline*. London: Methuen.

Hourdequin, M. & Havlick, D. (2016) Introduction: Ecological restoration and layered landscapes. In: M. Hourdequin & D. Havlick (Eds.) *Restoring layered landscapes*. New York: Oxford University Press, pp. 1–10.

Hudson, J. (2014) The affordances and potentialities of derelict urban spaces. In: B. Olsen & Þ. Pétursdóttir (Eds.) *Ruin memories: Materialities, aesthetics and the archaeology of the recent past*. London: Routledge, pp. 193–214.

Huyssen, A. (1995) *Twilight memories: Marking time in a culture of amnesia*. London: Routledge.

Ingold, T. (2012) Introduction. In: M. Janowski & T. Ingold (Eds.) *Imagining landscape: Past, present and future*. Farnham: Ashgate Publishing Company, pp. 1–18.

Joint nature conservation committee (2016) *UK BAP list of priority habitats*. DEFRA. Available from: http://jncc.defra.gov.uk/page-5706 [Accessed 30 November 2016].

Jorgensen, A. (2012) Introduction. In: A. Jorgensen & R. Keenan (Eds.) *Urban wildscapes*. London: Routledge, pp. 1–14.

Jorgensen, A., Dobson, S. & Heatherington, C. (2017) Parkwood Springs – A fringe in time: Temporality and heritage in an urban fringe landscape. *Environment and Planning A*, 49 (8), pp. 1867–1886.

Jorgensen, A. & Lička, L. (2012) Anti-planning, anti-design: Exploring alternative ways of making future urban landscapes. In: A. Jorgensen & R. Keenan (Eds.) *Urban wildscapes*. London: Routledge, pp. 221–236.

Jorgensen, A. & Tylecote, M. (2007) Ambivalent landscapes – Wilderness in the urban interstices. *Landscape Research*, 32 (4), pp. 443–462.

Kirkwood, N. (2001a) Manufactured sites: Integrating technology and design in reclaimed landscapes. In: N. Kirkwood (Ed.) *Manufactured sites: Rethinking the post-industrial landscape*. London: Spon Press, pp. 3–11.

Kirkwood, N. (2001b) *Manufactured sites: Rethinking the post-industrial landscape*. London: Spon Press.

Lien, M. E. & Davison, A. (2010) Roots, rupture and remembrance: The Tasmanian lives of the monterey pine. *Journal of Material Culture,* 15 (2), pp. 233–253.

Lynch, K. (1972) *What time is this place?* Cambridge, MA: MIT Press.

Mah, A. (2010) Memory, uncertainty and industrial ruination: Walker Riverside, Newcastle upon Tyne. *International Journal of Urban and Regional Research,* 34 (2), pp. 398–413.

Melnick, R. Z. (2014) Cultural landscapes and climate change. In: M. Roe & K. Taylor (Eds.) *New cultural landscapes.* London: Routledge, pp. 223–240.

Olwig, K. (2016) Virtual enclosure, ecosystem services, landscape's character and the 'rewilding' of the commons: The 'Lake District' case. *Landscape Research,* 41 (2), pp. 253–264.

Orange, H. (2015) Introduction. In: H. Orange (Ed.) *Reanimating industrial spaces: Conducting memory work in post-industrial societies.* Walnut Creek, CA: Left Coast Press, pp. 13–27.

Orton, J. (2006) *East London Green Grid.* London: Greater London Authority, pp. 16–51.

Pirzio-Biroli, L. (2004) Adaptive re-use, layering of meaning on sites of industrial ruin. *Arcade,* 23 (Winter), pp. 28–31.

Poller, T. (2012) Scottish blackhouses: Archaeolgical imaginings. In: M. Janowski & T. Ingold (Eds.) *Imagining landscapes: Past, present and future.* Farnham, Surrey: Ashgate Publishing Ltd., pp. 39–58.

Qviström, M. (2012) Network ruins and green structure development: An attempt to trace relational spaces of a railway ruin. *Landscape Research,* 37 (3), pp. 257–275.

Read, K. (1969) The ghostly gas works. *Seattle Magazine,* 11, pp. 42–45.

Relph, E. (1976) *Place and placelessness.* London: Pion.

Robins, J., Hensall, S. & Farr, A. (2013) *The state of brownfields in the Thames Gateway.* Buglife. Available from: www.buglife.org.uk/sites/default/files/The%20 State%20of%20Brownfields%20in%20the%20Thames%20Gateway_0_0.pdf [Accessed 30 November 2016].

Rodwell, J. (2007) *Remembering the land.* MB Reckitt Lecture, Mirfield, Yorks.

Roe, M. (2014) Exploring future cultural landscapes. In: M. Roe & K. Taylor (Eds.) *New cultural landscapes.* London: Routledge, pp. 241–269.

Roe, M. & Taylor, K. (2014) New cultural landscapes: Emerging issues, context and themes. In: M. Roe & K. Taylor (Eds.) *New cultural landscapes.* London: Routledge, pp. 1–23.

Ruelle, C., Halleux, J. M. & Teller, J. (2013) Landscape quality and brownfield regeneration: A community investigation approach inspired by landscape preference studies. *Landscape Research,* 38 (1), pp. 75–99.

Schneekloth, L. (2007) Unruly and robust: An abandoned industrial river. In: K. A. Franck & Q. Stevens (Eds.) *Loose space.* London: Routledge, pp. 253–270.

Shields, R. (1992) *Places on the margin: Alternative geographies of modernity.* London: Routledge.

Shoard, M. (2002a) A call to arms. *Urban wildscapes.* pp. 1–11. Available from: www.urbanwildscapes.org/wp-content/uploads/2011/09/UW-Marion-Shoard-A-Call-to-Arms.pdf [Accessed 18 November 2014].

Shoard, M. (2002b) Edgelands. In: J. Jenkins (Ed.) *Remaking the landscape: The changing face of Britain.* London: Profile Books, pp. 117–146.

Smith, L. (2006) *Uses of heritage.* London: Routledge.

Smithson, R. (1996) A tour of the monuments of Passiac, New Jersey (1967). In: J. Flam (Ed.) *Robert Smithson: The collected writings*. Berkeley, CA: University of California Press, pp. 68–74.

Spirn, A. W. (2002) The granite garden (1984). In: S. Swaffield (Ed.) *Theory in landscape architecture*. Philadelphia, PA: University of Pennsylvania Press, pp. 173–175.

Summerby-Murray, R. (2007) Interpreting personalized industrial heritage in the mining towns of Cumberland County, Nova Scotia: Landscape examples from Springhill and River Hebert. *Urban History Review-Revue D Histoire Urbaine*, 35 (2), pp. 51–59.

Swaffield, S. (Ed.) (2002) *Theory in Landscape Architecture*. Philadelphia, PA: University of Pennsylvania Press.

Swanton, D. (2012) Afterimages of steel: Dortmund. *Space and Culture*, 15 (4), pp. 264–282.

Swensen, G., Jerpåsen, G. B., Sæter, O. & Tveit, M. S. (2013) Capturing the intangible and tangible aspects of heritage: Personal versus official perspectives in cultural heritage management. *Landscape Research*, 38 (2), pp. 203–221.

Treib, M. (2002) Must landscapes mean? (1995). In: S. Swaffield (Ed.) *Theory in landscape architecture*. Philadelphia, PA: University of Pennsylvania Press, pp. 89–101.

Treib, M. (2005) Inflected landscapes (1984). In: M. Treib (Ed.) *Settings and stray paths: Writings on landscapes and gardens*. London: Routledge, pp. 52–73.

UK Biodiversity Partnership (ed. A. Maddock) (2007) *UK Biodiversity Action Plan; Priority Habitat Descriptions*. Biodiversity Reporting and Information Group Available from: www.ukbap.org.uk/PriorityHabitats.aspx [Accessed 24 May 2010].

UNESCO World Heritage Centre (2015) *Operational Guidelines for the Implementation of the World Heritage Convention*. UNESCO.

Vergunst, J. (2012) Seeing ruins: Imagined and visible landscapes in North-East Scotland. In: M. Janowski & T. Ingold (Eds.) *Imagining landscapes: Past, present and future*. Farnham: Ashgate Publishing Company, pp. 19–38.

Walsh, K. (1992) *The representation of the past: Museums and heritage in the postmodern world*. London: Routledge.

Ward-Thompson, C. (2012) Places to be wild in nature. In: A. Jorgensen & R. Keenan (Eds.) *Urban wildscapes*. London: Routledge, pp. 49–64.

Ward-Thompson, C., Aspinall, P., Bell, S., Findlay, C., Wherrett, J. & Travlou, P. (2004) *Open space and social inclusion: Local woodland use in central Scotland*. Edinburgh: Forestry Commision.

Waterton, E. & Smith, L. (2010) The recognition and misrecognition of community heritage. *International Journal of Heritage Studies*, 16 (1–2), pp. 4–15.

Wildlife and Countryside link (2015) *Open mosaic habitats high value guidance: When is brownfield land of 'high environmental value?'*. Available from: www. wcl.org.uk/docs/Guidance%20for%20brownfield%20land%20of%20high%20 environmental%20value.pdf [Accessed 30 November 2016].

Worpole, K. (2006) *East London Green Grid: Strangely familiar*. London: Greater London Authority, pp. 10–11.

3   Eleven landscapes and their qualities

In this chapter I outline a diverse range of case study sites selected from Europe, the USA, Australia and China that demonstrate the different ways in which designers incorporate the qualities of the DUN site in the developed landscape. The intention is to give the reader background information about each site in order to set the following chapters in context. The sites were selected by reviewing journals, academic papers, photographs, websites and through personal recommendation. Rather than attempting to select landscapes with a view to obtaining a representative sample, I have chosen sites for their variety and my aim was always to find places and interviewees that would help me to understand the case study sites (Stake, 1995). However, there were also various practical aspects to take into consideration: accessibility, the existence of information in English about the site, and the availability of evidence of the history of the site whilst operational, and prior to and during dereliction.

The eleven case study sites

Ballast Point Park

The 2.5 hectares site now known as Ballast Point Park is situated on the Sydney Harbour, Australia, in the suburb of Balmain, a short ferry ride west of the Harbour Bridge. The name is a clue to the former use of this headland; prior to colonisation it was aboriginal land occupied by the Eora tribe, but with the arrival of the Europeans this woodland was substantially altered as visiting ships took on sandstone, hewed from the site, as ballast for the return journey to Britain. In 1864 a grand villa was built on the cliff and from 1928 until its closure around 50 years later, it was an oil processing and storage depot, owned by Caltex (Reynolds, 2008). As might be expected with such prime waterfront real estate there was a long battle between local campaigners, who wanted to retain the site for the community, and the owners before the site was compulsorily purchased by the New South Wales Government in 2002. The original master planning was by Anton James (now JMDD), Context Landscape Design and Craig Burton but it was landscape architects McGregor Coxall who completed the detailed master planning and implemented the project. The park opened in 2009 and is managed by the Sydney Harbour Foreshore Authority (SHFA).

This very visible site was highly contaminated and contained various structures including the remains of oil storage tanks and buildings. It was the topography that was the most distinctive feature, bearing the scars of recent history. Sydney Harbour is bounded by steep sandstone cliffs and, as well as being hewn for ballast, these were cut and benched and ramped in order to create flat surfaces for the oil tanks and to provide access to the water. Concrete bund walls still stood along the boundaries but when the designers were allowed access to the site they found that the extent of contamination had necessitated the removal of many of the other structures and buildings (McGregor Coxall, 2010; McGregor Coxall, 2011).

Scott Hawken describes Ballast Point Park as a landscape that is a 'muscular fusion of natural and artificial topographies' (Hawken, 2009a: 46). The design builds on the existing topography of cliffs and ramps and highlights the contrast between the natural sandstone of the Harbour and the dramatic changes made by industry. The designers have created vistas, drawing attention to the topography of the Harbour itself and its relationship with the site. The materials also emphasise contrasts, juxtaposing different textures and finishes, and combining concrete and metal with gabions filled with waste (from this and other sites) and intriguing relics including tiles, shells, hard hats, springs and other found objects (Harding and Hawken, 2009: 44). Openings incised through the original structures reveal their construction – including entangled and rusting reinforcing rods – and create disjunctions and discontinuities. The simplest of interventions is one of the most cogent; the frame of a doorway cut in the concrete has been polished smooth and glossy to contrast it with the rough concrete aggregate around it. Inside the green painted concrete bund wall (which the designers have retained) the circular footprints of the oil tanks are replaced with steel rings simply planted with grass, creating an enclosed almost garden-like space. There is also a display case memorialising the Villa Menevia that occupied the site prior to its industrial incarnation, containing artefacts found during excavations (Harding and Hawken, 2009).

The landscape architects' fundamental concern was to create and showcase sustainable design as is evident in the retention, reclamation and reuse of materials and structures (Coxall, 2017). The new uses to which they are put subtly indicate an interest in the processes that have shaped this landscape. One example is the repurposing of the skin of an oil tank found on site to create the sculptural form of a gas cylinder (Simon, 2010). Eight wind turbines are fixed in a ring atop this structure and stamped in the circular metal frame, outlined against the sky, are what appear to be large rivet holes (Harding and Hawken, 2009). These form the first two lines of a poem by the Australian poet, Les Murray: 'Stone statues of ancient waves/tongue like dingoes on shore'.

Figure 3.1 Ballast Point Park: Top row – repurposed oil tank, cuts through concrete walls; bottom row – gabions filled with remnants, grass-filled footprints of tanks

Cockatoo Island

Cockatoo Island, a world heritage listed UNESCO site, is also in Sydney Harbour west of Ballast Point Park (Fletcher, 2011). It has had a chequered history over the centuries since the British fleet arrived in Australia to establish a penal colony in 1788. From 1839 it was primarily a prison and at times housed the most intransigent convicts who would not cooperate with the system. During the nineteenth century the prisoners worked on the island in the docks, shipyards and grain storage facilities. Later there was a women's prison on site and an industrial school for girls. In 1913 Cockatoo Island became the Commonwealth Naval Dockyard and was a major shipbuilding and dockyard facility during World War II (Fletcher, 2011). The site was finally abandoned in 1992 but these varied layers of history are evident across the whole island, in the docks and warehouses, the huge cranes, the prison buildings and the many different surfaces and walkways, including two tunnels hewn through the sandstone cliffs from one side of the island to the other. Like Ballast Point, the sandstone has been blasted away to create flat surfaces for warehouses and machinery and to facilitate the loading and unloading of ships. There are also remnants and bits and pieces of rubble dotted around and in one section there is evidence of the huge grain silos that the prisoners carved out of the rock wall. The author, Peter Carey, describing the wealth of complex historical layers embedded in this island, points out the indiscriminate ways in which they have been cavalierly changed, destroyed and reappropriated over the decades (Carey, 2008).

The Sydney Harbour Federation Trust (SHFT) now manages the site and maintains it as a tourist attraction: there is a campsite and cafes; there are concerts and art exhibitions; films are shot in the atmospheric warehouses. With such a varied and conflicted history and with the many possibilities for the future development of the island, SHFT needed to allow visitors access but wanted to retain the site with little change at present and so commissioned James Mather Delaney Design (JMDD) to design a linear walkway that would 'facilitate the appreciation of the site as both a sequential experience and a journey through the layers of the island's history' (JMDD, 2008: 1). The walkway was completed in 2008 and uses the existing structures and topography to define the routes and paths taken by the visitor; it is a 'clip-on landscape' (Hawken, 2008: 56), in places attached to and suspended from the cliffs or fixed into the concrete bases and fabric of the infrastructure (Figure 3.2). The structures, topography and surfaces of the island are integrated through this path of galvanised steel, whilst the sense of disjunction between the old and the new is enhanced. The mix of metal handrails with steel mesh treads and mown grass with decking creates 'a montage that confuses the domestic and the industrial.' (Hawken, 2009b: 59). The visitor, standing on the walkway high on the sandstone cliff, is suspended between the different histories of the site looking down to the footprints of buildings

Figure 3.2 The clip-on walkway at Cockatoo Island

and the outlines that formerly marked the position of oil tanks. In places the path disappears and visitors wander over the historic structures before joining the walkway again to climb the staircases up the cliff or alongside the grain silos (JMDD, 2008: 3). In fact, in much of the site, the visitor is free to explore without constraint. They can roam the atmospheric warehouses and industrial buildings with their diffused light and abandoned machinery and can cautiously find their way across the island through the damp sandstone tunnels before imagining life in the tiny prison cells.

Duisburg Nord Landscape Park

Duisburg Nord in Germany is considered by many as a forerunner, and indeed an exemplar, of an approach to the adaptive reuse of industrial sites that attempts to reveal the recent history of the landscape. The project was initiated under the auspices of the International Building Exhibition (IBA) Emscher Park, and landscape architects, Latz and Partners, worked with the local council as part of a large team of specialists and citizen groups. At the time the Ruhr district was undergoing severe economic problems, 'the coal, iron and steel industries … have left behind a bizarre landscape: spaces torn to pieces and environmental damage' (Latz, 2001: 150) and the IBA was looking for a new and innovative way in which to regenerate this extensive post-industrial landscape (Pirzio-Biroli, 2004). The result is a project that takes a 'path towards dirt, dust and work rather than from them' (Leppert, 1998: 34).

The 230 hectares Thyssen-Meiderich site on the Emscher River in Duisburg, Germany was decommissioned in 1985 with the loss of about 8000 jobs (Weilacher, 2008). The large industrial complex was dominated by the two huge sculptural blast furnaces. In addition there were bunkers, chimneys, turbines, cooling towers, foundries, gas tanks, walkways, walls, water collection pools, water channels and abandoned machinery. Opportunistic plants had started to take over, including birch trees growing high on the furnaces, and steppe-like vegetation had colonised the areas of wasteland. Weilacher (2008: 105) explains that local people saw this place as a '"terra incognita" and an ecological disaster area which nature was slowly winning back for herself'.

The recreation park opened in 2000. Visitors can make the exhilarating climb up through the rusting 80 metre high structure, once known as blast furnace five, from where they can trace the course of the railway line and the paths and cycle routes out into the flat expanse of the surrounding area. Below, in the area known as Cowperplatz, is a planted grid of ornamental fruit trees and close by is the Piazza Metallica with its centrepiece of 49 cast iron plates, each 2.2 × 2.2 metres, set out in a square on the ground plane. These plates, found in the pig-iron casting works, had to withstand molten iron temperatures of over 900 degrees Celsius (Latz, 2001) and traces of these extreme temperatures are written in their surfaces. The area around the blast furnaces is sometimes lit at night in a light show of bright washes of colour designed by Jonathan Park; apparently local people missed the sight of the fiery furnaces working through the night.

Latz (Pirzio-Biroli, 2004: 31), explains that he works with the 'information layers' already present in the landscape integrating the material elements of the industrial site with open spaces, paths, cycle tracks, gardens and play-grounds. One layer consists of the raised walkways that follow the route of existing tracks and link with roads, pathways and bridges that cross the site. Visitors can follow this elevated promenade above the sintering and ore bunkers, allowing them to look down into smaller bunkers, some containing formally designed gardens planted in recycled material from the site (Weilacher, 2008). The tall ore bunkers have been transformed into climbing walls, there is also a play area with a giant tube that allows children to slide from the top of a bunker to the bottom, and the gasometer is transformed into an underwater diving pool. Vegetation forms another layer to the park; material from demolished structures on the site has been crushed and used as a substrate thus encouraging and supporting rare and unusual plants (Beard, 1996). More than 200 foreign plant species have been identified, accidentally brought to the site in the iron ore imported from South America. Opportunist plants, primarily native birches, have also established themselves on and amongst the rusting buildings (Kirkwood, 2001). However, although this approach to the site's redevelopment is now known as 'industrial nature', Latz had no intention of allowing nature to regain control: 'then we have lost society as a whole. We have to keep a hold on technology and integrate it into our environment' (Weilacher, 2008: 129).

Much of the contamination in the areas of the site most used by the public has been capped and in other places there is an attenuating landscape strategy in place. However, Hargreaves (2007) notes that the approach to remediation is somewhat relaxed the further one strays from the central focus of the site and suggests that the availability of finances might have played a role in these decisions. Contamination prevents there being any natural running water on the site (Krauel, 2008), and water runoff is collected from buildings and runs through open channels and overhead pipe systems. Many of these pipes form part of the existing infrastructure of the industrial site; former cooling ponds now support lilies, fish and dragonflies, and in places water trickles from an overhead pipe, transformed into a rudimentary water feature (Figure 9.5).

The Hidden Gardens

Railway lines and two main roads bound the site of the former Coplawhill Tramworks in Pollockshields, on the south side of Glasgow. Parts of the original buildings have been converted into the Tramway Arts Centre and a new building for the Scottish Ballet School adjoins this. The 5,000 square metres that now encompass the Hidden Gardens are behind the arts centre (public access is only through the Tramway building) overlooked on one side by high-rise housing, and on the other adjoining what was the final derelict section of the Tramworks site. This has now been redeveloped as a Sikh Temple. The Hidden Gardens was designed by the City Design Cooperative and completed in 2003.

From 1820–1862 the site was partially occupied by a 40 acre market garden (Scotland's Places, Not known). The Coplawhill Tramworks (Transport Trust, Not known) were constructed during the latter half of the nineteenth century and opened in 1899 shortly before the electrification of the tramway system, although it appears that there were buildings used for the repair of horse-drawn trams on the site for several years prior to this date (Semple and Semple, 2014). A shallow ramp led to the first floor where there were the stables for housing the horses. In 1902 it was noted that at the Coplawhill works the tramways department had built around 400 electric cars (as trams were known) and converted about 100 horse drawn cars to electric, making the works reputedly the largest of their kind in the city (Semple and Semple, 2014). By 1910 they were being further extended and in particular a new paint shop was added with six tracks able to accommodate 30 cars at a time (Semple and Semple, 2014). A plan of the site from 1959 shows the extent of the buildings including the paint shop, a body shop, overhaul shop, machine shop, brass foundry, smithy and stores (Semple and Semple, 2014).

The Tramworks were closed in 1962 and some of the buildings were converted into the Glasgow Museum of Transport. However, in the 1980s, after the transfer of the museum to Kelvinhall, the site fell into dereliction and was threatened with demolition. It was in the late 1980s and early 1990s that parts of the building were taken over as arts venues and in 2000 the Tramway Arts Centre opened (Glasgow Architecture, 2014) However, much of the site remained derelict and there was no public access to the section that now forms the gardens. I have however found photos online taken in the 1980s of the derelict buildings, and blogs also imply that some people did access the site (Glass, 2006a; PaulK, 2011; Royal Commission on the Ancient and Historical Monuments of Scotland, 2014). One blogger, who visited some of the still un-renovated buildings in 2006, was unimpressed by the site, commenting on the need to wear protective clothing because of the dirt (Glass, 2006b: post 12 of 15). The consultant (Hunter, 2011) employed by the team developing the gardens to undertake consultation and outreach work told me that a group of youngsters from the Govan Hill area, 'were using it as a den and to hang out, they just got in over the fence'.

The name, the Hidden Gardens, perfectly describes this small site and, unlike the other case studies, this is indeed a garden with spaces for growing vegetables and flowers, bird feeders and compost heaps. Community based groups use the space to run workshops and there is a team of active volunteers. The Tramway café looks out over the garden and it is a safe place for children to play whilst their parents chat over coffee. The design works around structures and materials found on the site including: the boiler-house chimney, which forms a focal point dominating the more intimate spaces in the garden; the facade of the Tramway; a small section of tram track;

concrete factory floors; cobbles and materials such as slate shale; gabions filled with bricks from the demolished boiler house and recycled timber (Coultart, 2010). Throughout the design the integration of a simple palette of industrial materials – corten, galvanised metal, reclaimed timber and concrete – creates links between the old and the new (Figure 6.2).

Some successional silver birches have been retained and native Scottish plants added, whilst in more formal areas ornamental trees are laid out in grids making symbolic reference to the time when the site was a nursery (Roscher, 2011). Collaboration with artists was an important aspect of the design brief, and works include Alec Finlay's Xylotheque sited on a mound in a small wooded area. This gazebo-like enclosure, hidden in the trees, is reminiscent of Japanese architecture in its roof shape and open structure (The Hidden Gardens, 2011–2014). It houses a tiny 'library' of Scottish trees represented by carved 'books' each fabricated from a particular wood. A circular rill by Julie Brook runs through the lawn in the back of the garden and harks back to the water channels in traditional English and Islamic gardens; however on my first visit I interpreted this as a symbolic reference to a tram turntable.

The High Line

Probably the best known and the most visited of the sites discussed here, the High Line runs through what was once the meat packing district in Lower West Side, Manhattan, New York. It was designed by James Corner Operations with Diller, Scofidio and Renfro, with planting designed by Piet Oudolf. It opened in three phases in 2009, 2011 and 2014 and runs for approximately 2.4 kilometres through the city.

The linear site was originally an elevated railway, approximately 9 metres above street level, that had not been used since 1980 and had fallen into disrepair and become colonised by a myriad of opportunistic planting; a report in 2004 lists lichens, bryophytes and 161 species of vascular plants (Stalter, 2004). Described as 'a rust-caked dragon's tail of black-iron urban blight, blotting out the sky' (Martin, 2009: 41), the derelict railway was considered a barrier to regeneration that should be destroyed. However, others saw beauty and possibility in this lost landscape and in 1999 Robert Hammond and Joshua David formed Friends of the High Line, dedicated to redeveloping the elevated tracks rather than erasing them (David and Hammond, 2012). The photographer Joel Sternfeld recorded the ethereal vegetation that had established above the heads of the New York inhabitants and his book, published in 2000 (Sternfeld, 2000), helped to spark interest in developing this landscape; people began to see it as more than merely a blight on the local area.

The design for the linear park makes reference to its history in the reinterpretation of the existing form of the railway line; it is a 'landscape that is designed for a journey' (Ulam et al., 2009: 94). In places the rail tracks are visible running like ghostly echoes through the planting. It was necessary to remove and number all the tracks before cleaning them and carefully replacing them in their original positions. The palette of materials is a contemporary take on the industrial aesthetic and includes corten and stainless steel, glass and bespoke precast concrete 'planks', up to four metres long (Pearson *et al.*, 2009). The linear surface of these planks references the railway tracks and the tapered ends feather into the planting, merging hard and soft landscaping (Figure 3.3). The planks become more abstract as they peel upwards to form fixed seating (Pearson *et al.*, 2009). In places beside the walkways there are sunbeds that can be pushed slowly along short sections of rail tracks. The third phase of the project makes more overt reference to the site's history; the steel beams that support the track are exposed and contrast with the sleek concrete and ephemeral planting (David and Hammond, 2012). In one area these beams are encased in a soft play surface and children can play, clamber and balance on the structure of the track itself (Figure 3.3).

Oudolf has designed the planting with careful consideration of the original vegetation and some species are varieties of those that were found on the derelict site (Martin, 2009). The hard and soft landscaping form a continuous surface; each element flows in and out of the other. In some areas there are large blocks of planting, in others the plants have been designed to grow between the gaps in the bespoke paving: a reminder of the previous ephemeral vegetation on the railway tracks (Ulam *et al.*, 2009).

Figure 3.3 Play surface and bespoke paving on the High Line

Source: photos by Stephen Walker and Alex Johnson

Middlesex Filter Beds

The Middlesex Filter Beds lie in a triangle of land bounded on two sides by the River Lea and the Navigation (sometimes known as the Hackney Cut) and adjacent to the Hackney Marshes. In the distance across the marshes is the 2012 London Olympic site, now the Queen Elizabeth Park, and just beyond the north west corner of the site is a busy road. Two sets of filter beds, the Essex and the Middlesex, were built on opposite banks of the River Lea by the East London Waterworks Company in 1853 following a cholera epidemic in London. They provided East London with drinking water until they closed in 1969. The Middlesex site covers six acres and comprises six separate beds arranged around a circular collection area. The sloping sides of the beds were constructed of brick and concrete, and water taken from the River Lea was filtered through gravel and sand and then passed along a network of brick pipes before collecting in the central well. Photos from the Thames Water archive show workers accessing the beds from the raised walkways to remove, replace and rake the layer of sand at the top of the beds. It took between six and eight weeks to 'sand a bed' and one worker, Bill Whitehead, explained that the process left such a smooth surface, 'you could roll a billiard ball across [it]' (Pike, 1991).

Although several buildings, including the Victorian pump house, were demolished before the site was leased by Thames Water to the Lee Valley Regional Park Authority (LVRPA),[1] much of the structure and spatial arrangement of the site remains, including walkways, walls dividing the beds, a brick boundary wall and a variety of surfaces and artefacts. In 1988 it appears that rubble from demolition remained on the site and successional vegetation was already taking hold (LVRPA, 1988). There was also extensive colonisation of the beds themselves, each one taking on a different appearance dependent on the depths of retained sand and gravel. The crumbling walls between the beds were becoming covered with a patchwork of lichens and mosses and vegetation was taking a foothold in breaks in the concrete (LVRPA, 1988). Photographs from the LVRPA's archive show how during the 1970s and early 1980s the open site became completely overgrown with what appear to be mature trees established in the beds. During the period of dereliction the site was used by a diverse range of people: children were playing in the beds; there was shooting; people lit fires and barbeques; egg collectors ransacked nests; young people were sniffing glue (LVRPA, 1988). The site was also used by both amateur and professional naturalists and ecologists, dog walkers and anglers taking a short cut to the river (LVRPA, 1988). The Filter Beds eventually opened to the public as a nature reserve in the late 1980s.

The LVRPA recognised that the future of the Filter Beds was of concern to local people and that the site should not be seen in isolation but should be considered in the context of the area around the Lea Bridge as a whole (LVRPA, 1988). Their management plan in 1988 indicates that they consulted with local and London-wide public bodies and community groups. From an early stage they recognised the difficulties that would be involved in maintaining the ruined aesthetic of the site whilst also considering public safety (LVRPA, 1987). Perhaps surprisingly they decided against fencing in the beds thus leaving a drop of around one and a half metres from the walkways and they stressed that the landscape architects should ensure 'the variety, jumble and informality of the floorscape' was enhanced rather than erased. (LVRPA Countryside Officer, 1989). The industrial artefacts were considered a significant and valuable resource and it was noted that the cost implications of making safe the artefacts and preventing them from decaying further would not be prohibitive (LVRPA Countryside Officer, 1989). Ideas of education and interpretation were a central feature of the initial management plan but it was also recognised the site would need to be managed carefully to retain the diversity of flora and fauna (LVRPA, 1988). In 2012 a Park Development Framework (LVRPA, 2012) indicates that this requirement to balance both the historic significance of the site and its wildlife value remains largely unchanged.

There has been little formal design input to the Filter Beds and both spatially and structurally they remain much as they were before they were abandoned. The site is enclosed on one side by the repaired original brick wall and on the other by the River Lea. Pathways circumnavigate the site above the beds themselves and surface materials such as cobbles, terracotta tiles, concrete, bricks and tracks all remain in situ. In the centre of the site the covered central well, approximately 30 metres in diameter, forms a horizontal open plane; the crumbling walls of the beds with their encroaching vegetation radiate from this circle. The LVRPA continue to manage each bed for different stages of succession and to ensure there is a range of habitats on the site. Industrial artefacts – hoppers and sluices – have been painted in black gloss paint and are found beside the paths, and a rusty pipe runs through one bed and across the River Lea. The granite foundations of the pump house originally on the site have been reused to create an artwork by Paula Haughney colloquially known as the Hackney Henge (Figure 5.2).

RSPB Reserve, Rainham Marshes

The site known as Rainham Marshes is actually part of the Rainham, Wennington and Aveley marshes on the north bank of the Thames, bounded to the north by a high speed train line, the Channel Tunnel Rail Link (CTRL) and busy roads, and to the south by the river. To the east is a landfill site that has traditionally served North London and there are numerous industrial complexes in the area. Purfleet and the Thames estuary have long been home to industry and the Tilbury Docks and the new DP World container port are only a few miles downstream. The area is used to changes; 'farmlands were erased to allow for industries and now industries are being erased to allow for housing' (Thurrock Council, 2004).

The Rainham Marshes Nature Reserve is on the site of the former Ministry of Defence site, the Purfleet Rifle Range established in 1909. The site was used by the military during World War I and II and for National Service training in the 1950s (Beard, 2011) and by the army and other organisations as a shooting range. I found anecdotal reports of life on the ranges online in the *Great War Forum*. In 1914 soldiers arrived to find that they were billeted in tents on marshland, 'there were not enough blankets to go round; the food was coarse, there were no recreation huts, no dining halls, no canteens' (Great War Forum, 2004: post 3 of 7). The RSPB archive contains a postcard sent in 1917 showing the lines of tents and entitled 'musketry camp' (Vaughan, 2011). Another former serviceman commented that he had visited the site in the 1980s when in the Territorial Army and it was also pointed out that the Metropolitan Police used the site for target practice (Great War Forum, 2004: posts 4 and 5 of 7). It is difficult to be specific about when the military finally left the site; another writer on the forum talks of visiting in the 1990s when 'it always rained and was windy, a right miserable place' (Great War Forum, 2004: post 6 of 7). Nevertheless, as I discuss later, interviewees described the site falling into dereliction and in use for various alternative practices throughout the 1990s.

Although the MOD was present on the site for much of the twentieth century, it also had other uses. The Purfleet Heritage Centre has information about a Scottish shepherd who arrived in the 1930s and stayed on the marshes with his dogs and a herd of sheep (Beard, 2011). I was told he used the US Airforce World War II billets as shearing sheds. There was also a herd of cows on the marsh (Beard, 2011). People were permitted on the site when the red flags were down signalling that shooting was not in progress and local people and bird watchers made full use of this permitted access and continued to visit when it was abandoned.

There were various proposals for the site's future including the idea of building a theme park (Harrison and Burgess, 1994) but in 2000 it was purchased by the RSPB and the process of creating a bird reserve commenced. There was some conflict with a few local residents; interviewees described how the RSPB suddenly fenced off the site leading to protests from people who had previously had free access. However, staff and volunteers at the RSPB explained that this was essential due to the fact that the site had become a free-for-all with motorbiking and car dumping, two of the many antisocial activities. The RSPB's aim was to manage the site to restore and develop various important habitats to 'transform a former wasteland into an important natural asset' (RSPB, 2011). The clean-up operation was extensive as the derelict site was scattered with large quantities of spent ammunition and the occasional unexploded bomb. One bird watcher remembered the 'bright blue soil' and the RSPB described the site as 'that rubbish tip with burnt out cars, piles of tyres, bubbling chemical pools, rats, guns, motorbikes and whizzing bullets ... oh and water pipits' (Vaughan, 2005). Various structures also remained including parts of the rifle range, a submarine lookout tower, ammunition stores and the thick walls of a large building used for storing cordite. An archaeological report commissioned by Essex

County Council[2] notes the main military features on the site 'were three lengths of stop butt with targets and protective mantlet, primarily constructed of concrete and brick' (Field Archeology Unit, 2010: 3). The butts stretched across the marsh for 500 metres (RSPB, Not known). Now only a small section of these stop butts remain, just outside the public area of the reserve, although long lines of mantlet banks gradually rotting into the marsh are visible from the path. There are also parallel ridges in the landscape, only apparent from the air, stretching at intervals across the site; soldiers lay behind these ridges for protection during target practice.

Rainham Marshes opened in 2006 and various design interventions have been made over the last decade, including the opening of the award winning visitor centre designed by van Heyningen and Haward. The RSPB (2011) states that their main objectives are to create an accessible site for everyone whilst maintaining their conservation priorities. Early in the development process they worked with English Heritage (Beard, 2011) with the aim of protecting the archaeological heritage and have offered guided walks of the military remains (RSPB, Not known).

The main landscape design was undertaken by Peter Beard who has taken a minimal intervention approach explaining, 'generally speaking in lots of cases we try and do as little as possible and try not to brand things' (Beard, 2011). He has interpreted the forms of the existing site through a circular route that follows old pathways, the route of the trams which were used for moving munitions on the military site and, in places, the original railway tracks (Worman, 2012). Low wooden boardwalks allow visitors access to the reedbeds forming part of the simple horizontal ground plane in the flat landscape. There is minimal detailing, handrails are only incorporated where necessary, and materials include wooden screens and blocks of reclaimed oak to make rough seats. A bird hide and the Marshland Discovery Zone are constructed of rusting reclaimed shipping containers with, in places, a floor of steel mesh revealing the water beneath.

The RSPB display a small selection of the artefacts found on the site in the education centre, and commissioned an artist to recycle MOD bicycles, unearthed during the clean-up, as dragonfly and kingfisher artworks that they have now sited in the entrance to the Discovery Zone and in nearby ponds. There is little attempt to integrate the remaining military history with the new landscape, although a path leads into and around the cordite store. There is no evidence of the rail tracks that once took munitions from the main line directly into the store, although an OS map from the 1930s clearly shows how the line branched off from Purfleet Riflerange Station into the site. The shooting range (comprising the mantlet banks and stop butts), cordite and ammunition stores and lookout tower, are unobtrusively interpreted with signs beside the paths and boardwalks; however, vegetation is gradually engulfing these features and birds and wildlife are appropriating the decaying structures.

Südgelände Nature Park

Südgelände Nature Park was originally a freight railway yard until the partition of Berlin after the war led to its closure; the abandonment of the site to all but a few trains which were repaired there, allowed the process of natural succession to continue undisturbed amongst the railway tracks and derelict buildings. The neglect was compounded by the fact that although sited in West Berlin, it was under the jurisdiction of East Germany (Langer, 2012). The site itself was relatively inaccessible, surrounded by railway tracks and busy roads and protected by guard dogs; consequently it 'was removed from the consciousness of the population' (Langer, 2012: 153). In 1980 there was a proposal to redevelop the area; however, local people blocked the plans (Burg, 2010), and instead persuaded the city authorities to commission a survey of the successional ecology. The results showed the high levels of diversity at Südgelände and eventually led to the agreement to develop a nature park (Langer, 2012), however, it was not until the reunification of Germany in 1989 that the development of the park became a possibility. The State of Berlin acquired the site as ecological compensation for the large amount of building work in the city (Langer, 2012) and in 2000 it opened as a nature park, designed by OkoCon and Planland with the artist group ODIOUS.

Designers faced the challenge of creating a park that could be open to the public whilst protecting the vegetation and wildlife and also allowing natural succession to continue (Langer, 2012). Surveys indicated that if left unchecked, succession would soon result in a completely forested area, therefore it was decided to 'combine both natural dynamics and controlled processes' to 'demonstrate the transformation from railway yard to wilderness over time' (Langer, 2012: 155–156). The designers have ensured that different stages in succession are present at the same time in different sections of the site, thus visitors can experience these processes as they explore the park (Grosse-Bächle, 2005). Three forms of succession are demonstrated in this system: in the first, the process is stopped and a constant state maintained; in the second, processes are modified to some extent, and the third is left to its own devices (Grosse-Bächle, 2005).

The problem of allowing people access to the site whilst still protecting the ecosystems which had established (Langer, 2012) has been partially solved by the installation of a linear metal walkway, raised about 50 centimetres above the ground plane and cutting through the most sensitive section of the site (Figure 3.4). The elevated track allows visitors to walk just above the grassland and self-seeded birches. Metal side tracks and bridges branch off and connect with dirt paths running alongside the existing railway tracks, ramped areas and underpasses in the less sensitive parts of the site where the visitor is free to walk amongst the well-established acacias and birches growing through the infrastructure (Kowarik and Langer, 2005).

Figure 3.4 The walkway at Südgelände

The approach taken to cultural artefacts on the site varies; a restored locomotive is situated in a grove for children (and adults) to play on, but the railway tracks which cross and wind amongst plants and paths are often grown over and concealed amongst planting, sometimes reappearing as ghostly traces. 'Thus the processes and cycles of cultural and ecological production and evolution are clearly evident throughout the landscape.' (Lamb, 2007: para. 1 of 4). The contested history of the city can be read in the site; its very existence is due to firstly the division of Berlin and subsequently to its reunification. At the entrance is a long wall, painted orange on the outside but transformed inside with extensive and changing graffiti; this is a gritty reminder of the graffiti adorning the Berlin Wall which divided the city for 28 years.

Turning the Tide

The Turning the Tide partnership was responsible for cleaning and decontaminating 225 hectares of beach and clifftop along a 12 kilometre stretch of coastline in County Durham, extending from Seaham in the north to Blackhall Colliery in the south (English Nature, 2003). In the middle is Easington Colliery, in its heyday one of the biggest coal mines in Europe. Easington was the last pit to close along this stretch of coast, in 1993, and work started on the project in 1997 with the major clean-up phase completed in 2002. Considering the extent of the industrialisation and pollution involved it is unsurprising that erasure was considered the only option for regeneration of this area. English Nature, a partner in the Turning the Tide project, identified their objectives as:

- To restore, enhance and conserve the environmental quality of the Durham Coast.
- To encourage access to, enjoyment of and sustainable use of the Durham Coast.
- To rekindle local pride and a sense of ownership of the Durham Coast.
  (English Nature, 2003: case study 1)

The pollution along this length of coastline was considered the worst in the world; spoil and waste were tipped on the beach, in some places to a depth of 10 metres and extending up to 7 kilometres into the North Sea (Durham Heritage Coast, 2006). The black beaches feature memorably in a scene from a 1971 British crime film, *Get Carter*, starring Michael Caine – a chase scene plays out along the bleak, blackened wasteland. During the life of the Turning the Tide project 1.3 million tonnes of colliery waste were removed from the beaches and 225 hectares of cliff-top arable land were purchased and seeded with wild flowers and grasses to create a seemingly natural meadow (English Nature, 2003: case study 1). Cycle and footpath routes were implemented to connect local people back to the sea and the installation of artworks and other local community projects was undertaken (English Nature, 2003: case study 1). The beaches and clifftops are now restored and accessible to local people and tourists and in 2001 the area was awarded Heritage Coast status (Davies, 2014).

When I visited in 2005 I could wind my way down the cliffs to the beach surrounded by a mass of meadow grasses. To all appearances any visible evidence of the former uses of this vast area of industrial landscape at Easington has been erased, although a local retired miner took me to see some hidden remnants – a blocked tunnel entrance concealed amongst the meadow grasses and traces of spoil on the beach.[3] The Turning the Tide project does make some reference to the history of the site through its artworks; on the cliff top at Easington, markers on a historical timeline for the area lead to a lone and isolated memorial consisting of a static pit cage similar to those once used to transport the miners underground.[4]

The Litmus Garden, Vintondale

Vintondale is a small community surrounded by the wooded slopes of the Appalachian Mountains in Pennsylvania, in the USA. This area was the site of extensive mining leaving a legacy of severe contamination and pollution, in particular acid mine drainage (AMD) seeping from the abandoned mines into the water courses which ran orange with the high concentration of iron and aluminium. The mine at Vintondale was closed in the 1960s leaving a washer, power plants, 152 coke ovens, derelict structures and the footprints of buildings (Comp, 2004). The Treatment and Litmus Garden and the Emergent History Wetlands were completed in 2001, as part of a community based project run by the historian T. Allan Comp, artist Stacy Levy and landscape designer Julie Bargmann (Kirkwood, 2004). Bargmann, explains her approach to such polluted landscapes, 'I feel committed to giving the landscape a voice … That voice may whisper of abuse, but it also speaks of the people who spent their lives in the factories, mines and industries that have shaped the country' (Pell, 2002).

The Litmus Garden has water treatment as its focus; the acid discharge from the mines is piped through a series of six ponds each lined with limestone which gradually absorbs the iron from the water (Kapusta, 2005). The water enters the final pond clear and at a neutral pH before flowing into a wetland for final purification and entry back into the river system (Kapusta, 2005). The woodland which runs alongside the treatment pools has been planted by volunteers with 1,000 native trees arranged in blocks; each group of trees has a different autumn leaf colour to correspond with the colour of the water as it turns from reddish-orange through yellow to silvery-green (Reece, 2007). These design interventions use the form of the new landscape as both a metaphor for the purification process and as a means by which to remember the industrial history of the area. Bargmann and Levy also make reference to the site's history in the way they evoke the coke ovens that used to stretch for nearly 430 metres across the site. All the buildings had been removed and any evidence of footprints or foundations was buried beneath piles of mining waste, colloquially known as bony. Therefore, rather than attempting to excavate or reinstate the industrial traces, Bargmann and Levy (Kirkwood, 2004) mounded the bony into long thin earthworks that recall the extent of the industrial buildings. These hummocks in the new wetland will eventually become wildlife habitats. Bargmann explains 'Stacy and I were interested in the evocation, particularly spatial, of the occupation of this forty-acre site by the coke works over 100 years' (Kirkwood, 2004: 75). Planting also traces visible footprints of derelict buildings in other parts of the site, adding to the strategy of 'emphasizing, celebrating and abstracting the significant history embedded in industrial remains' (Kapusta, 2005: 72).

Comp believes that involving the community is crucial to the redevelopment of these landscapes in order to 're-instil a sense of place and pride, allowing community members to forge new connections to the local environment and history' (Comp, 2004: para. 18 of 21). Reece agrees, writing that 'by laying claim to the past, a community has laid claim to a revived sense of place' (Reece, 2007: para. 24 of 34), going on to point out that after 30 years of inactivity the residents have decided to restart the Town Planning Committee. Sue Thering, from the University of Wisconsin, who studied the project at Vintondale, suggests that it was the design team's willingness to collaborate with the local people that eventually led to a change in attitude and a belief in the success of the park (Reece, 2007).

Zhongshan Shipyard Park

The 11 hectare Zhongshan Shipyard Park, completed in 2001, was built on the site of an abandoned shipyard and is situated in the Guangdong province of China on the Qijiang River. The owners were declared bankrupt in 1999 and the docks, cranes and water towers gradually fell into disrepair (Saunders, 2012). The site was polluted and the rusting infrastructure and machinery were considered a blight on a local area that was itself under-developed and viewed as dirty and unsafe (Yu, 2016). When landscape architect, Kongjian Yu, and his team at Turenscape were first involved in the site it was already being dismantled with a view to erasing all evidence of its industrial history. Originally the plan was to build a traditional Chinese garden and Yu's concept of preserving and reusing existing structures was considered too 'modern and western', and his design was rejected by experts from around China (Yu, 2016). However, Yu persevered and convinced the Mayor (the head of the region) and the community to take a different approach: one that valued the ordinary and started from the premise that 'socialist industrial heritage of the 1950s, 1960s, and 1970s [is] ... as precious as that of ancient traditional culture' (Saunders, 2012: 20).

The landscape architects have focused on enhancing native habitats and preserving cultural elements as well as reusing existing structures, such as the cranes, rail tracks, water towers and some of the machinery, for new purposes. The huge dock buildings have been left as stripped back steel frames (Saunders, 2012). Two water towers were also left on site; one is encased in a glass box, creating the impression of a precious object on display in a museum, whilst the other takes the form of a skeletal steel tower (Figure 9.2). The latter is in reality new, made to appear as if the concrete of the original has been removed from its supporting structure. Unfortunately it was not possible to actually dismantle the concrete from the existing tower, hence the replica (Saunders, 2012).

New elements include green boxes made of hedging and designed with the same spatial dimensions as the dormitories once used to house the factory workers. The shipyard in its heyday employed and housed 1,300 workers on this site (Padua, 2003). Two diagonal paths lead through the green boxes and converge in a steel box, painted bright red, a colour that makes reference to the Mao era. Within the box is a text written by Yu including a phrase, reputedly of Lenin – 'to forget is to betray' (Beardsley, 2012: 13). One route winds around the lake but the pathways mainly follow a linear grid-like pattern, in one case running along the rail tracks, and in places bringing the visitor close to the tidal water's edge in a series of accessible terraces, some of which are covered by water twice a day (Beardsley, 2012). At the entrance is a fountain plaza edged with steel plates recycled from the site and this edging continues along several of the granite paths (Saunders, 2012).

Yu also introduced a new way of using plants and vegetation in Shipyard Park; his philosophy is to 'value the ordinary and discover the beauty of weeds' (Yu, 2016). This new aesthetic is very different from traditional Chinese planting design. Yu's 'weeds' are low maintenance and comprise wetland plants, local wild grasses and vernacular Chinese vegetation commonly found on the edge of rice paddies and fish ponds in the region (Beardsley, 2012). Yu also saved ten ancient banyan trees that were destined to be cut down to widen the river and help with flood mitigation. Instead he created a channel around the trees thus forming an island accessed by two bridges that link it to the main park (Saunders, 2012).

A typology of qualities

Table 3.1 outlines a typology of qualities that designers incorporate into the developed landscape and is drawn from my detailed analysis of the 11 case study sites. Qualities fall into three categories, material, spatial and temporal, and categories are also connected; when discussing qualities in the temporal category reference is made to the material and spatial qualities through which the temporality is made visible. In the typology I subdivide the qualities into practical categories that relate to the discourse around the derelict industrial site discussed in Chapter 2 and also make sense when applied to landscape architectural practice.

The material qualities are straightforward descriptions of objects that were once part of the DUN site. These can be structures and buildings or rail tracks and surfaces that become a visible reminder of the pastness of the site.

There are also smaller material artefacts, relics and fragments evident in most derelict sites that are incorporated in some way into the new landscape. A further category describes objects that have been made of materials from the DUN site: either reused as they are or repurposed. Finally there are qualities relating to the vegetation or planting; this is closely linked to the temporal qualities, as successional vegetation is indicative of the processes that take place when a site is abandoned.

I have included the use of an industrial palette of materials and textures in the typology; however, this quality differs from the others in that it does not explicitly take something from the DUN site for use in the new landscape. The textures and patinas of these materials echo those found in the industrial and DUN landscapes: rusty and galvanised metals and meshes; broken concrete and exposed aggregates; chunks of wood that were once beams or structures. Often designers who use these materials also recycle materials from the site as part of their palette.

Spatial qualities concern the topography of the landscape and the relationships between the landscape, the visitor and the surroundings. Often landscapes were changed dramatically and violently: cliffs blasted away and huge waste tips created. Past usage also dictated the ways in which the site related to its surroundings: some were enclosed and access was forbidden; others changed the surrounding infrastructure; many contributed to the pollution of the local area. I discussed in Chapter 2 the ways in which the topography of the DUN site is described in terms of the breakdown of structures and infrastructure that results as ruination progresses, and the corresponding freedom of movement that is experienced by visitors (Armstrong, 2006; Edensor, 2005a). However, although designers sometimes work with existing landscape forms, the new designs necessarily impose restrictions, and there is no obvious correlation between the freedom of movement suggested in the literature of the derelict site and the uses made of topography in the new landscape.

I arrived at the categories for the temporal qualities by returning to the literature around the derelict site and examining the ways in which temporality is discussed. Processes and rhythms of change are evidenced in the gradual decay of the material artefacts, the ruination of buildings and infrastructure, the growth of successional vegetation and the action of external agencies. There are also processes that highlight the discontinuities in the history of the landscape. As sites become ruined and derelict, layers and juxtapositions of materials become more chaotic. I have identified this juxtaposition or layering of materials and plants as an important temporal quality of the derelict site, which can be intentionally or unintentionally incorporated into the designed landscape. More difficult to identify as qualities specifically incorporated in the new landscapes are concepts such as indeterminacy and disorder: aspects of the derelict site that figure prominently in the theory (Doron, 2007; Edensor, 2005b; Jorgensen and Tylecote, 2007). I suggest that these qualities can, however, be perceived through the quality of juxtaposition and I discuss this aspect in more detail in Chapters 8 and 9. The final two temporal qualities I identify are those that refer to concepts of remembering and recollection and those that look towards future change. These temporal experiences are mediated through material and spatial qualities and both occur in the discourse around the derelict site (Edensor, 2005a; Garrett, 2011).

Finally, I should mention one aspect discussed extensively in the theory that is not specifically incorporated in the case studies discussed here: the potential for temporary and possibly illegal activities (Franck and Stevens, 2007; Swanton, 2012). By their very nature such activities are seen as alternative and out of the mainstream; if a site is designed in order to incorporate these sorts of engagements there is, by definition, an element of control or intention and as a result the possibility for alternative activities is undermined. I therefore do not directly consider this aspect of the derelict site, although it is addressed indirectly in a discussion of the heterogeneity and indeterminacy of the new landscapes.

Table 3.1 gives the reader an indication of the range of qualities found in the 11 case study sites. It is not an exhaustive list and detailed exploration on site would produce further evidence. The three case studies that form the focus of Chapters 5, 6 and 7 are the Hidden Gardens, the Middlesex Filter Beds and the RSPB Rainham Marshes. I have therefore included more detailed descriptions of the qualities found in these sites and, where they occur in Table 3.1, they are highlighted.

Table 3.1 A typology of qualities

Material qualities	
Structures and footprints of buildings	
Ballast Point Park	Footprints of oil tanks planted with grass, rusting smaller tanks, bund walls.
Cockatoo Island	Many, including buildings, footprints of structures, walls, grain silos, tunnels.
Duisburg Nord	Many, including blast furnaces, bunkers, water cooling systems, walls, towers, chimneys.
Hidden Gardens	Chimney, boiler house wall, Tramway facade with evidence of former buildings, doorways and windows, the horse ramp in the Tramway building which was once the paint house.
The High Line	The elevated railway line.
Middlesex Filter Beds	Six filter beds, brick walls, central collecting well, boundary wall, inaccessible and dilapidated covered bridge across the River Lea, empty pylon plinth.
Rainham Marshes	Shooting range – stop butts and mantlet banks, cordite and ammunition stores and lookout tower.
Südgelände	Boundary wall.

(continued)

Table 3.1 A typology of qualities *(continued)*

Material qualities	
Vintondale, Litmus Garden	Footprints of buildings.
Zhongshan Shipyard	Water towers, cranes, dockyard structures.
Relics and artefacts	
Ballast Point Park	Found objects and fragments used in gabions, pottery from Villa Menevia.
Duisburg Nord	Many, including pipes, iron plates forming Piazza Metallica.
Middlesex Filter Beds	Rusty pipes running across filter bed and River Lea, black-painted hopper and sluices around the central well, concrete and brick structures sealed off in beds, small signs on surfaces, some showing initials of various water companies.
Rainham Marshes	Benches and unidentifiable equipment under mantlet banks lying in water and vegetation. Shed at end of mantlet banks that was once a lavatory for the soldiers.
Südgelände	Steam engine.
Tracks and surfaces	
Cockatoo Island	Many different surfaces in disrepair including brick, concrete and sandstone.
Duisburg Nord	Many, including paths following railway tracks and walkways.
Hidden Gardens	Tram tracks in undergrowth at the end of the garden. Original cobbles and several runs of tracks in the entrance to the ballet school. Remains of concrete floor.
The High Line	Rail tracks.
Middlesex Filter Beds	Cobbles, tiles, terracotta, including some from inside buildings that were once on the site, broken concrete, metal tracks and concrete channel.
Rainham Marshes	Rectilinear concrete surfaces at intervals in front of mantlet banks.
Südgelände	Paths follow existing rail tracks, tracks emerge from grassy meadow.
Zhongshan Shipyard	Rail tracks.
Reused and repurposed materials	
Ballast Point Park	Skin of existing oil tanks cut and formed into a replica with wind turbines and artworks.
Duisburg Nord	Many, including water-cooling systems repurposed as ponds and bunkers as climbing walls.
Hidden Gardens	Cobbles for paths, bricks in gabions.
The High Line	Girders covered with soft material to form play area.
Middlesex Filter Beds	Granite foundations of pumping house form artwork with traces of ground out holes, apertures and pieces of rusty metal.

Material qualities

Rainham Marshes	MOD bicycles as artworks, blocks of timber as benches.
Turning the Tide	Pit cage memorial.
Zhongshan Shipyard	Steel plates form edgings to fountain and paths.

Industrial palette of materials and textures

Ballast Point Park	Polished and rusty metal, rough and worked concrete, exposed aggregate, gabions, meshes.
Cockatoo Island	Steel walkway, metal meshes.
Hidden Gardens	Corten, metal, concrete, gabions, timber.
The High Line	Steel, concrete, wood, mesh, consolidated gravel.
Rainham Marshes	Metal, shipping containers.
Südgelände	Metal and mesh raised walkway and bridges.

Vegetation and planting

Ballast Point Park	Seeds taken from local sources.
Cockatoo Island	Planting palette informed by existing vegetation.
Duisburg Nord	Successional vegetation.
Hidden Gardens	Birch trees retained.
The High Line	Planting evocative of spontaneous vegetation.
Middlesex Filter Beds	Successional vegetation differs in each bed depending on depths of sand and gravel that were left on site.
Rainham Marshes	Existing marshland now managed as a grazing marsh.
Südgelände	Successional vegetation.
Turning the Tide	Meadow planting.
Vintondale, Litmus Garden	Autumn colours of trees reference the water treatment process.
Zhongshan Shipyard	Local grasses and water-loving plants, traditionally thought of as weeds.

Spatial qualities

Topography

Ballast Point Park	Cut and blasted sandstone cliffs of the Sydney Harbour and concrete bund walls used as layers in new landscape.
Cockatoo Island	The island, changes made to the sandstone cliffs, walkway attached to and traversing existing structures and landscape forms, tunnels.
Duisburg Nord	Existing infrastructure used as layers in new landscape.
Hidden Gardens	Spatial layout of nursery and of factory floor inform design.
The High Line	Existing infrastructure (the elevated railway).
Middlesex Filter Beds	Topography of original site retained.
Rainham Marshes	Walkways follow old paths and tram tracks. Old maps show the lines of stop butts and ten rows of ridges at 100 yard intervals. Soldiers lay behind the ridges when shooting at the targets. The ridges are still visible on satellite images of the site.

(continued)

Table 3.1 A typology of qualities *(continued)*

Spatial qualities	
Südgelände	Pathways follow existing railway lines dictating the site layout.
Vintondale, Litmus Garden	Mounded hummock evokes the line of coke ovens.
Spatial relationships	
Ballast Point Park	Views through the cut sandstone and the concrete walls to the Harbour and down to the grass circles, visitors brought into contact with past landscape layers.
Cockatoo Island	Clip-on walkway allows visitor access to decaying and ruined parts of the site, views into the grain silos, and out from the cliff over the Harbour.
Duisburg Nord	Access to blast furnaces, vista to surrounding infrastructure and landscape, views from walkways into bunkers, pathways follow existing routes and infrastructure.
The High Line	Linear structure of park and materials make reference to transportation history, phase 3 runs through adjacent rail yards towards the river.
Middlesex Filter Beds	Boundary wall and river enclose site, paths around site allow visitor access whilst discouraging access to beds. Steps down to beds closed off with railings but can be circumnavigated as evidenced by informal tracks through the reeds.
Rainham Marshes	Open, flat and exposed marshland is visible from the road and railway. Panoramic vistas from the Visitor Centre across the site to the roads and railway, the surrounding industrial sites and to the Thames and London Docklands.
Südgelände	The site is surrounded by railway lines and busy roads and now by mature trees, thus feeling hidden and enclosed.
Zhongshan Shipyard	Tidal terraces bring visitors in contact with the river, walkways run though the green box dormitories.

Temporal qualities	
Processes and rhythms of change	
Ballast Point Park	Reuse of found materials and wind turbines on replica oil tank reference the changes in energy production.
Cockatoo Island	Decaying structures remain on site.
Duisburg Nord	Decaying structures, successional vegetation, complex water treatment systems.
The High Line	Seasonal and ephemeral planting design.
Middlesex Filter Beds	Successional vegetation and decaying and crumbling structures. Maintenance is sometimes dramatic. Working parties cut down all the vegetation in one bed over a weekend. Changes in the seasons open up views across the site.

Temporal qualities

Rainham Marshes	Decaying structures and artefacts some of which have become new habitats, vegetation and water levels managed for key wildlife species. Cattle graze the site as part of this management process.
Südgelände	Examples of successional and managed vegetation.
Vintondale, Litmus Garden	Autumn colours of trees reference the water treatment process. Mound following line of coke ovens gradually becomes wildlife habitat.
Zhongshan Shipyard	Tidal terraces and banyan tree island make links between site and sea.

Juxtaposition

Ballast Point Park	Layers of past landscapes, sandstone cliffs, concrete bund walls, old and new materials, polished and rough concrete.
Cockatoo Island	Old and new materials, structures and surfaces.
Duisburg Nord	Successional vegetation growing on decaying industrial structures.
Hidden Gardens	Old and new materials and structures.
The High Line	New materials, reused rail tracks, ephemeral planting, views into the city and to adjacent buildings.
Middlesex Filter Beds	Vegetation engulfing the structures and crumbling brickwork. Mix of textures and patinas.
Rainham Marshes	Vegetation and decaying structures, old and new materials.
Südgelände	Rail tracks and successional vegetation, graffiti within a nature park.
Zhongshan Shipyard	Concrete water tower encased in a glass box.

Possibilities for recollection

Ballast Point Park	Display case for the Villa Menevia, found objects in the gabion walls, views down to footprints of buildings, views to the Harbour.
Cockatoo Island	Structures and artefacts retained and walkway allows access, views down to footprints of buildings.
Duisburg Nord	Structures and artefacts retained, light show, views to surrounding landscape.
Hidden Gardens	The Tramway Arts Centre was used as the Museum of Transport and many local people visited. The Rill and Xylotheque.
The High Line	Linear nature reminiscent of transportation system, designed linear surfaces, moving sunbeds.
Rainham Marshes	Military structures and artefacts.
Südgelände	The graffiti wall, artefacts and the new walkway as a metaphorical reminder of the rail tracks.
Turning the Tide	The artworks make reference to the industrial history.

(continued)

Table 3.1 A typology of qualities *(continued)*

Temporal qualities

Vintondale, Litmus Garden	The process of cleaning the polluted water and the evocation of the history of the site.
Zhongshan Shipyard	The green boxes in the shape of the dormitories and the red box reminder of the Cultural Revolution.

Expectation of future change

Ballast Point Park	Changes in views to the Harbour as vegetation is established.
Cockatoo Island	Temporary nature of walkway to allow further development.
Duisburg Nord	Vista from blast furnace to the river encompasses the industrial nature of surrounding landscape.
The High Line	Views into the city and the development of the local area.
Middlesex Filter Beds	Obvious decay and encroachment of vegetation is undermining the structures and walls.
Rainham Marshes	Views along boardwalk to the west towards new wind turbines.
Südgelände	Understanding of succession.
Vintondale, Litmus Garden	Visible remediation of the polluted water systems.

Notes

1   In the 1940s Professor Abercrombie produced the Greater London Plan, a blueprint for the future of London; he radically suggested that the Lea Valley should become a green corridor connecting Essex and Hertfordshire to the slums in the East End. However it was not until 1967 that the Lee Valley Regional Park Authority was formed through an act of parliament.

2   The archeological report also notes that an earlier survey undertaken between 2004–6 whilst the reserve was in the development stage revealed practice trenches and shelters and late medieval drainage features as well as evidence of the submerged Purfleet Neolithic forest, including 'trunks and roots of trees such as alder, ash and yew' (Field Archeology Unit, 2010: 4).

3   I interviewed the former miner at Easington in 2005 for part of my MA at Middlesex University.

4   Davies (2014) suggests that the involvement of the local community is crucial when incorporating artworks in new developments on former industrial sites and that local people are interested in celebrating their industrial history in this way. I have not examined the place of art in any depth in this book, although I do mention the artworks at the three main case study sites. My anecdotal evidence from interviewees' comments about these works is that they rarely see them as having any relationship with the history of the site.

References

Armstrong, H. (2006) *Time, dereliction and beauty: An argument for 'landscapes of contempt'*. IFLA, Sydney: The landscape architect.

Beard, P. (1996) Life in the ruins. *Blueprint,* 130, pp. 32–35.

Beard, P. (2011) *Personal communication – Rainham Marshes*. To: C. Heatherington.

Beardsley, J. (2012) Popular aesthetics, public history. In: W. Saunders (Ed.) *Designed ecologies, the landscape architecture of Kongjian Yu*. Basel: Birkhäuser, pp. 10–19.

Burg, A. (2010) Natur-Park Südgelände: An unexpected victory. *Lotus*, 144 (Dec.), pp. 2–6.

Carey, P. (2008) *30 days in Sydney*. London: Bloomsbury.

Comp, T. A. (2004) *AMD&ART: Founder's statement, A challenge to creativity in reclamation*. greenmuseum.org. Available from: www.greenmuseum.org/generic_content.php?ct_id=189 [Accessed 15 June 2011].

Coultart, D. (2010) Industrial integration. *Garden Design Journal*, June 2010 (95), pp. 27–30.

Coxall, P. (2017) *Personal communication, Ballast Point Park*. To: C. Heatherington.

David, J. & Hammond, R. (2012) *The uncut story of the High Line: Josh and Rob in conversation*. High Line Symposium, The Garden Museum, London.

Davies, C. (2014) *Old culture and damaged landscapes*. In: M. Roe & K. Taylor (Eds.) *New cultural landscapes*. London: Routledge, pp. 41–48.

Doron, G. (2007) *Badlands, blank space …* Available from: www.field-journal.org [Accessed 24 January 2010].

Durham Heritage Coast (2006) *Turning the Tide*. Durham County Council. Available from: www.durhamheritagecoast.org/dhc/usp.nsf/pws/Durham+Heritage+Coast+-+Durham+Heritage+Coast+-+Videos+-+Turning+The+Tide [Accessed 4 June 2011].

Edensor, T. (2005a) The ghosts of industrial ruins: Ordering and disordering memory in excessive space. *Environment and Planning D: Society and Space*, 23 (6), pp. 829–849.

Edensor, T. (2005b) Waste matter – The debris of industrial ruins and the disordering of the material world. *Journal of Material Culture*, 10 (3), pp. 311–332.

English Nature (2003) *Memorandum by English Nature (COA 18)*. Select Committee on Office of the Deputy Prime Minister: Housing, Planning, Local Government and the Regions Available from: www.publications.parliament.uk/pa/cm200203/cmselect/cmodpm/1169/1169we19.htm [Accessed 18 November 2014].

Field Archeology Unit (2010) *Butts hide RSPB Rainham Marshes Nature Reserve, Purfleet, Essex. Archaeological monitoring and recording*. Essex: Essex County Council. Available from: http://archaeologydataservice.ac.uk/archiveDS/archive Download?t=arch-439-1/dissemination/pdf/essexcou1-75223_1.pdf [Accessed 12 August 2014].

Fletcher, P. (2011) *Cockatoo Island, Dictionary of Sydney*. Available from: http://dictionaryofsydney.org/entry/cockatoo_island [Accessed 26 June 2017].

Franck, K. & Stevens, Q. (2007) Tying down loose space. In: K. A. Franck & Q. Stevens (Eds.) *Loose space*. London: Routledge, pp. 1–33.

Garrett, B. (2011) Assaying history: Creating temporal junctions through urban exploration. *Environment and Planning D: Society and Space*, 29, pp. 1048–1067.

Glasgow Architecture (2014) *Tramway theatre Glasgow*. Available from: www.glasgowarchitecture.co.uk/tramway-theatre [Accessed 14 June 2014].

Glass, A. (2006a) *Past present*. The Hidden Glasgow Forums. Available from: www.hiddenglasgow.com/forums/viewtopic.php?f=15&t=681&start=600 [Accessed 14 November 2014].

Glass, A. (2006b) *Past present*. The Hidden Glasgow Forums. Available from: www.hiddenglasgow.com/forums/viewtopic.php?f=3&t=4452&start=75 [Accessed 22 November 2014].

Great War Forum (2004) *Remembered today: Purfleet, Essex*. Available from: http://1914-1918.invisionzone.com/forums/index.php?showtopic=8223 [Accessed 15 June 2014].

Grosse-Bächle, L. (2005) Strategies between intervening and leaving room. In: I. Kowarik & S. Körner (Eds.) *Wild urban woodlands: New perspectives for urban forestry.* Berlin: Springer, pp. 231–246.

Harding, L. & Hawken, S. (2009) Ballast Point Park. *Landscape Architecture Australia,* 124 (November), pp. 42–51.

Hargreaves, G. (2007) Large parks: A designer's perspective. In: J. Czerniak & G. Hargreaves (Eds.) *Large parks.* Princeton, NJ: Princeton Architectural Press, pp. 120–173.

Harrison, C. & Burgess, J. (1994) Social constructions of nature: A case study of conflicts over the development of Rainham Marshes. *Transactions of the Institute of British Geographers,* 19 (3), pp. 291–310.

Hawken, S. (2008) Flooded valleys and exploded escarpments: material cycling and Sydney Harbour's new landscapes. *Topos,* 63, pp. 48–57.

Hawken, S. (2009a) Ballast Point Park in Sydney. *Topos,* 69, pp. 46–51.

Hawken, S. (2009b) Cockatoo Island; Landscape architects: James Mather Delaney Design. *Landscape Architecture Australia,* 124 (November), pp. 56–59.

Hunter, C. (2011) *Consultation for Hidden Garden development.* To: C. Heatherington.

JMDD (2008) *Cockatoo Island Clifftop Walk, Sydney Harbour.* Sydney, JMDD. Available from: www.jmddesign.com.au/wordpress/wp-content/uploads/2009/04/cockatoo-island-clifftop-walk_72dpi.pdf [Accessed 17 June 2011].

Jorgensen, A. & Tylecote, M. (2007) Ambivalent landscapes – Wilderness in the urban interstices. *Landscape Research,* 32 (4), pp. 443–462.

Kapusta, B. (2005) Second nature: Seeing the blight. *Azure: Design Architecture and Art,* 21 (162), pp. 72–73.

Kirkwood, N. (2001) *Manufactured sites: Rethinking the post-industrial landscape.* London: Spon Press.

Kirkwood, N. (2004) *Weathering and durability in landscape architecture: Fundamentals, practices and case studies.* Hoboken, NJ: John Wiley & Sons.

Kowarik, I. & Langer, A. (2005) Natur-Park Südgelände: Linking conservation and recreation in an abandoned rail yard in Berlin. In: I. Kowarik & S. Körner (Eds.) *Wild urban woodlands: New perspectives for urban forestry.* Berlin: Springer, pp. 287–299.

Krauel, J. (2008) *Urban spaces: New city parks.* Barcelona: Links.

Lamb, Z. (2007) *Backlands post-industrial urban wildlands in Berlin.* Zachary Lamb, MIT. Available from: http://architecture.mit.edu/class/nature/student_projects/2007/zlamb/urban-nature/sudgelande/culturallandscape.html [Accessed 15 June 2011].

Langer, A. (2012) Pure urban nature: The Südgelände Nature Park, Berlin. In: A. Jorgensen & R. Keenan (Eds.) *Urban wildscapes.* London: Routledge, pp. 152–159.

Latz, P. (2001) Landscape Park Duisburg-Nord: The metamorphosis of an industrial site. In: N. Kirkwood (Ed.) *Manufactured sites: Rethinking the post-industrial landscape.* London: Spon Press, pp. 150–161.

Leppert, S. (1998) Landscaftspark Duisburg-Nord, Germany. *Domus,* 802, pp. 32–37.

LVRPA (1987) *Lee Valley Regional Park Authority, Development Committee 5 Feb. 1987, paper no. D345. Middlesex Filter Beds – Management Plan. Report by the Chief Executive.* LVRPA.

LVRPA (1988) *A Management Plan for the Middlesex Filter Beds, Lee Valley Regional Park Authority, Countryside Service.* LVRPA.

LVRPA (2012) *Lee Valley Regional Park: Park Development Framework. Thematic Proposals for Community, Landscape and Heritage and Environment.* LVRPA.

LVRPA Countryside Officer (1989) *Lee Valley Regional Park Authority, 31/1/1989, internal memorandum, from Countryside Officer to senior landscape architect, acting head ranger.* LVRPA.

Martin, G. (2009) New York's hanging gardens. *The Observer*, Sunday 8 November 2009. Available from: www.theguardian.com/world/2009/nov/08/highline-new-york-garden-martin [Accessed 22 November 2014].

McGregor Coxall (2011) *Personal communication, Ballast Point Park.* To: C. Heatherington.

McGregor Coxall (2010) *Ballast Point Park.* Available from: www.mcgregorcoxall. com [Accessed 22 April 2010].

Padua, M. (2003) Industrial strength. *Landscape Architecture,* 93 (6), pp. 76–86.

PaulK. (2011). Pollokshields, mid-eighties. *The Hidden Glasgow Forums.* Available from: www.hiddenglasgow.com/forums/viewtopic.php?f=31&t=10939 [Accessed 3 March 2013].

Pearson, L., Clifford, A. & Minutillo, J. (2009) Two projects that work hand in hand, the High Line and the Standard New York bring life to New York's West Side. *Architectural Record,* 197 (10), pp. 84–95.

Pell, S. (2002) *From refuse to refuge.* Charlottesville, C-Ville Holdings. Available from: www.dirtstudio.com/press_allpress.php [Accessed 13 June 2010].

Pike, K. (1991) *Notes made for research for Middlesex Filter Beds Site Guide.* LVRPA Archive.

Pirzio-Biroli, L. (2004) Adaptive re-use, layering of meaning on sites of industrial ruin. *Arcade,* 23 (Winter), pp. 28–31.

Reece, E. (2007) *Reclaiming a toxic legacy through art and science.* Great Barrington, Orion Magazine. Available from: www.orionmagazine.org/index.php/articles/article/460 [Accessed 8 August 2011].

Reynolds, P. (2008) *Ballast Point, Dictionary of Sydney.* Available from: http://dictionaryofsydney.org/entry/ballast_point [Accessed 26 June 2017].

Roscher, R. (2011) *Personal communication, The Hidden Gardens.* To: C. Heatherington.

Royal Commission on the Ancient and Historical Monuments of Scotland (2014) *Glasgow, 552 Pollokshaws Road, Coplaw horse-tram depot.* Available from: http://canmore.rcahms.gov.uk/en/site/150610/digital_images/glasgow+522+pollokshaws+road+coplaw+horse+tram+depot/ [Accessed 14 June 2012].

RSPB (2011) *Rainham Marshes, our work here.* RSPB. Available from: www.rspb. org.uk/discoverandenjoynature/seenature/reserves/guide/r/rainhammarshes/work. aspx [Accessed 18 November 2014].

RSPB (Not known) *The rifle range story.* RSPB, pp. 1–4.

Saunders, W. (Ed.) (2012) *Designed ecologies, the landscape architecture of Kongjian Yu.* Basel: Birkhäuser.

Scotland's Places (Not known) *Glasgow, 522 Pollokshaws Road, Coplaw Horse-tram Depot.* Available from: www.scotlandsplaces.gov.uk/record/rcahms/150610/glasgow-522-pollokshaws-road-coplaw-horse-tram-depot/rcahms?item=1027168#carousel [Accessed 14 June 2014].

Semple, I. & Semple, A. (2014) *Glasgow transport 1871–1973, Glasgow car works and depots.* Available from: www.semple.biz/glasgow/copelawhill%20depot.shtml [Accessed 14 June 2014].

Simon, K. (2010) Ballast Point Park. *Architecture Australia,* 99 (No. 3 May/June), pp. 95–102.

Stake, R., E (1995) *The art of case study reseach*. Thousand Oaks, CA: Sage Publications.

Stalter, R. (2004) The flora on the High Line, New York City, New York. *Journal of the Torrey Botanical Society,* 131 (4), pp. 387–393.

Sternfeld, J. (2000) *Walking the High Line*. The official website of the High Line and Friends of the High Line. Available from: www.thehighline.org/galleries/images/joel-sternfeld [Accessed 27 April 2010].

Swanton, D. (2012) Afterimages of steel: Dortmund. *Space and Culture,* 15 (4), pp. 264–282.

The Hidden Gardens (2011–2014) *Artworks*. Available from: http://thehiddengardens. org.uk/artwork-of-the-hidden-gardens.php [Accessed 30 November 2016].

Thurrock Council (2004) *Visionary Thurrock*. Available from: www.visionarythurrock. org.uk/docs/examples/landpark/index.html [Accessed 22 January 2010].

Transport Trust (Not known) *Coplawhill Tramcar Works and Depot, Glasgow*. Available from: www.transportheritage.com/find-heritage-locations.html?sobi2Ta sk=sobi2Details&catid=128&sobi2Id=793 [Accessed 14 June 2014].

Ulam, A., Cantor, S. L. & Martin, F. E. (2009) Back on track: Bold design moves transform a defunct railroad into a 21st century park. *Landscape Architecture,* 99 (10), pp. 90–109.

Vaughan, H. (2005) *RSPB Rainham Marshes: A potted history*. Available from: www.elbf.co.uk/rainham.htm [Accessed 18 June 2012].

Vaughan, H. (2011) *Back in the day*. Available from: www.rspb.org.uk/community/placestovisit/rainhammarshes/b/rainhammarshes-blog/archive/2011/12/02/back-in-the-day.aspx [Accessed 16 June 2014].

Weilacher, U. (2008) *Syntax of landscape: The landscape architecture of Peter Latz and Partners*. Basel: Birkhäuser.

Worman, M. (2012) *Personal communication: Interview at RSPB site*. To: C. Heatherington.

Yu, K. (2016) *Personal communication – Zhongshan Shipyard Park*. To: C. Heatherington.

4 Designing to reveal change

In this chapter I examine three overarching ways in which landscape architects incorporate the qualities of the derelict, underused and neglected (DUN) site to reveal the changes that have taken place in post-industrial landscapes. The most straightforward technique is to use materials and processes to make reference to the past, sometimes symbolically or metaphorically. Then there is a palimpsest approach in which historic layers in the landscape form part of a temporal collage. Finally, designers draw attention to changes in the landscapes through the relationships they create between the visitor and the site. Often these approaches are used in combination. However, first I consider designing from the perspective of the *tabula rasa* where practically all evidence of the previous landscape is removed, lost or hidden.

The *tabula rasa* approach

Dirlik suggests that the compulsion to erase history is an inevitable by-product of modern capitalist economics that 'has rendered places into inconveniences on the path of progress to be dispensed with, either by erasure, or ... by rendering them into commodities' (2001: 42). The *tabula rasa* approach, or the complete erasure of all evidence of the history of the site, is often precipitated by the need to remove or contain extensive contamination. In the UK in the latter part of the last century a 'dig and dump' approach predominated as is made clear in the case studies described in the Brownfields Guide (English Partnerships, 2006b).[1] Although, more recently, advances in technology have enabled remediation to take place on-site rather than removing the problem elsewhere, English Partnerships acknowledge the difficulty of meeting the expectations of developers whilst still conforming to government policy in the fields of planning and environmental regulations (English Partnerships, 2006a).

Nevertheless, it is evident that the ability to deal with contamination successfully *in situ* does not always lead to a change in attitude towards the qualities of the DUN site; the Olympic Delivery Agency, a public body responsible for all development on the high profile Olympic 2012 site in London, coined the slogan 'DEMOLISH, DIG, DESIGN' (Marrero-Guillamon, 2011), and displayed this prominently on hoardings around the site, thus implying the designer must start with a blank canvas. However, this was an extremely contaminated site, a place of heavy industry and landfill sites, criss-crossed with water channels and railways and the remediation requirements were extensive. Recent promotional material published by the UK Government points to the leading role taken by UK companies in the regeneration work: 'In total, 2.2 million square metres of soil was excavated, of which 764,000 square metres was treated by soil washing, chemical stabilisation, bioremediation or sorting. 80% of the excavated material was re-used on site as engineering fill' (Department for International Trade, 2015) (section: Case study Olympic achievement).

In fact 98% of the materials from demolition of structures and buildings were recycled (Lass and Oliver, 2012) and yet, in spite of this ability to contain and remediate contamination and to reclaim and reuse materials, there appears to be no understanding that any of the industrial heritage of the area might be worth acknowledging in the new landscape.[2]

The degree of ruination of the site when redevelopment commences can also affect the ways in which the buildings and infrastructure are treated. The further along the gradient towards complete ruination the more difficult it is to reuse material elements of the site. Peter Latz describes how, when first visiting Duisburg Nord Landscape Park, he found that the railway lines were operational, the blast furnaces had only recently been decommissioned and the iron in the foundries was still liquid (Pirzio-Biroli, 2004), even though other parts of the site were falling into ruin.

The sheer scale of the site, of the contamination and the size of the industrial buildings may also dictate how the regeneration process proceeds; the Turning the Tide project was required to address the problem of massive contamination from several mines over a large area (Durham Heritage Coast, 2006). In Country Durham when coal mining was at its peak in the 1920s there were around 300 mines (Durham Mining Museum, 2008) and it would obviously be undesirable to retain remnants of the mining industry across so many sites. J.B. Priestley, writing in 1933, described the impact on the east Durham landscape: 'darkly studded here and there with pitheads and tips' (1968: 335). A former miner, who had worked at the Easington pit on this stretch of coast for forty years, vividly described to me his journey to work, the short distance from the village to the pithead, the long descent underground in the pit cage and then being transported through tunnels to the coalface several miles out under the North Sea. He could not conceive of a scenario in which any of this vast conglomeration of industry and infrastructure could be saved or adapted for other uses; it was too all encompassing, too close to the town and too dirty.

As well as being a practical decision, the removal of all evidence of the industrial history of the site may also be dictated by a communal desire or agreement to forget. There is an assumption that in order to move away from these traditional industries and their concomitant social and political histories requires a 'modernisation of communities and removal of the vestiges of this culture from the landscape' (Davies, 2014: 41). Connerton (2008: 59) introduces the term 'prescriptive forgetting' to describe a form of forgetting that is precipitated by governments, or groups in power, for the good of the public. He suggests that this form of erasure, rather than being about loss, can be understood as 'constitutive in the formation of a new identity' (Connerton, 2008: 63). Easington is an example of how this form of forgetting is manifested; in 2005, more than a decade after the closure of the pit, Alan Burnip from the District Council proudly stated 'we have the Dalton Park retail and shopping complex built on old colliery ruins' (Northern Echo, 2005). Nevertheless, at this time, there was a high level of disillusionment, especially amongst the young men of the town, and drug use was rife.³ In spite of the promise of new landscapes and the commitment of the local council to creating jobs, Professor Ray Hudson of Durham University commented in 2002, 'it's difficult to imagine east Durham will be turned around in the foreseeable future – it's difficult to see where alternative jobs are going to come from' (Northern Echo, 2002), and in 2005 Channel 4, a UK terrestrial channel, featured Easington as one of the ten worst places to live in Britain (Hartlepool Mail, 2005).

The process of prescriptively forgetting an industry that was the focus of people's lives over many generations is not necessarily straightforward. It might seem perverse that anyone would want to be reminded of the hardships of an industrial past that often led to illness or premature death. A quote in the Guardian from 1973 seems to sum this up: '... preserve a steel mill. It killed my father, who wants to preserve that?' (Lowenthal, 1985: 430). However, Randolph Langebach when researching the history of the Lancashire cotton mills, observed that after the closure of the mills 'the dislocation and sense of loss can break down the pride and respect that ordinary citizens may have in their hometown. What they identified as being their world ceases to be a part of them' (Binney *et al.*, 1977: 25). Priestley wrote, 'I cannot help feeling that I shall be told that there is no such place' (1968: 336) when faced with the horror of the mines at Shotton, a village 20 kilometres from Easington. Perhaps, decades later, some of those left behind after the closure of the mines also feel they are being told 'there is no such place'.

Revealing the past through the use of materials and processes

A much-used way of referencing the history of a landscape is to use a palette of materials that makes reference to the site's industrial past. This is evident at Ballast Point Park where the landscape architects explained that they 'aimed to have all the detailing be fairly raw...in the vein of the Caltex engineering solutions.' (JMDD, 2011). The result is a combination of new and recycled materials; shiny metals are contrasted with rusting steel, and broken and exposed reinforced concrete with polished surfaces, creating a juxtaposition of textures and patinas. Remnants and artefacts mingled with waste in the gabion walls become intricate surfaces for visitors to explore (Harding and Hawken, 2009), much as explorers of abandoned sites search out artefacts in the debris (Edensor, 2005; Garrett, 2011). There are even metal signs mixed with the rubble; one proclaims 'manufactured by Cockatoo Dock' and another mysteriously cautions, 'check with grease plant before switching off compressor' (Figure 3.1). On a tour of Ballast Point Park led by landscape architect, Phillip Coxall, informal feedback about the park confirmed that visitors appreciated the historical elements made visible through the use of materials and signalled out the gabions for praise (Anderson, 2010).

Other sites such as Cockatoo Island, The Hidden Gardens and Rainham Marshes all draw on an industrial palette, and in the Hidden Gardens gabions filled with bricks from the demolished buildings form retaining walls. Designers of the High Line had hoped to recycle the timber and ballast from the old railway tracks but found it to be so contaminated with asbestos that it needed to be removed from the site and washed before being made safe, so they made the decision to use new stone and timber (Martin, 2009). Nevertheless rather than using wood chippings as a mulch they have chosen a volcanic stone to echo the qualities of the original ballast (Ulam *et al.*, 2009). In phase three, the section of the site most recently opened in 2014, a consolidated gravel surface merges with the bespoke stone paving, inlaid in places with the original rail tracks, thus making more explicit reference to the site's history than is seen in earlier phases of the project.

Although the use of an industrial palette of materials is commonplace, there has been little research into how visitors to these sites make sense of these ways of revealing the past. Treib (2002, 2011), when referring to the use of vernacular materials and buildings, points out that the appropriation and reframing of materials in a new context divorces them from their original meanings; one cannot predict how such metaphors and symbols will be understood. It is reasonable to suppose that this might also apply to the industrial palette. In a plural society where we come from diverse backgrounds with multiple cultural reference points, it is not possible for a designer to imbue a landscape with meaning; meaning is always personal (Treib, 2002).[4] Lynch (1972), however, suggests there is value in retaining landmarks and topographical forms as familiar elements to anchor the mind in an otherwise changing landscape. Perhaps these very visible and structural material qualities are comparable to a monument: inducing a collective remembering. However, monuments are often in danger of becoming a part of everyday life, something to walk past and ignore (Crinson, 2005, p. xvii). It is only by re-remembering, for example at an anniversary, that they can retain their mnemonic power. DeSilvey (2010) suggests that research into the memories engendered by preserved and displayed historical artefacts demonstrates that such memories cannot be controlled. It is not always possible to contain 'the practice of memory with any precision' (DeSilvey, 2010: 492). This raises questions about the use designers make of material or spatial qualities to make symbolic reference to past histories; are these symbols, like the monument, in danger of being overlooked or ignored?

The Turning the Tide pit cage memorial is an example of the symbolic monument, standing as a reminder of the industrial history of the area. However, the link is tenuous between this sanitised, static structure placed on the cliff top and the erased pithead and extensive mining works. The former miner, who had started his shift at the pithead for so many years, commented 'I don't know what the bugger that's about!' Similarly, the chimney at the Hidden Gardens is also intended as a reminder. However, although the retention of an artefact can be seen as a way of maintaining continuity and familiarity, work ceased at the Tramworks in the early 1960s and it seems unlikely that many people will remember the working site and the chimney, or have any understanding of its original purpose.

A more complex use of the material qualities is to repurpose them: creating new features that make metaphorical reference to the processes that have shaped the sites' histories. At Ballast Point Park the sculptural representation of the oil tank, complete with its poetical inscription, uses wind turbines to make reference to the changes in the processes of energy production from oil and gas to wind (Simon, 2010). In a similar vein at Südgelände the linear walkway of rusting steel and metal mesh is reminiscent of the ghostly traces of the original railway lines that can be glimpsed running through the tall grasses and between the silver birches on either side (Figure 3.4). Both the past and the future are referenced in the Zhongshan water tower that is trapped in its solar glass box; the preserved concrete structure reminds us of the site's history whilst a glimpse of the future is reflected in the glass case that absorbs solar energy in order to light the structure at night (Saunders, 2012). Many of the design interventions at Duisburg Nord also involve the repurposing and recycling of materials and just one is singled out here to illustrate again the idea of process. The iron plates in the Piazza Metallica are grooved, chipped and distorted by the processes that they underwent in the casting works where they had to withstand extreme temperatures, and Latz's (2001) intention is that these processes will continue, albeit at a much less intensive pace.

Designers also repurpose material structures, tracks and artefacts for more playful uses: here the revealing and interpretation of history is of secondary interest. The sunbeds move along rail tracks on the High Line (Pearson *et al.*, 2009) with a nod to the transportation history of the site and the exposed steel girders that support the park itself are playfully encased in colourful plastic to allow children to indulge in slightly risky play activities (David and Hammond, 2012) (Figure 3.3). The stone circle known as the Hackney Henge is much used by visiting children for climbing, jumping and imaginary games (Figure 4.1) and at Duisburg Nord the ore bunker walls

Figure 4.1 The 'Hackney Henge' at the Middlesex Filter Beds

have become 'rock faces of a mountain scenery' (Kirkwood, 2001: 151). As well as adding climbing holds to the walls of the bunkers, free-climbers can ascend using just the 'cracks and scars formed by the ore ripping the surfaces of the concrete' (Kirkwood, 2001: 151).

Vegetation and decaying material structures and artefacts are incorporated in the developed landscapes to signal the ways in which processes make reference to past histories, particularly in those sites that retain the vegetation that established during the period of abandonment. The indeterminate nature of Südgelände and the Middlesex Filter Beds is reinforced through the temporal qualities of the DUN landscapes; process and rhythms of change are made visible to the visitor through the retention and management of this successional vegetation. Both sites also strive to maintain a balance between the decaying material qualities and the encroaching vegetation and in Chapter 9 I discuss the implications that this approach to temporality entails.

An unexpected example of process made visible through vegetation, whilst also referencing the site's history, is found at Duisburg Nord where seeds, brought in with the iron ore have established themselves to form an important element of the ecology of the site (Pirzio-Biroli, 2004). However, it is not only spontaneous vegetation that can make reference to these tem-poral qualities; on the High Line, Piet Oudolf evokes the wild communities of the original DUN site – 'nature appears in a seemingly random and untamed fashion' (Ulam *et al.*, 2009: 92). As James Corner explains, Oudolf 'sort of dismembered the original meadow … and then put it back,' (Martin, 2009: 42). The designers have used the spatial qualities of the derelict site – the linearity and the way in which the landscape is raised above the city – as the basis of an innovative landscape design that makes visible the interweaving of material qualities and temporal processes.

Cathy Dee, in her paper examining the teaching of design, puts forward the suggestion that designers should 'treat landscape forms as *trajectories*' (2010: 28); they are created by processes and have the potential to continue changing in the future. Within landscapes 'form has the potential to speak of multiple timeframes' (Dee, 2010: 28). These changes may be natural, seasonal and climatic, or they may be wrought by individuals. Dee sets a challenge to designers to work with such dynamic forms that reveal processes through their materiality, maybe in exaggerated or abstract ways, to 'throw into relief time, whether of cosmological, geological, hydrological, vegetative, or human lifespan' (Dee, 2010: 29). Latz's eroded iron plates in the Piazza Metallica epitomise this but a more immediate example is found at Zhongshan where the tidal terraces change their form twice each day (Beardsley, 2012), drawing attention to the natural processes whilst also reminding the visitor that this site is connected by the river to the sea and is also therefore connected to its history as a shipyard.

In a similar fashion at Vintondale the forms of the trees – specifically their autumn colour – and the earthworks draw attention to both historic and present processes; the temporal qualities are evident in both the seasonal and the remediation processes. There is also an implied trajectory into a future where the land is less polluted and has taken on new forms and new processes; the dramatic discontinuity caused by the extreme contamination of the landscape, is referenced – and partially healed – in the new design, as the process of water purification is made explicit. Bargmann does not see these new forms and processes in juxtaposition to the previous industrial uses of the site but as a continuation of this history. She explores the ways such sites were 'wired with interesting flows of raw and manufactured materials' (Kirkwood, 2004: 70) and is concerned with rewiring the flows in the developing landscape through an examination of both the site and its context. However, I do not suggest that all visitors to the Litmus Garden will recognise and understand these particular processes through the forms of the landscape. For the local community this is part of their history and as such is one stage on a continuous trajectory, but for people visiting the area for the first time it may be understood as a beautiful and seemingly natural landscape.

Incorporating time layers – the palimpsest approach

Traditionally a palimpsest is defined as a paper or parchment where the old writing has been scraped off to make room for the new layer, sometimes leaving traces of the initial writing behind (Shorter Oxford English

Dictionary, 1993). The archaeologist O. G. S Crawford applied this idea to landscape comparing it with:

> A document that has been written on and erased over and over again ... But it is not always easy to read ... because, whereas the vellum document was seldom wiped clean more than once or twice, the land has been subject to continual change throughout the ages.
>
> (1953: 51)

As the concept of the landscape as palimpsest has been extended and utilised by archaeologists, anthropologists and geographers, the definition needs refining. For the archaeologist the geological layers of a landscape are read in order to understand the history of the area, however, any reading of landscape in this way is dependent on the individual layers remaining intact and decipherable (Bailey, 2007). If the palimpsest metaphor for landscape is to be useful it is necessary to move away from a chronological layering to a more intertwined entanglement of incomplete material traces, both natural and cultural, from different temporalities. Crang (1996) explores a practical application with reference to the city of Bristol, suggesting that history is inscribed in the urban landscape through a continuous stream of cultural and natural processes. He underlines the role that can be played by both the expert and the ordinary person in interpreting everyday landscapes: 'the past remains in the detail of the present and can be retrieved from the everyday world' (Crang, 1996: 430).

In addition to this understanding of landscape as an intermingling of tangible activities and materials, any reinterpretation of the palimpsest metaphor must consider the intangible memories and experiences that form a significant part of people's understanding and perception of a place. In Cormac McCarthy's novel *The Road* Godfrey (2011) describes how memories are graphically emplaced in a post-apocalyptic landscape through which a father and son are travelling. Blackened stumps and grey empty tracts of land evoke memories of former meadows and orchards, but 'these things exist only in the father's mind, creating a scene before him that is indeed a haunting topographical palimpsest' (Godfrey, 2011: 170).

This expanded metaphor of the palimpsest is particularly appropriate to a discussion of former DUN landscapes where dramatic changes have had an impact on local residents' lives giving rise to diverse and multiple narratives (Heatherington et al., 2017). Lynch's (1972) term 'temporal collage', rather than palimpsest, makes clear the intermingling that occurs between time layers and he cautions us to 'expect to see conflicting views of the past, based on the conflicting values of the present' (Lynch, 1972: 53). This raises the question of choice and intention; the designers and developers of these landscapes must take potentially controversial decisions about which elements of the history of the site to make visible and which to leave hidden. There may also be a question, when restoring a landscape, of how far back to go; which layer of history is the one of value that should be displayed? Natural processes also affect this temporal collage; the erasing of evidence of change is not exclusively a human action and in DUN sites processes of decay and ruination leave tangible marks on the landscape that contribute to the changing narratives. Summing up the value of the palimpsest metaphor, Layne writes:

> If human stories are indeed written into landscape stories, and vice versa, then the palimpsest can serve as a powerful rhetorical device to bring the multiple stories at work under consideration, without dictating that one aspect be subservient to another.
>
> (Layne, 2014: 67)

The political nature of choices made by a designer is especially evident in the Chinese case study; Padua writes that 'episodes like the Cultural Revolution and Tiananmen Square have left the Chinese people with historical blind spots ... there is a collective effort to banish them from memory' (2003: 78). At Zhongshan Shipyard Park, Yu is attempting, through design, to make aspects of twentieth century history visible again (Beardsley, 2012). He challenges the prevailing view that the industrial past is not important with his presentation of structures and artefacts and he includes the dramatic red box as a place to contemplate the impact of the Cultural Revolution (Padua, 2003).

This reference to such a controversial period of history could be considered bold; at Duisburg some have questioned whether the new landscape has effectively erased, or at the very least selectively avoided, a history some would prefer to forget – the links between the Thyssen steelworks and the Nazi era. There have been suggestions that Jews were compelled to work as slave labour (Berger, 2009) and Fritz Thyssen is known to have provided finance for Hitler during the 1930s before falling out with him in 1941 (Aris and Campbell, 2004). Hargreaves too suggests Duisburg tells an incomplete narrative thus becoming a 'troubling celebration of the industrial sublime' (Hargreaves, 2007: 165). Nevertheless, Langhorst maintains that the region's industrial history can be read in the park (2004). The dramatic rusting structures and artefacts are very visible reminders and there is an interweaving of old and new evident in the bunkers, for example, where Latz has designed gardens and climbing walls. He confirms the palimpsestic nature of his work asserting that 'landscape is composed of a wealth of selectable information layers covering one another up and presenting themselves as coincidental images only to the beholder,' (Pirzio-Biroli, 2004: 31). Processes are also revealed in the juxtapositions of successional vegetation and rusting metal, and in the water recycling systems. These allude not only to the past but also to the ways the site might develop in the future; the vegetation and water systems are helping to mitigate the contamination of the site. This is a landscape open to change and to new ways of understanding the relationships between the human and the non-human (Langhorst, 2004). It is important to embrace the possibility of future change rather than attempt to stifle it. As Lynch reminds us, 'an environment that cannot be changed invites its own destruction (1972: 39).

At Ballast Point Park the designers aimed to 'use the site's identifying components and work with them to keep the entire history of the site visible' (McGregor Coxall, 2011). The palimpsestic nature of the site is made evident in the relationships the designers have created between the material, spatial and temporal qualities and new layers in the landscape. The concrete foundations of structures and buildings on the site and the cuts in the sandstone cliffs of the harbour are exposed (Hawken, 2009) and thus retain the potential to remind the visitor of the changes wrought by the industrial past. The oil tanks have been removed but are remembered by their grass footprints and the display case holds material remnants and artefacts from the Villa Menevia, presenting the past in an almost museum-like fashion. However, the creation of this palimpsest landscape at Ballast Point Park has not been without controversy. Former Australian Prime Minister Paul Keating, a strong voice in planning issues concerning sites around the Sydney Harbour, believes that rather than revealing the relatively recent history, sites should be taken back to their pre-European forms. In a speech in 2007 he asserts that the foreshore should be returned to: 'That which most approximates the natural environment as it might have obtained before 1788 ... I believe there's only one compelling heritage interest ... the pre-colonial configuration of the foreshore' (DHub, 2007).

Aside from the obvious fact that to attempt to reinstate sandstone cliffs that have been blasted and hewn away would be impossible, we must also question whether we want these sites and their difficult pasts to be sanitised or 'are we interested in all of the competing truths of their history?' (Harding and Hawken, 2009: 44). The choice of which time layers and which material, spatial and temporal qualities should be included in the new landscape becomes a choice of which stories to tell, which histories to reveal and which to suppress or ignore.

Designers create palimpsests landscapes in two ways; I call these natural and abstracted palimpsests. In the former, designers choose to leave material and spatial qualities from the DUN site *in situ* and create the new landscape around them. Natural palimpsests include those at the Middlesex Filter Beds, Rainham Marshes and Südgelände where the topography of the DUN site and the material structures and artefacts are largely unchanged. New interventions are designed to be separate from these remnants of the past. Peter Beard (2011), designer of parts of the Rainham Marshes site, described to me his philosophy for working with DUN sites: 'If you're talking about derelict buildings you just let them get on with what they do, [there are] other places where you make obviously new gestures, other places where you modify or adjust or seek to repair'.

These sites most closely relate to the derelict landscape, where the material structures gradually decay and there is a merging of the natural and the cultural worlds. I also place Cockatoo Island into this category, walkways are constructed as an explicit new layer on top of or adjacent to the existing spatial qualities and material structures of the industrial landscape, leaving them relatively unchanged. These natural palimpsests contribute to the possible stories that comprise a place at any one time (Massey, 2005). However, as the sites are subject to processes of decay and succession, evidence of pastness is obscured and even eventually lost, thus the stories also change, vanish, and are replaced and invented anew.

In creating an abstracted palimpsest the designer makes a choice about which material, spatial and temporal qualities of the DUN site to use within the new design, creating intentional juxtapositions between the old, the new and the invented, sometimes making these contrasts explicit and at others blurring the boundaries of the time layers. As I have mentioned above they are also making a choice about the inclusion of possible stories that might then contribute to an understanding of the place. Ballast Point Park, the High Line and Zhongshan Shipyard Park exemplify the abstracted palimpsest with their combination of existing structures and new interventions. Duisburg Nord straddles both categories of palimpsest; successional planting, rusty decaying buildings and old walkways over the existing bunkers remain much as they were in the DUN landscape. However, there are new interventions that make explicit the boundary between the time layers: the metal plates at the Piazza Metallica; the mix of new gardens and successional planting; the grid of ornamental trees planted in recycled rubble.

Revealing the past through relationships

In both the natural and the abstracted palimpsest the juxtapositions between the intermingled elements of the temporal collage contribute to the complexity of the design and are open to different interpretations. I use the term *time edge* to describe these juxtapositions. This word is mentioned by Relph when referring to research carried out by a graduate student; he explains that a time edge occurs when there is a 'abrupt juxtaposition' (2004: 114) between one time period and another. The palimpsest at Ballast Point Park contains many explicit time edges: the juxtapositions between the footprints of the oil tanks and the grass lawns; the rough concrete next to the cut sandstone; the polished concrete door frame beside the rough aggregate; the gabions filled with rubble and artefacts next to sleek concrete and metal (Figure 3.1). In contrast with these abrupt juxtapositions there are other sites where the time edges become gradually blurred, for example at Rainham Marshes where vegetation managed primarily to attract wildlife gradually encroaches on and slowly destroys the mantlet banks and the cordite store.

However, the juxtapositions between time periods evident in these detailed and usually smaller-scale time edges are just one form of relationship to be found in these landscapes. There are relationships between the site and its surroundings, between visitors and the site and between different elements within the site. International designer, George Hargreaves, is partly known for his innovative work with post-industrial and former military sites such as Byxbee Park and Crissy Field.[5] Anita Berrizbeitia describes how, for Hargreaves, relationships between the landscape and its surroundings are fundamental to an understanding of the site: 'The meaning of the work is not to be found within it, but relocated to the outside, to those things and attributes of the surrounding world that explain the work and give it its logic and poetics' (Hargreaves *et al.*, 2009: 62).

Raxworthy (2008) is interested in the way designers create landscapes that place the visitor in a relationship with the site's history – in this book's terminology, its material, spatial and temporal qualities. He examines in detail the concept of a place being formed through relations between the human and the non-human in both space and time and suggests that by determining the ways in which visitors move through the landscape, designers can encourage engagement with the 'histories and processes that developed the material qualities' (Raxworthy, 2008: 74) of the site. Raxworthy gives, as an example, another park on Sydney Harbour, BP Park, where McGregor Coxall have suspended a curved metal walkway above the sandstone cliffs that were once cut to contain an oil tank. The view is to the Harbour Bridge. Raxworthy explains that the 'site's history is present in this act because changing environmental worldviews would make such a violation of the Harbour today unthinkable' (2008: 76). In later chapters I examine this concept in more detail and explore how visitors interpret these relationships and use them to create a frame for reading through which to interpret the history of the site (Treib, 2002).

Raxworthy's relationship approach can be used to describe aspects of the design of the High Line, Zhongshan Shipyard Park, Ballast Point Park, Cockatoo Island and Duisburg Nord as well as, to a lesser extent, the Middlesex Filter Beds and Rainham Marshes. At Ballast Point the designers have sliced through the existing bund walls of the industrial site to reveal their construction and to create entrances and access routes (Hawken, 2009). A slab of concrete is felled like a tree and then placed on the ground as a step and walkway between the cut walls (Figure 4.2). The designers lined up the opening with a remaining oil tank on the opposite side of the Harbour. By this means the visitor experiences the time edge between old and new materials as they walk through the opening whilst also having their gaze directed to the history of the Harbour beyond. The designers of the landscape on Cockatoo Island also acknowledge the importance of relationships between the visitor and the old and new layers. The walkway forms an explicit time edge, drawing attention to the spatial qualities of the site, the different time layers, and also, by its temporary nature, points to the possibility of future changes. In projects of this type the designers told me that they seek to:

> Maintain the scale, eccentricity and matter of factness of these spaces. The journey through these spaces then becomes very important, how one interacts, moves through, over and around these spaces is the way in which we can allow the sites to reveal their qualities and that is how we gain meaning from [them].
>
> (JMDD, 2011)

Cockatoo Island, with its multiple intertwining layers of history, does not reveal its meanings easily. The walkway raises the visitor up to the level of the grain silos, hewn high in the sandstone cliff by convicts, and we can read the stories of how they were built, but we are left to ask why these silos are sliced through vertically. Peter Carey (2008) explains, when an extra building was needed a new slice of sandstone was hacked away, cutting the silos in half, and paradoxically leaving them open and visible to any present-day visitor. When Carey visited there was no walkway and he had to squash up against the now abandoned machine shop and strain the eye upwards to make out the sliced silos.

At Zhongshan Shipyard Park, visitors walking through Yu's green boxes are able to reimagine the lives of workers living there: to experience the spatial qualities of these hedged enclosures that make reference to former dormitories. The designers have also created relationships between the visitor and the site that draw the surrounding landscape into the park. This is particularly evident in the tidal terraces and the island of banyan trees; relationships are created between the visitor and the wider riverine landscape and ultimately, the sea. Although the paved terraces flood twice a day with the tides, visitors can walk close to the water's edge along paths that are sometimes under water (Figure 4.3) (Saunders, 2012). Some visitors, crossing to the island, may also be aware of how the channel between the park and the banyan tree island helps with flood mitigation.

At Rainham Marshes, Beard dictates the ways in which people move around the site through a system of paths and decked walkways.[6] Although these walkways run close to material qualities such as the shooting range, mantlet banks and lookout tower, the visitor cannot experience these artefacts directly; they are visible over fences or through the reeds. It is only the roofless enclosure of the cordite store that is accessible. However, the paths and boardwalks do serve to highlight the relationship between the site and the wider landscape. The horizontal marshland and estuarine nature of the surroundings gives the impression that this is a landscape without borders, one where marsh merges with industry and transportation. The linear boardwalks within the site reflect the forms of this surrounding transport infrastructure, and vistas along the long straight walkways seem to draw disparate signs of the twenty-first century into the RSPB site. Rising in

Figure 4.2 Cuts in concrete bund wall to create entrance and step at Ballast Point
Park

Figure 4.3 The tidal terraces at Zhongshan Shipyard Park

Source: photo by Yu Kongjian

the west is a working landfill site formed of much of the waste of North London and to the north, above the reeds, is the busy A13 and the Channel Tunnel Rail Link. The sound of trains and trucks is a constant backdrop to the birdcalls. The visitor walks under humming pylons that stretch across the site from east to west taking energy to London. A possible future is also visible further beyond the marshes to the west in the form of a group of wind turbines and within a decade the landfill site will be closed and a gradual process to return it to a natural landscape will commence.[7]

At Duisburg the relationship between the site and its surroundings also clearly tells the story of the history of the area. This relationship becomes visible when experiencing the material qualities of the rusting blast furnace; at the summit the visitor is greeted with views clearly revealing how the rail tracks running through the site traverse the landscape before connecting with the River Emscher (Latz and Latz, 2001). In places close to the site these tracks form the new cycle paths and walkways leading into and through the park; in the distance they point to the industrial history of the area – on the horizon there are still working factories and furnaces. To ensure that the rail tracks continue to contribute to the narrative, Latz has instructed that they should be mown and kept clear of opportunist vegetation (Weilacher, 2008).

The spatial qualities of the derelict landscape at the Middlesex Filter Beds and Südgelände dictate the relationship between the visitor and the site. The decaying walls and walkways that make up the Filter Beds and the minimal use of railings to prevent access (LVRPA, 1987) contribute to the site's indeterminate nature and encourage diverse uses. However, the topography counteracts this by dictating the routes taken by the visitor and discouraging entry to the beds themselves in order to protect the vegetation and wildlife. Visitors are raised up above the beds and walk on the existing walls and paths, thus the spatial relationship allows them to experience temporal qualities evident in the establishment of different types of successional vegetation whilst also imparting a sense of the importance of protecting these habitats. Similarly at Südgelände, the pathways and access routes, that in places follow the existing topography of the DUN site, place people in relationships with the temporal processes of succession and decay.

In this chapter I have explored in detail some of the material, spatial and temporal qualities that I discussed in Chapter 3 and I have discussed the different ways in which designers seek to incorporate these into their redeveloped landscapes. I now turn to the experiences of the visitors and examine their interpretations in order to evaluate how successful these different approaches to the inclusion of the qualities might be. I begin with the first interlude 'Musing on the Tracks', in which I describe my encounters with the Middlesex Filter Beds and, whilst pondering on the function of some of the artefacts I found there, I examine the process of my own thinking and engagement with these remnants.

Notes

1 Although this document was published in 2006 it includes comprehensive information about the problems facing developers of brownfield sites, case studies and advice about good practice. It can be accessed through the Cl:aire website, an industry organisation for sustainable land reuse (English Partnerships, 2006b).

2 In fact there is mention of the cultural heritage of the area prior to industrialisation and an archaeological investigation that unearthed four bodies in an Iron Age cemetery and 4,000-year-old flint axes, gunning posts from the First World War and a Roman era wall (Lass, M. & Oliver, K., 2012).

3 Statistics for the Easington Local Authority (Nomis, 2005) showed that 45.8% of those claiming Job Seekers Allowance were aged 18–24 compared with a national average of 29.7% and Easington had one of the highest rates of economic inactivity in Britain at 32% compared with 22% nationally. Economically inactive people are those who are neither employed nor registered as unemployed, however, it does not necessarily indicate that they do not want to work.

4 Treib (2002) notes that referencing the vernacular is seen as a way of focusing on the world around about as it really is, but suggests that designers take no account of the makeshift nature of the vernacular building and the fact that often they have not been designed to last. This suggests an interesting parallel with the ruin, rather than with the industrial buildings when they were in use. The quotidian nature of the derelict and the temporality of the ruined site are qualities that are not necessarily evidenced in industrial materials such as galvanised steel and polished concrete.

5 At both Byxbee Park and Crissy Field, Hargreaves and his team (Hargreaves *et al.*, 2009) have focused on the spatial qualities of the abandoned sites. Byxbee is a capped former landfill site and interventions include a series of hillocks stretching across the open landscape and a field of telegraph poles that reference the former power lines crossing the site. The intention was that as the landfill decomposed and settled the height of the poles would change, thus reflecting the changing topography. Unfortunately this did not happen. This use of changing material forms to reflect both the history of the site and the processes that shaped and are still shaping the landscape is a compelling example of Dee's (2010) assertion that material forms can be designed to allude to different time frames. Crissy Field in San Francisco was a historic military aviation site and an important marshland ecosystem with views to the Golden Gate Bridge. Here Hargreaves Associates (Hargreaves *et al.*, 2009) used juxtapositions and the form of the airfield itself to create meaning and to highlight the interrelationships between the natural processes, history and culture.

6 Beard has also designed a series of simple footpaths and metal bridges outside the RSPB site itself that lead from Rainham Village, across the railway tracks by means of a sweeping footbridge, and through the marshes to the River Thames. This has ensured that the people of Rainham can again access the river, something that has not been possible for decades due to the military presence and the industrialisation of the area. At points on the walk there are simple blocks of concrete that form seats and also large mysterious carved numbers – 100, 200, 300 etc. – that lie in the long grass. These numbers mark the 100-yard intervals at which the ridges occur. Soldiers used these ridges for protection when they were shooting at the distant targets. Similar ridges are visible on the RSPB site – see Chapter 3.

7 When the landfill site closes there are proposals to develop the site as open space. The closure and gradual greening of the site will also affect the RSPB's

management of the surrounding areas. The landfill attracts a large number of corvids (crows, rooks, magpies etc.) that find the nesting birds on the wetland to be a source of convenient snacks. Initially the policy was to manage the site to increase the numbers of lapwings, however this policy has been revised; lapwing chicks were constantly predated and often none survived the nesting season.

References

Anderson, L. (2010) *Peninsular Precinct News Birchgrove.* Sydney. Available from: www.leichhardt.nsw.gov.au/IgnitionSuite/uploads/docs/Peninsula%20Precinct%20 News%20Dec.pdf [Accessed 11 January 2011].

Aris, B. & Campbell, D. (2004) How Bush's grandfather helped Hitler's rise to power. *The Guardian,* Saturday 25 September 2004. Available from: www.guardian. co.uk/world/2004/sep/25/usa.secondworldwar [Accessed 8 August 2010].

Bailey, G. (2007) Time perspectives, palimpsests and the archaeology of time. *Journal of Anthropological Archaeology,* 26 (2), pp. 198–223.

Beard, P. (2011) *Personal communication – Rainham Marshes.* To: C. Heatherington.

Beardsley, J. (2012) Popular aesthetics, public history. In: W. Saunders (Ed.) *Designed ecologies, the landscape architecture of Kongjian Yu.* Basel: Birkhäuser, pp. 10–19.

Berger, A. (2009) *Keynote speech: Scalar ruins: 4 systemic projects.* Eclas, Landscape & Ruins, Planning and design for the regeneration of derelict places, September 2009, The University of Genova.

Binney, M., Fitzgerald, R., Langebach, R. & Powell, K. (1977) *Satanic mills: Industrial architecture in the Pennines.* London: SAVE Britain's Heritage.

Carey, P. (2008) *30 days in Sydney.* London: Bloomsbury.

Connerton, P. (2008) Seven types of forgetting. *Memory Studies,* 1 (1), Elsevier B.V., pp. 59–71. Available from: www.scopus.com/inward/record.url?eid=2-s2.0-405490 93962&partnerID=40&md5=2f88ad157671d58e569ca8567c6f1900 [Accessed 8 August 2011].

Crang, M. (1996) Envisioning urban histories: Bristol as palimpsest, postcards, and snapshots. *Environment and Planning A,* 28 (3), pp. 429–452.

Crawford, O. (1953) *Archaeology in the field.* London: Phoenix House.

Crinson, M. (2005) Urban Memory: An introduction. In: M. Crinson (Ed.) *Urban memory: History and amnesia in the modern city.* London: Routledge, pp. xi–xxiii.

David, J. & Hammond, R. (2012) *The uncut story of the High Line: Josh and Rob in conversation.* High Line Symposium, The Garden Museum, London.

Davies, C. (2014) Old culture and damaged landscapes. In: M. Roe & K. Taylor (Eds.) *New cultural landscapes.* London: Routledge, pp. 41–48.

Dee, C. (2010) Form, utility, and the aesthetics of thrift in design education. *Landscape Journal,* 29 (1), pp. 21–35.

Department for International Trade (2015) *Land remediation: Bringing brownfield sites back to use.* www.gov.uk. Available from: https://www.gov.uk/government/ publications/land-remediation-bringing-brownfield-sites-back-to-use/land-remediation-bringing-brownfield-sites-back-to-use [Accessed 30 November 2016].

DeSilvey, C. (2010) Memory in motion: Soundings from Milltown, Montana. *Social and Cultural Geography,* 11 (5), pp. 491–510.

DHub (2007) *Paul Keating on the design of East Darling Harbour.* Sydney, Powerhouse Museum. Available from: www.dhub.org/articles/932 [Accessed 17 June 2011].

Dirlik, A. (2001) Place-based imagination. In: R. Praznaik & A. Dirlik (Eds.) *Places and politics in an age of globalization.* Lanham, MD: Rowman and Littlefield, pp. 15–51.

Durham Heritage Coast (2006) *Turning the Tide.* Durham County Council. Available from: www.durhamheritagecoast.org/dhc/usp.nsf/pws/Durham+Heritage+Coast+-+Durham+Heritage+Coast+-+Videos+-+Turning+The+Tide [Accessed 4 June 2011].

Durham Mining Museum (2008) *1921 list of mines under the Coal Mines Act – Durham.* Available from: www.dmm.org.uk/lom/1921_202.htm [Accessed 8 January 2010].

Edensor, T. (2005) *Industrial ruins.* Oxford: Berg.

English Partnerships (2006a) *Brownfield strategy: Policy and consultation workshop.* London: English Partnerships Department for Communities and Local Government.

English Partnerships (2006b) *English Partnership's brownfield guide.* Available from: www.claire.co.uk/index.php?option=com_content&view=article&id=196:english-partnerships-brownfield-guide&catid=81&Itemid=662 [Accessed 30 November 2016].

Garrett, B. (2011) Assaying history: Creating temporal junctions through urban exploration. *Environment and Planning D: Society and Space,* 29, pp. 1048–1067.

Godfrey, L. G. (2011) "The world he'd lost": Geography and "green" memory in Cormac McCarthy's the road. *Critique – Studies in Contemporary Fiction,* 52 (2), pp. 163–175.

Harding, L. & Hawken, S. (2009) Ballast Point Park. *Landscape Architecture Australia,* 124 (November), pp. 42–51.

Hargreaves, G. (2007) Large parks: A designer's perspective. In: J. Czerniak & G. Hargreaves (Eds.) *Large parks.* Princeton, NJ: Princeton Architectural Press, pp. 120–173.

Hargreaves, G., Czermak, J., Berrizbeita, A. & Campbell-Kelly, L. (2009) *Hargreaves: The alchemy of landscape architecture.* London: Thames and Hudson.

Hartlepool Mail (2005) *Easington one of worst place to live claim.* Available from: www.hartlepoolmail.co.uk/news/easington-one-of-worst-place-to-live-claim-1-983640 [Accessed 2016].

Hawken, S. (2009) Ballast Point Park in Sydney. *Topos,* 69, pp. 46–51.

Heatherington, C., Jorgensen, A. & Walker, S. (2017) Understanding landscape change in a former brownfield site. *Landscape Research.* Available from DOI 10.1080/01426397.2017.1374359

JMDD (2011) *Personal communciation, Ballast Point Park.* To: C. Heatherington.

Kirkwood, N. (2001) *Manufactured sites: Rethinking the post-industrial landscape.* London: Spon Press.

Kirkwood, N. (2004) *Weathering and durability in landscape architecture: Fundamentals, practices and case studies.* Hoboken, NJ: John Wiley & Sons.

Langhorst, J. (2004) *Rising from ruins: Postindustrial sites between abandonment and engagement.* Open Space: Tourist places/Theories and Strategies 2004, Edinburgh.

Lass, M. & Oliver, K. (2012) *From brown to green: Transforming London's 2012 Olympic park.* Centre for a Better Life. Available from: http://livebettermagazine.com/article/atkins-from-brown-to-green-transforming-londons-2012-olympic-park/ [Accessed 30 November 2016].

Latz, A. & Latz, P. (2001) Imaginative landscapes out of industrial dereliction. In: M. Echenique & A. Saint (Eds.) *Cities for the new millennium.* London: Spon Press, pp. 73–78.

Latz, P. (2001) Landscape Park Duisburg-Nord: The metamorphosis of an industrial site. In: N. Kirkwood (Ed.) *Manufactured sites: Rethinking the post-industrial landscape*. London: Spon Press, pp. 150–161.

Layne, M. K. (2014) The textual ecology of the palimpsest: Environmental entanglement of present and past. *Aisthesis. Pratiche, linguaggi e saperi dell'estetico; Vol 7, No 2 (2014): Formare per metafore. Arte, scienza, natura*, pp. 63–72.

Lowenthal, D. (1985) *The past is a foreign country*. Cambridge: CUP.

LVRPA (1987) *Lee Valley Regional Park Authority, Development Committee 5 Feb. 1987, paper no. D345. Middlesex Filter Beds – Management Plan. Report by the Chief Executive*. LVRPA.

Lynch, K. (1972) *What time is this place?* Cambridge, MA: MIT Press.

Marrero-Guillamon, I. (2011) The convenience of public art. *The Hackney Wick*, Summer 2011.

Martin, G. (2009) New York's hanging gardens. *The Observer*, Sunday 8 November 2009. Available from: www.theguardian.com/world/2009/nov/08/highline-new-york-garden-martin [Accessed 22 November 2014].

Massey, D. (2005) *For space*. London: Sage Publications.

McGregor Coxall (2011) *Personal communication, Ballast Point Park*. To: C. Heatherington.

Nomis (2005) *Annual Populations Survey 2004–05 and the Local Area Labour Survey 2003–04*. Available from: www.nomisweb.co.uk/reports/lmp/la/2038432084/report.aspx?town=easington [Accessed 1 January 2006].

Northern Echo (2002) With one swift blow, the miners' way of life was axed. *The Northern Echo*. Available from: www.thisisthenortheast.co.uk [Accessed 1 June 2005].

Northern Echo (2005) Colliery town "worst place to live". *The Northern Echo*. Available from: www.thisisthenortheast.co.uk [Accessed 3 July 2005].

Padua, M. (2003) Industrial strength. *Landscape Architecture*, 93 (6), pp. 76–86.

Pearson, L., Clifford, A. & Minutillo, J. (2009) Two projects that work hand in hand, the High Line and the Standard New York bring life to New York's West Side. *Architectural Record*, 197 (10), pp. 84–95.

Pirzio-Biroli, L. (2004) Adaptive re-use, layering of meaning on sites of industrial ruin. *Arcade*, 23 (Winter), pp. 28–31.

Priestley, J. B. (1968) *English journey*. London: Heinemann.

Raxworthy, J. (2008) Sandstone and rust: Designing the qualities of Sydney Harbour. *Journal of Landscape Architecture*, 3 (2), pp. 68–83.

Relph, E. (2004) Temporality and the rhythms of sustainable landscapes. In: T. Mels (Ed.) *Reanimating places: A geography of rhythms*. Aldershot: Ashgate Publishing Limited, pp. 111–122.

Saunders, W. (Ed.) (2012) *Designed ecologies, the landscape architecture of Kongjian Yu*. Basel: Birkhäuser.

Shorter Oxford English Dictionary (1993) Oxford: Clarendon Press.

Simon, K. (2010) Ballast Point Park. *Architecture Australia*, 99 (No. 3 May/June), pp. 95–102.

Treib, M. (2002) Must landscapes mean? (1995). In: S. Swaffield (Ed.) *Theory in landscape architecture*. Philadelphia, PA: University of Pennsylvania Press, pp. 89–101.

Treib, M. (2011) Commentary 2: Must landscapes mean? Revisited. In: M. Treib (Ed.) *Meaning in landscape architecture and gardens: Four essays, four commentaries.* London: Routledge, pp. 126–133.

Ulam, A., Cantor, S. L. & Martin, F. E. (2009) Back on track: Bold design moves transform a defunct railroad into a 21st century park. *Landscape Architecture,* 99 (10), pp. 90–109.

Weilacher, U. (2008) *Syntax of landscape: The landscape architecture of Peter Latz and Partners.* Basel: Birkhäuser.

Musing on the tracks

The first interlude

My first memory of the Filter Beds dates from some time in the early 1990s when I was living in Hackney, East London. I have an image in my mind of a causeway running through the site, set with a concrete channel and tracks, surrounded by vegetation (Figure i). It was that memory that sent me back to the Lea Bridge to see whether this would be a suitable case study site for my research. From the start I was puzzled by the tracks but initially I didn't question them; they were rail tracks weren't they? That's what they looked like to me and they led along the central causeway and perhaps with a bit of imagination, they could extend to run outside the site. The proximity of the Navigation (the Hackney Cut) also lent weight to the idea that the tracks were for bringing in something – I knew the Navigation was a transport

Figure i The concrete channel and tracks at the Middlesex Filter Beds

link, canal barges travelled up and down from the Thames. So the tracks must be to do with that mustn't they?

> There were loads and loads of different barges dropped off stuff in Hackney ... my recollection for instance of Hackney Cut would be from Lea Bridge to Old Ford ... the barges bringing in coal and taking out rubbish.
>
> (Space Studios, 2011: 6)

There were inconsistencies with the account that I told myself, why were the tracks so narrow? It must have been a narrow gauge railway then. What was the concrete channel? Why was there a concrete barrier at one end of the tracks? These questions were too hard to answer; perhaps parts of the infrastructure had been removed and if they had remained, all would be clear.

Then people started to talk to me about the tracks; a woman interested in local history, who I interviewed early on, asked me:

> *have you looked at historical maps for the filter beds? ... You should, if you get hold of a copy of you know pre 1900 maps you'll be able to see the railway lines.*

So they were railway tracks then ...

Other people questioned what they were for, asking if they were railway or tram tracks and one told me, *it's like all the railway lines, I've been told about that a couple of times, but I couldn't tell you about them.* Obviously they were confusing for others as well as for me, but for some it was obvious; *train tracks to bring in the sand,* one told me. Another reinforced my first impressions:

> *I thought there was a bit of track that I was interested in on the towpath ... there was a little bit of railway track, I think there was a small narrow gauge railway, probably just trucks, rather than a train and it used to meet the canal and I think it's where they unloaded and loaded from the canal ... They obliterated it when they put the new path in, which was annoying.*

That sounded convincing to me and yet when I looked at photos of the towpath taken in the 1980s by Berris Conolly (Not known), there was no sign of a railway track.

I then came across photos from the LVRPA (1988) archive showing the causeway in 1972 and 1984 demonstrating the extent of plant colonisation. When I first looked at these I was not thinking about tracks but about successional vegetation; I succeeded therefore in overlooking what was staring me straight in the face – a sand washing machine on tracks in the middle of the filter beds. And so I went on for another period, ignoring the tracks.

An interviewee explained why he had taken a photo - *because of the tracks, which you know look original, I think*. He went on to imagine uses for the hopper fixed at one end of the concrete channel; *this is almost like ceremonial ... it's like well, what happens in that? Something, a process happens in that, in that... trough there, er ... some sort of ritual maybe*. A mother described her children's reactions to the tracks and concrete channels, *first they played on it then it was like oh what's it for and then we'd go out and find what it's for*. But what was it for? I looked at the interpretation signs but they didn't really explain it.

A young woman liked them because *every time I'm here they always play on those bits ... it's nice how it's turned into a little playground* and a father pointed to the channel explaining, *this is quite nice ... my kids think this is a train ... they would sit in there*. A train again - time to examine the historical maps of the area. The OS map from 1894 showed no evidence of the tracks, but one from 1966 had two lines, either side of the central collecting well, which could indicate the sections of concrete channel and tracks. But there were no other tracks leading out of the site. So maybe these were not train tracks at all. In that case, what were they?

A few interviewees saw the tracks, concrete and hopper as aesthetic forms. One explained that they

> *reminded me of the sort things that they might have at Chelsea [the Flower Show], the kind of rill type thing ... [it] has a got little dog leg in it for some reason and I don't know why. But that makes it better I think.*

I contacted Thames Water to ask to see their archive and spent some time looking through their photographs and glass plate negatives. At last I found a new explanation (the one I should have noticed earlier): two photos dated from the 1940s, of different sand washing machines running on narrow tracks in the nearby Essex Filter Beds. Finally I had an idea of the real use of the tracks and also I suddenly had real people in my reimaginings of the history of the site; one, in long coat and official cap, stands to attention beside the machinery whilst other photos from the archive show workers with their sleeves rolled up as they shovel new clean sand across the beds. And these photos show two different types of hopper, one of which looks very like the fixed hopper still standing at the end of the tracks. Ah, I thought judgementally, they have just concreted a hopper there as a static, preserved artefact! But I was wrong. I found another photo from 1941 which shows the hopper already in position and looking through the LVRPA (1988) archive produced a second image from the 1970s of the abandoned hopper, labelled as a 'sand trolley', and surrounded by the beginnings of successional vegetation. I still have no idea what it is doing there. Nor do I yet know how the sand was brought into the site.

I thought that my exploration was finished and I had come to some conclusion but a few weeks later I found an annotated diagram of the

Middlesex Filter Beds with the words, 'fuel was delivered by barge and rail which branched off the Great Eastern Railway into the Essex works' (LVRPA archive, Not known). Around the same time, I was also looking at a new website about the history of the Filter Beds which showed a video of a narrow gauge train. The video was not taken at the Middlesex or the Essex beds but was included on the website as an example of the trains that were in use in waterboard properties (Lea Bridge Heritage, 2012). It seems there was a railway line into the Essex Beds, but so far I can find no evidence of one on the Middlesex side of the Lea.

References

Conolly, B. (Not known) *Hackney 1985–87*. Available from: www.berrisconolly.com [Accessed 13 June 2014].

Lea Bridge Heritage (2012) *The view from the bridge, waterworks railway*. Available from: http://leabridge.org.uk/gazetteer/archaeology/waterworks-railway.html [Accessed 13 June 2014].

LVRPA (1988) *A Management Plan for the Middlesex Filter Beds, Lee Valley Regional Park Authority, Countryside Service*. LVRPA.

LVRPA archive (Not known) *The Middlesex Filter Beds in Operation*. LVRPA, p. 1.

Space Studios (2011) *The Cut: Interview Barry Milsom*. London, Space Studios. Available from: www.spacestudios.org.uk/wp-content/uploads/2014/11/450_TheCut_Catalogue_Q_low2.pdf [Accessed 18 December 2014].

5 Perceptions of material and spatial qualities in developed sites

Corner (2002: 148) writing about landscape asserts that 'the disclosure of meaning ... can only occur when the subject is present, moving through it, open to sensation and experience'. We see, touch, smell, hear and taste things as we move around and it is through these senses that we perceive and comprehend the world. This is a phenomenological perspective that stresses the value of embodied engagement through sensory experiences whilst also foregrounding the materiality of landscape (Tilley, 2006). As Bender says 'although our engagement with the land is subjective, the land itself, because of its materiality, "talks back" – it sets up resistances and constraints' (2006: 303).

This physical aspect – the 'thingyness' of places – is often overlooked in the discourses that focus on the relationship of people with the landscape: theories such as place attachment and place identity.[1] The embodied experience of derelict landscapes is a fundamental part of their attraction and any discussion of how the qualities of these sites might be reinterpreted and reimagined must necessarily focus on materialities. Without doubt these sites contribute to people's sense of place attachment and place identity; however, there is little research into the types of material, spatial and temporal qualities that people respond to, or into how the ways in which such qualities are incorporated into the designed landscape affect these responses. The geographer Doreen Massey's theories of place and space are particularly suited to an examination of such heterogeneous sites, with their conflicting and contingent histories, the openness of meaning and uncertain identities, the changing materialities, the multiple temporalities and the possibilities they raise for future change. Massey (2005) conceives of place as a simultaneity of on-going and ever-changing stories that take into account a diverse range of voices, many of whom may not previously have been considered as having contributions of any value to make to discussions of landscape. For Massey, place is the here and now, conceived of as an intertwining of histories, 'where spatial narratives meet up or form configurations, conjunctions of trajectories which have their own temporalities' (2005: 139). It is the returning, the meetings and the accumulation of encounters that lend continuity to place.

This way of conceptualising landscape results in a place that is always in flux, constantly changing, nonetheless Massey stresses that she is not arguing for a rejection of the specialness of places, which she conceives of as formed by ongoing relations and interactions – an 'event of place':

> What is special about place is not some romance of a pre-given collective identity or of the eternity of the hills. Rather, what is special about place is precisely that throwntogetherness, the unavoidable challenge of nego-tiating a here-and-now (itself drawing on a history and a geography of thens and theres); and a negotiation which must take place within and between both human and non-human.
>
> (Massey, 2005: 140)

Place, when understood from this perspective, is not part of a coherent narrative, it is unfinished, it is open, it is woven together out of multiple on-going stories (Massey, 2005). Its character is a product of these stories and their interaction with the wider setting. It is also a product of the exclu-sions, the relations not established; these all contribute to the specificity of place. Individuals revisit the places in their lives, picking up where they left off, finding out what has happened whilst they have been away, weaving together 'stories-so-far' (Massey, 2005: 130). Massey's conception of place puts a responsibility on the individual, who becomes implicated in both the lives of others and in relationships with the non-human agencies; it challenges us to be aware of how we might respond to encounters with both humans and the non-human in our everyday interactions (Massey, 2005).

In this chapter, and Chapters 6 and 7, I draw on research I carried out between 2011 and 2013 in which I examined visitors' responses to three case study sites: the Middlesex Filter Beds, RSPB Rainham Marshes and the Hidden Gardens. I recruited participants at the three sites and, in order to remain as true as possible to the concept of the embodied engagement with landscape, I usually interviewed them whilst we were walking around the site. Appendix A gives brief demographic information about the participants[2] and in what follows I have used italics to indicate when I am quoting directly from the interviewees' own words. The idea of walking whilst interviewing is not new; Pink (2007) discusses the benefits of videoing a subject and points out that this form of interview necessarily includes the relationship between the subject and the materiality of the landscape itself (Pink, 2009). Interviewing the visitor whilst they are experiencing the landscape has the potential to produce varied and interesting data, 'heightened reflections and new ways of knowing' (Pink, 2009: 86–87). Deming and Swaffield (2011) also suggest that people can begin to articulate their feelings about landscapes whilst sharing activities with the researcher and Rishbeth and Powell (2013) explain in detail the value of understanding people's embodied experiences in order to further research in the field of landscape architecture. Orange (2015) also successfully uses this methodology in her research into the memories of people in the former Cornish copper mining landscapes.

At each of the three case study sites participants were able to dictate the route they wished to take, the speed, or indeed whether to sit and talk rather than walk. In practice it was sometimes necessary, if the weather was very bad, for the interview to take place inside, overlooking the site, and a number of the volunteers interviewed at Rainham were working in the visitors' centre whilst being interviewed. There is no visitor centre at the Filter Beds but at the Hidden Gardens a café in the Tramway borders the garden with a good view of the central area and the chimney, and at Rainham the visitors' centre is raised above the site with a view across the marshland and over the Thames. I also interviewed staff members at the three sites and two military history enthusiasts at the Purfleet Heritage Centre.

In this chapter I examine visitors' interactions with, and responses to, material and spatial qualities in the three case study sites. I explore whether these qualities of the DUN site, when retained in the developed landscape, give rise to similar forms of re-engagement with the past as those discussed in Chapter 2.

Reinterpreting the past – history, mystery and imagination

In both the Filter Beds and Rainham Marshes the structures, artefacts and surfaces are in a state of decay and their original function is partially, or completely, obscured. This, together with the breakdown of the contextualising framework that once surrounded them, leads to uncertainty (DeSilvey, 2006) and a struggle to understand or imbue the objects with meaning (Edensor, 2005c). Like the tracks and concrete channel at the Filter Beds, the cordite store, stop butts and mantlet banks at Rainham Marshes are examples of artefacts and structures that have become divorced from their original uses, resulting in them having no clear or understandable purpose. In the first interlude I described the confusion and misconception engendered by the tracks, and the erosion of the spatial relationship between the mantlet banks and the stop butts also obscures their original function leading to a sense of uncertainty (Figure 5.1). In fact, there is an existing mantlet bank in front of the section of remaining stop butts but this is not visible from inside the site and was only evident when I climbed over the perimeter fence and found myself standing on top of it. If meaning is fragmented in this way, how do visitors to these sites attempt to understand and relate to these artefacts?

Walking around the Filter Beds is not akin to a curated trip around historical relics, instead, from the moment they first glimpse the site from over the wall or through the gate, visitors are free to choose how they might engage with the apparently randomly-placed material qualities of the landscape. It was a man, who sometimes moored his canal boat outside, who encapsulated the possibilities this sense of arrival had for future mysteries and storytelling; *I think for me … it's to do with that idea of the gate being a sort of portal … a separation, a distance. I think when you go through that gate you're somewhere else.* Several interviewees likened the site to *The*

Soldiers fired from behind the ridges on the marsh - over
the mantlet banks - at the targets on the stop butts

MANTLET BANK

The soldiers sat under
the bank and relayed
information about which
targets had been hit.

The line of mantlet banks
was about 20m. from the
line of stop butts.

STOP BUTTS

Figure 5.1 The relationship between the stop butts and the mantlet banks at Rainham Marshes

Secret Garden, a children's book about a place with a mysterious past – gradually uncovered as the story progresses – and the promise of a future for the book's young characters, expressed metaphorically through the seasonal regrowth of the garden. Other participants spoke of creating their own stories about possible presents: the rusty pipes that could *burst open and make loads of stuff come out of them* and the track and concrete channel that *my kids think is a train.* Understanding the original functions of these objects was not necessarily the important factor; artefacts revealed and stumbled across when walking have become fragments, divorced from the whole, and as such they hold out possibilities for speculation, questioning and reimagining.

It is these senses of indeterminacy and mystery, of not knowing, that are important aspects of participants' perceptions; one local artist commented, *I really don't know anything about it ... and I kind of quite like the mystery of it actually.* Nonetheless for others it was a puzzle to be solved, a first step to delving more deeply into the history of the site in order to come to an understanding about its past. A first-time visitor closely examined the Hackney Henge whilst musing about its purpose, observing, *the holes have*

Figure 5.2 Middlesex Filter Beds: Top row – view to collecting well with hopper in the foreground, preserved sluice machinery; bottom row – grinding lines in surface, remnants in the granite foundation stones that comprise the Hackney Henge

rust stains – it implies they were definitely in use for something. Another interviewee questioned the original purpose of the mosaic of surfaces asking, *was there a building or a house or something over there?* Occasionally visitors read the interpretation signs to try to understand how the filtration system worked, but engaging with the material and spatial qualities was more often an opportunity to use their imagination and create their own stories, much as explorers describe in a ruined site (DeSilvey and Edensor, 2013; Garrett, 2011). A few interviewees were also interested in the fact that the stories they told themselves about the site could change from visit to visit as the original purposes of the artefacts and structures became unrecognisable. An artist in her sixties reflected on this aspect – *I think I prefer that it just sort of is suggestive and you can write your own ... which you can rewrite every time you come.*

The sense of not knowing, coupled with discovery, was an important factor in the attraction of the site, and the diverse range of material qualities allowed 'the viewer to substitute invented traditions and imaginary narrations' (Boyer, 1996: 19) rather than 'read' a coherent historical narrative. As one of the interviewees said, *it's not just a kind of historical narrative, it's a place that you could make up any story, isn't it, there's a real kind of mystical fantasy narrative that could go with it.* After one visit I made a note of my own feelings when, against the unwritten rules, I ventured over the fairly basic railing and down the steps into one of the beds:

> *I decide to go down into the filter beds. Immediately everything is different. You are surrounded by the landscape – old and new – within it rather than perched above it. The black winch-type structures are above me. My slight feeling of guilt and unease makes me imagine they are tall, black-clad figures.*

In this sense the Filter Beds can be understood in the light of Massey's discussion of place as a collection of stories that are open to change or might only be perceived in one specific interaction with the place – one particular 'conjunction[s] of trajectories' (Massey, 2005: 139).

However, in contrast with these perceptions of mystery, at Rainham interviewees had a more matter-of-fact response to the structures and artefacts. They barely referred to the historical remains unless asked specifically and there was little mention of their mysterious nature: no sense of discovery or wonder about their purpose. Many local people have grown up in the area and were very familiar with the local landscape and the military presence. Peter Beard (2011) pointed out to me that in the past they could look across the marshes from their homes to the places where they worked, and several interviewees spoke of taking the train across the marsh, next to the MOD site, on their daily commute. A young father who had been coming to the area to bird watch for 28 years, since he was a child, summed up this sense of matter-of-factness: *I mean all of this is what I grew up with. It's all very natural to me.* For him, and many of the other interviewees, the site was a part of his everyday life.

Nevertheless, a few interviewees did create imaginative stories relating to the people who had worked for the MOD during the war. One volunteer who took visitors on historical walks around the site spoke of the cordite store – *the walls are about three, four foot deep. You put your hand on them, they're so cold. You can feel, I don't know, you can feel history.* He described to me in vivid detail how the women would have worked at night during the war loading up shells while bombers flew overhead. It was also the cordite store that engendered discussion about its present value; the huge walls, overtaken by vegetation, create a microclimate with its own ecology and it is the place to come to see butterflies, insects and songbirds. Similarly, people told me how the mantlet banks are now a habitat for rare bees and used by nesting shelduck.

There is no overt attempt in the design and management of the landscape at Rainham to create a historical narrative of the recent past; structures are encountered seemingly at random at wide-spaced points around the site, although each artefact has an interpretation board and there is sometimes a leaflet available in the Visitor Centre, which guides walkers around the military history. The ways in which visitors can engage with the material qualities differ from those at the Filter Beds with most structures remaining behind post and rail fences or inaccessible amongst the reeds. The exception is the cordite store with its two deep entrances in the thick ivy-clad walls. Although people can walk close to the mantlet banks, a simple fence keeps them apart, and they can only view the ammunition store, stop butts and lookout tower from a distance. The sense of engagement with the material qualities is very different at the Filter Beds, where one interviewee commented; *it really feels you are involved in it. You can touch and walk on things.* This may account for the difference in the responses of the two groups of interviewees and for the fact that at Rainham there was little mention of alternative narratives or of imagining, nor was there the sense of playful engagement that some interviewees spoke of at the Filter Beds. It is worth noting that the two interviewees who spoke of imagination and mystery at Rainham did so mainly in relation to the cordite store, the one structure that is accessible to the public.

However, there are other reasons that could explain the differences in responses between the two sites. The Filter Beds is a wooded site where seasonal and maintenance changes can affect visibility. This is conducive to experiences of 'stumbling upon' artefacts. Rainham Marshes in contrast, is an open, horizontal marshland where changes of vegetation have less impact. The wider landscape forms a permanently visible backdrop to the site and, when within looking out, the boundaries are unclear. However, although the military remains can hardly be said to be 'stumbled upon', they do merge with the landscape when viewed from a distance, only becoming distinct when approached. This also applies to views from the road and railway; the site merges into one panoramic vista, as was pointed out by one interviewee who had often driven past but not registered its separate existence. Clearly perceptions of the remains differ depending on the context; Rainham is more easily perceived on the large scale whereas the Filter Beds lend themselves to detailed observation.

Differences in interviewees' perceptions might also be due to the intentions of the owners and managers of the sites. Rainham is primarily designed and marketed as an RSPB reserve; nevertheless there are schemes to attract visitors who may not necessarily be interested in bird watching and some of the interviewees were not visiting with the primary aim of seeing birds, but used it as a place to walk, to keep fit or just to wander. In contrast, at the Filter Beds the aim of the LVRPA (2012) is to balance the historical significance of the site with its role as a nature reserve. A further reason for the difference between the two sites could be due to the fact that the majority of the interviewees at Rainham were local people who were very familiar with the history of the site; the past was an integral part of their present lives.

In contrast with these two case studies, the way in which the material qualities are incorporated at the Hidden Gardens is very different: most are in a state of arrested decay, preserved at a particular point in the decaying process (see DeLyser (1999), Oakley (2015) and DeSilvey (2006) for further

Figure 5.3 The boardwalk and view to the north at Rainham Marshes

information on the policy of maintaining structures in a state of arrested decay). They appear placed in fixed positions as a cohesive element of the garden design, rather than giving the impression that they occur randomly or by chance. The most conspicuous structure is the chimney, however, in spite of its visibility, I usually had to ask interviewees directly for their thoughts and opinions about it. Some said that it was a significant landmark and reminder of the history of the site, but a few felt it was irrelevant in the wider scheme of the garden and most had little understanding of its original function. Lynch suggests that commonplace landmarks can serve as 'psychological anchors' (Lynch, 1972: 198), creating stability whilst change continues around them. However it is clear from the comments of the interviewees that at the Hidden Gardens the chimney rarely functions in this way; removing it from its surrounding systems and framework resulted in a loss of understanding of its original function. It was left to one young man to give a more imaginative interpretation, describing it with reference to the Batman stories – *it's like a bat-signal, … so now when I'm going to be in the Southside, whenever I look at that, … I'd be drawn here.*

However, some interviewees were more responsive to the facade of the Tramway, pointing out the visible traces of doors and windows that hinted at the other buildings that must once have existed on the site; the huge paint shop and stores that now form the art centre were only a small part of the Coplawhill Works. There is also one remnant of the Tramworks that appears to have been almost forgotten and unconsidered during the design process: the small section of tramway track confined to the very end of the garden. Unfortunately this was closed to the public during my visits; nevertheless many of my interviewees were frequent visitors and had had access to this part of the garden, and yet there was little mention of these tracks. A few interviewees did question whether the spatial layout of the central section of the garden followed the original tramlines and footprints of buildings, and a volunteer who had trained in landscape design went further: *I suppose they've used the original base – the tramway/the trams – the straight lines of the design hint at this.* There was also a suggestion from one elderly woman, who remembered the site as the Transport Museum, that the Hidden Gardens should give the historical context greater attention. She explained how when it was first opened people entered through a separate entrance from Pollokshaws Road where *it's all the old cobblestones, it's all your old tramway lines … it's amazing.* Nevertheless, if the whole of the Tramway itself is understood as an entrance to the garden then it is clear that the history is well signposted and there are also large interpretive boards with photos and a timeline in the foyer, although many of the interviewees did not appear to have read them.

The design of the garden is conceived as a 'celebration of a specific, given landscape … plant nursery, chimney and factory floor' (The Hidden Gardens, 2011): an interpretation of the past that is reinforced in the heritage narrative of the site set out in the informative interpretation panels. Although the designers did not intentionally take a museum-like approach to the displaying of the material qualities, it is clear that they function in much the same way as is suggested by Ingold's (2012) materialising mode, discussed in Chapter 2: as reminders of a past that is over and to some extent lost and forgotten. In contrast, at the Filter Beds and to a lesser extent, Rainham, the ways in which participants relate to the past through the material qualities is similar to experiences of derelict sites described by Edensor (2005a, 2005b) and Garrett (2011) that I outlined in Chapter 2. It is clear that there is a difference between these artefacts that have the potential to engender imaginings that bring the past into the present and suggest possible futures, and an object that is displayed purely as part of a heritage landscape with a clearly defined, and usually official, narrative. The most obvious difference is their state of decay, and I will discuss the temporality of these sites in more detail later. However, as I have shown at Rainham, many of the structures, although decaying, do not engender diverse responses and although I have noted several possible reasons for the differences between the two sites, it is possible that the physical engagement with the artefacts at the Filter Beds is a contributory factor in the imaginative responses of the interviewees, particularly with respect to the imagining of possible futures. The separation of the visitor at Rainham from most of the mantlet banks, the look-out tower and the stop butts results in a museum-style presentation – the materialising mode. Despite this, the artefacts are not preserved or protected, rather they are in danger of gradually becoming invisible.

I described in Chapter 4 how Rainham Marshes and the Filter Beds can both be thought of as taking a relationship approach to their design, and it might therefore be possible to view the ways in which visitors relate to the past in terms of Ingold's (2012) gestural mode; they interact with the landscape following historic routes and paths. In the case of the Filter Beds the spatial arrangement of the boundary walls, the entrance and the paths remain exactly as they were when the site was a working filter beds. At Rainham some of the new paths and boardwalks follow the original access routes and rail tracks on the site, and the entrances to the cordite store were originally on the route of a small railway that connected with the main line to bring in explosives. However, there is no visible evidence of this railway line and only a small number of visitors were aware of how the topography of the site was dictated by these historic structures. One interviewee, who did have prior knowledge of these parts of the site, imagined stories about the past that could perhaps be said to follow old paths taken by our ancestors (Ingold, 2012) when he eloquently described the women working in the dark moving between the cordite and ammunition stores:

> *How frightening that must be? They had wooden trucks, and they had to manhandle the explosive kegs onto the trucks and then they had to pull them all the way to the little explosive store, glass roof one, to fill up the bullets, ready for the men to use the next day for the target shooting. Whilst the bombers were literally flying over the top.*

However, in spite of describing the steps, movements and emotions of the women, the interviewee is telling a story, rather than having an embodied experience. I suggest that in general the cordite store and the other material qualities at Rainham can be understood in terms of Ingold's (2012) quotidian mode. Although the ruins at Rainham can hardly be described as part of everyday life in the way a house can, they did indeed form a background to the lives of many of my interviewees, whether they were bird watchers or local residents. During the period of dereliction these structures became part of a landscape of recreation, used by many in the local community, and now they are places for wildlife, and this has informed the ways many of my interviewees viewed and engaged with them.

In the Filter Beds, in spite of the relationship approach to its layout, it is also difficult to see how the gestural mode can account for visitors' responses to the site. Although they are following what could be described in Ingold's terms as ancient routes, none of the interviewees had been to the site when it was a working filter beds and nor did they have experience of what working there would have entailed. In fact I found that interviewees showed very little interest in the working lives of those who had been employed there. This is in contrast with Edensor's (2005a) descriptions of retracing the movements of the vanished workers in derelict sites. For some however, the relationship approach to the spatial layout of the site led to embodied and imaginative responses that helped them to make sense of what they were seeing. One example was an interviewee who took a photo of himself looking down into one of the filter beds; *I deliberately included my feet. It's like diving into a pond.* The composition of his photo referenced the watery history of the beds whilst including himself and his experience in a new imagining.

In the first interlude, 'musing on the tracks', I demonstrated the diverse interactions possible with just one grouping of material artefacts – the tracks, concrete channel and hopper. There is the interpretation sign that tells an official story about the filter beds – the materialising mode – and I have an engaged interaction with the qualities, as do several of the interviewees quoted, who imagine the past in diverse ways. Then there are also the games children play and the talk of possible rituals and processes that might take place there, bringing the past into the present and imagining possible different presents and potential futures. It is also clear from 'musing on the tracks' that prior knowledge is a significant factor in my and the interviewees' embodied perceptions; maps and photographs play their part in the possible imaginings, as do past perceptions and understandings of the history of the wider landscape surrounding the site.

The fluidity and contingency of the interviewees' imaginings at the Filter Beds demonstrate in practice the relevance of Massey's concept of the 'thrown-togetherness' (2005: 140) of space. Reimaginations of the past add to the range of possible stories that, for Massey, contribute to the specificity of place. However, as with the other two sites, Ingold's (2012) quotidian mode is also present here; the everyday present takes precedence over the imagined past. On one visit I observed an example of this. Someone had rearranged a broken section of coping stone to form a step down into one of the filter beds, where there was an old mattress, possibly for use as a comfy seat or even a bed. The quotidian mode is also evident in the imaginative playfulness that is a part of visitors' experiences in the Filter Beds. Edensor (2005c) explains how a sensual engagement arises between the body and the materiality of the ruin; visitors are 'playfully drifting, even risking encounters with the unpleasant, in contrast to the re-assuring promenades created by planners and designers' (Armstrong, 2006: 119). The spatial layout of the site, emphasised through the relationship approach, gives visitors the freedom to playfully and imaginatively interact with the material qualities, including sometimes taking the risk to venture off the paths and down into the beds themselves.

Relating to the past – frames for reading

The concept of 'framing the story' (Potteiger and Purinton, 1998: 42) when we 'read' the landscape has been used to describe the boundaries of the site that mark the beginning and end of the 'story realm', but here I take the phrase a 'frame for reading' from Treib (2002: 93) to describe the context in which we perceive a landscape.[3] Treib asserts that 'we are formed and circumscribed by our culture and our times, but we make interpretations based on our experience and our knowledge' (2011: 132). I use the term frame for reading therefore, to encompass cognitive and sensory experience, together with consideration of the surrounding landscape, rather than focusing on the bounded site.

Official and unofficial narratives

The concept of an 'authorised heritage discourse' (AHD) was introduced by Laurajane Smith (2006) to describe the way in which particular types of heritage are valued by experts and preserved, unchanged and unchallenged for the future:

> Heritage according to the AHD is inevitably saved 'for future generations' a rhetoric that undermines the ability of the present, unless under the professional guidance of heritage professionals, to alter or change the meaning and value of heritage sites or places. In disempowering the present from actively rewriting the meaning of the past, the use of the past to challenge and rewrite cultural and social meaning in the present becomes more difficult.
>
> (Smith, 2006: 29)

The AHD approach results in the promulgation of one official narrative about the history of a place: a narrative agreed by experts or by the present owners. The danger is that official narratives can dominate and sometimes close down alternative stories about a site. However, I found that interviewees do not only take account of the official reading; prior knowledge together with perceptions of the wider landscape form a general contextualising structure and added to this, in some cases, are memories of the site prior to development. I discuss the time layers in the landscape in more detail in Chapter 6 and here focus on the ways in which the interviewees use the site's surroundings and its material and spatial qualities in order to better understand it.

The official narrative of the Filter Beds is one that seeks to balance the demands of a nature reserve with the story of the historical remains, and there is a continuing commitment by the LVRPA (2012) to managing the site in this way. Although interpretive signs make an attempt at education, it is clear from some interviewees' responses that they do not take much notice of these, preferring to make their own stories and come to their own personal understandings about the site.[4] One interviewee, on his first visit, summed it up – *I did read a notice board that explained how they worked … it says the water went in here and then it went out again … But I wasn't really that interested anyway.* In contrast at Rainham, although the RSPB does offer some education about the military remains, the main focus of the official narrative is to describe how the site was once a medieval grazing marsh and how, with sensitive management, it is reverting back to this period in its history. Many interviewees understand and embrace this story and this might in part explain why the responses to this site were very different from those of interviewees at the Filter Beds.

The brief for the designers of the Hidden Gardens was primarily 'to create a space that would have spiritual resonance with the surrounding communities' (Roscher, 2011); consideration of the historic layers present and hidden within the landscape was of secondary importance. This emphasis has continued in the ways in which the site is viewed by its employees and by many of the interviewees I spoke to, who see the garden as a safe and peaceful place, and it is noticeable that the historic narrative is often overlooked or only read at a superficial level. The exceptions are those visitors who knew the site prior to its redevelopment and have memories of its life as a Transport Museum. I discuss this in more detail in Chapter 7, where I show that it is the building itself – now the Tramway – that serves as a frame for reading, and the historical references in the garden itself play only a minor role.

Understanding materials

The problem of the recontextualisation of material qualities discussed above appears to also apply to the recycling of industrial materials and the referencing of a history through an industrial palette. At the Hidden Gardens and Rainham it was often the case that interviewees viewed the rusting metal, concrete and gabions with matter-of-fact acceptance rather than seeing them as ways to connect with the previous histories of the site. One woman, visiting the RSPB reserve for the first time, thought the bird hide made from an old container looked a bit decrepit but then questioned her reaction – *why shouldn't it look decrepit? That's an urban bias isn't it you know?* For many, rust was not a problem or something out of the ordinary, the hide and the rusting containers that form the Discovery Zone just blended in – *it doesn't have to be painted red or yellow does it?* However, a few participants at Rainham did make observations about the links between the materials, the industrial surroundings and the new use to which the site had been put. One young woman volunteer spoke of the containers referencing the industrial history of area, *bringing in the industrial bit into the natural wildlife*, and a local birdwatcher, also referring to the containers, explained that *it's great having it, cos' this was really a brownfield site that's been reclaimed.* A student with a background in landscape design also pointed out *the way they've linked it all to the containers* going on to remark *it's that sense of this landscape – that no one's taken or hidden away these things, they're part of it.* Interviewees, however, did puzzle about the previous use of the blocks of granite that form the Hackney Henge at the Filter Beds and I was given various different stories about their origin. Although not all the interviewees liked the artwork, a large number did engage with it and it is especially popular with children; as one older volunteer said, the stones *can be whatever they want them to be.* A young playworker expressed her dislike of the work until I explained that the granite had been repurposed, when she changed her view, appreciating the fact that it now had a new use, not so much as an artwork or a reminder of the site's history, but as an exciting place for children to play.

Across all three sites there was evidence of a sensual engagement with the materials in their new context, some interviewees enjoying the contrasts between materials and the plants or the natural landscape, and others appreciating the ways in which these elements blend in with their surroundings. At the Hidden Gardens comments about both the recycled and the new materials included statements such as, *it's got the urban, gritty thing going on.* However, far from being a frame for relating to the historic layers of the landscape, these materials have become an integral part of a new design, engendering new sensual responses. For many they simply provide walkways and structures, seating areas and planting beds, whilst for others they become a way of creating something new and beautiful in their juxtapositions with the temporal elements of the landscapes. This matter-of-fact acceptance of the incorporation of the materials is also evident in interviewees' understanding of the importance of recycling and their expectations that this had taken place: something particularly noticeable at the Hidden Gardens.

Drawing on the surrounding landscape

There was evidence that some interviewees in all three case studies drew on the surrounding landscape as a way of conceptualising the sites. This was evident in their understanding of the treatment of the entrances. At the Filter Beds the long Victorian boundary wall, that is for many the first indication of the presence of the Filter Beds, contributed to the sense of a place with an important historical past. One woman on her first visit mused that it was obviously *something precious as it has significant walls and gate.* Similarly the Tramway building has become the grand entrance to the Hidden Gardens giving a sense of the scale and historical significance, as a professional woman described:

> *for me there's certainly a resonance of the kinda heavier industries, particularly around the transport museum and things ... you just need to go inside there and you can see, you know the whole history of the*

trams, you can just feel it in the building and you know, just the way in which it's such a heavy-duty building, they don't build buildings like this now.

At Rainham, however, one of the first actions of the RSPB when they took over the site was to install boundary fences to prevent vandalism, and access to the site is now across a contemporary drawbridge that leads to the Visitor Centre. Two local interviewees explained how the erection of these fences contributed to their feelings about the site – *I don't think … the old people around here, will forgive what was done … for closing it off … telling people they can't come.*

In the wider landscape there was an understanding that industry played a significant part in the history of the surrounding areas. This was particularly true of Rainham where it was noticeable that, without my asking any specific questions, industry and transport were often mentioned, in contrast with responses about the military history of the site. The flat landscape and visual permeability of the boundaries give a clear view of the transport infrastructure, the light industrial complexes and the breakers' yards surrounding the marsh-land, and there is the regular sound of trucks visiting the landfill site broken intermittently by the 'whoosh' of the high speed trains against a backdrop of other mechanical noises (Figure 5.3). A retired fireman from Kent took time to think about the view before saying:

> *I mean, you look at some of the like the flyovers and things and it looks a bit ugly. BUT, it's an urban reserve and I think it sort of adds to it a little bit. … You hear a little bit of train noise … as it whooshes by … they couldn't really do much more to hide it could they?*

This is perhaps one reason why, for many of the interviewees, it was natural to refer to the industrial connections between the site and the wider surroundings. However, this industry is also part of the social fabric, and informs stories told about the local area; as one retired local volunteer remarked – *they always say that Thurrock is one big landfill site.*

Although the Filter Beds is more enclosed than Rainham, there is an awareness that the site is surrounded on two sides by water and the sounds of the city are a constant presence. In summer it feels quite separate and enclosed whilst in winter there are vistas into the surrounding, partially industrial landscape, and interviewees spoke of the industrial history of the area and the importance of the River Lea and the Navigation as communication routes to the Thames. Even at the Hidden Gardens, where the surrounding area is more residential, there was an awareness, expressed by some, that the transport system had played a part in the history of the area with one professional woman commenting, *you can still hear the railway line for instance and that's nice, they're still about transport in some ways.*

Perceptions of dereliction and wastelands

An alternative frame for reading was also evident in the ways some interviewees at the Hidden Gardens and Rainham referred to derelict sites and wastelands. The evidence in the present of the past dereliction of these sites was often unremarked upon, however some interviewees had memories of and opinions about wasteland that influenced the ways in which they read the sites. Fairclough (2012), discussing landscape from an archaeological viewpoint, writes 'the remains, traces or influence of the past do not always need to be visible, but our knowledge of their hidden existence ... is an important aspect of perception' (2012: 94). For some interviewees the 'hidden existence' of the DUN site in their memories affected their present understandings of the new landscape and for others it was their imagination that conjured up this hidden existence from other experiences rather than any specific engagement with the site during abandonment.

Between the Hidden Gardens and the railway track there was, until 2012, a large area of barren wasteland, mainly consisting of concrete and scrubby low vegetation, that was originally part of the Coplawhill Tramworks and this, together with the knowledge of similar sites nearby standing empty beside new developments, led interviewees to the generic conclusion that wastelands had little value. As Lynch (1990) explains, there are wastelands that encourage exploration and inventiveness whilst others appear to serve no purpose and have no potential as 'loose space' (Franck and Stevens, 2007): space where unpredictable and unprogrammed events might happen. A young woman, newly arrived in Glasgow and on her first visit pointed out:

> *Yeah there's a lot of those new, new buildings ... sort of modern buildings but around it is just waste ground, you know. And it takes it away from like how nice the buildings are that there's just this big rubble area and fences around it and stuff.*

Other interviewees when discussing the transformation of the landscape used phrases such as *make a difference* and *put to good use,* and spoke of a sense of renewal and progress that appeared to come from understanding that the site had once been derelict. An unemployed young man, also visiting for the first time, was impressed saying, *it's really amazing seeing that they've done something with something that basically just could be a big pile of rubble.* A cleaner who sometimes helped in the garden explained in a similar vein:

> *instead of looking at a derelict thing. Think, well we can do something with this! And it's good for ... everybody. You know what I mean?... so yes, it's progress there, you know what I mean, er... instead of looking at a dump.*

However, interviewees' responses also demonstrated an appreciation of the importance of retaining some reference to the history of the site and they liked the way the industrial remains had been used as a backdrop for the new design. Although there was again little discussion of how this history could be read through the connections between old and new, there was an appreciation of how the site, rather than being saved, has been renewed. Although, as I show above, the material artefacts present in the gardens can be seen as examples of Ingold's (2012) materialising mode of thinking about the past, the concept of renewal and growth suggests the quotidian mode. However, this is a quotidian mode that is more than merely functional; it is creative and holds possibilities for different and exciting engagements with the landscape.

In contrast with interviewees at the Hidden Gardens who saw no value in a derelict site, at Rainham the interviewees specifically made many references to the state of the site during the time it was abandoned and awaiting redevelopment. Some in the local community stressed its importance; they had visited and trespassed there when it was operational and used it as their playground whilst it was derelict. One interviewee who had many memories from these years admitted, *it started getting used as a dump ... things got really bad ... that's one of the memories. ... I've got to admit this, we were one of the guilty ones.* The potential value of the site was also affirmed by the bird watchers, who had visited when it was MOD land and felt that the period of dereliction was detrimental to the wildlife and to their enjoyment. One participant who worked as an ornithological consultant explained:

> *that was a bad period in my eyes, because you had other people using the site, the motor cyclists, the falconers, it affected all the birds. So you had a period when potentially it could have been thriving, it could have been a great opportunity ... so it was a very frustrating period with all the high disturbance there and not actually being able to get in and have a look at stuff.*

At Rainham, valuing the derelict site provides a frame for reading that leads to two opposing understandings. One reinforces the official narrative by stressing that the landscape has been saved, restored to its former state prior to the MOD's residency and its subsequent abandonment, whilst also acknowledging that without the MOD's protection, it might have been lost completely to housing or industrial development. This official history is cyclical, returning the landscape to medieval grazing marsh, and there is pride in the fact that it now looks *how it should have done*. The second frame for reading also sees the period in which the site was derelict as a problematic one, and accepts that some, but not all, of the activities that took place were detrimental to the area. However, this unofficial narrative draws on memories of the wildlife on the site both before and during its wasteland period, to counter the RSPB's claim that they have saved the site. These two histories are epitomised in the story of the meadow ants, recounted to me by advocates of both narratives to strengthen their position. The mounds evident across the site indicate the presence of generations of ant colonies, thus demonstrating that the landscape must have remained for tens, or even hundreds of years, in much the same condition as it appears today. Thus the physical landscape and its wildlife are portrayed as emblematic of the site's history: it is who is perceived as the guardian and champion of that history that is contested. Are the RSPB the saviors of the site, guiding it to a 'natural' state that existed centuries ago? Or was the landscape already 'natural' with no need of intervention?

In fact these differing ways of relating to the past both lead ultimately to the same understanding of a quotidian future that allows the landscape to continue to be safe from development, a valued green space for the local people. However, the differences between the two views remain evident in the ways in which local people speak about the site and the uses they make of it; there are still some older residents who cannot forgive the RSPB for, as they see it, taking their land. Watts describes how futures are 'inseparable from the landscapes of their making' (2012: 59) and the quotidian futures for Rainham are indeed informed by its military and industrial pasts, and by the perceptions and understanding of the local people, both of this site and of others in the wider landscape.

The possibility of meaning

Meaning is personal; it 'results from a transaction between people and the landscape' (Treib, 2011: xii) and is gradually added to through the years (Treib, 2002). Our embodied experience of landscape changes with each visit and thus our understanding of the landscape and its temporal layers also changes. Corner (1999) questions how design can contribute to habitually used landscapes and suggests that there should be an emphasis on engagement and emotional involvement. However, although both Corner and Treib are acknowledging the temporal and the relational in their discussions of meaning, they are also envisaging specific physical landscapes: landscapes that have materiality. There is therefore an implied, and also common sense, assumption that these landscapes are there already and it is our embodied engagement with them that produces meaning. Corner writes 'the experience of landscape *takes time,* and results from an accumulation of often distracted events and everyday encounters' (2002: 148). This assertion that we experience the landscape over time also implies that everyday events and actions that take place add to that experience. Massey wants us to go further and to understand that every time we experience the 'thrown-togetherness of place' (2005: 141), we must also be open to the challenge of negotiation with others and with the non-human. It is the challenge to engage with the non-human that is perhaps most relevant when discussing the qualities of DUN sites.

It is clear from the responses of visitors to the three case study sites that they do indeed have multiple individual ways in which they might reimagine meaning. However, there is also evidence of a more generic understanding of the relationship between the site and its surroundings that makes reference to its past history, and is used as one strand of a frame for reading. Interviewees perceive interconnections between the site and the city and between the site and the history of the area, both locally and further afield. These under-standings also form part of an imagining of what might happen in the future to the landscapes. The different ways of contextualising the site that I des-cribe above demonstrate that prior knowledge has a bearing on our percep-tual engagement with the landscape, whether we are visualising a fixed history, an imaginative reconstruction of the past or a creative reimagining of the past in the present. The interviewees' responses also show that their experience of other local landscapes is an important factor in how they make comparisons and draw conclusions about a site. For a few interviewees this knowledge is gained from familiarity with the immediate surrounding area whilst also drawing on experiences of other landscapes from further afield, and even, in the case of the Filter Beds, from literature. Clearly relationships with these places are tempered with numerous other experiences, memories and references, made through engagement with other landscapes both real and imaginary. This accords with Massey's understanding of the particularity of place as being:

> Constructed not by placing boundaries around it and defining its identity through counterposition to the other which lies beyond but precisely (in part) through the specificity of the many links and interconnections to that beyond.
>
> (1994: 5)

A retired local volunteer at Rainham expressed this concept in his own terms when talking of how the site related to its surroundings, *you can't separate one from the other. It's all got to be part of the team … It's all got to be carefully managed, so each one has its own er, freedom to expand and manoeuvre, and be.*

Notes

1   Scannell and Gifford (2010) in their tripartite model of place attachment examine the specificity of the physical place and suggest that the physical attributes of a place contribute to the meanings it may have for the visitor. They suggest that this meaning may be symbolic or may contribute to a person's sense of identity. However, they do not consider in detail specific physical attributes, rather concentrating on general concepts such as wilderness, home and nature.

2   Initially I recruited people for interview by visiting the sites at different times of the day and asking people if they would be prepared to take part. This method was particularly useful in providing a selection of habitual visitors to the site. Regular users included dog walkers, retired friends socialising, volunteers, walking for health groups, mothers and children meeting for coffee, birdwatchers and artists, depending on the site. In order to extend the group of interviewees to

those who were not necessarily regular visitors, I asked people who had already participated, if they would pass on details of others who might be interested and I made contact with the staff at the three sites to ask them to pass on details of any potential interviewees. Consideration was given to contacting people who had no prior knowledge of the sites, however it was not obvious how I would select a group of interviewees from the wide range of diverse groups that lived in the surrounding areas and therefore I restricted myself to seeking out additional people for interview who could be considered to have a close interest in the site. At the Filter Beds there is a boat mooring outside the site and I therefore contacted and interviewed two canal boaters. The Hidden Gardens is situated behind the Tramway Arts Centre and I ensured that I also interviewed people whose primary aim was not to visit the gardens.

In addition to recruiting members of the general public I also made efforts to find people who lived in the area before the sites were redeveloped. At the Hidden Gardens I contacted volunteer groups who worked regularly in the gardens. These users were often referred to the garden by occupational therapists or social workers, and included many people who had lived in the area all their lives. Volunteers were also contacted at the RSPB Rainham Marshes and again these were mainly local people, some of whom had prior knowledge of the site. In the case of the Middlesex Filter Beds, attending the Lee Valley Regional Park Authority user group yielded valuable contacts who were able to put me in touch with other possible participants.

3　I discuss the ways in which narratives can form part of our understanding of place in 'Buried Narratives', a chapter in the book *Urban Wildscapes* (Heatherington, C., 2012). I suggest designers can use different narratives to increase the local distinctiveness of the landscapes they are working with and discuss the value of such approaches.

4　This accords with results observed during a research programme by students at UCL over the period 2008–2010 (Threpsiades, A. *et al.*, 2010). The research, which centred on the Hackney Marshes and included the Filter Beds, found that people enjoyed discovering the marshes for themselves and finding new things in a situation where the urban environment meets nature. This research also found that it was the over 50s who responded to this type of landscape, with teenagers preferring more structured and programmed environments.

References

Armstrong, H. (2006) *Time, dereliction and beauty: An argument for 'landscapes of contempt'*. The landscape architect, IFLA, Sydney.

Beard, P. (2011) *Personal communication – Rainham Marshes*. To: C. Heatherington.

Bender, B. (2006) Place and landscape. In: C. Tilley, W. Keane, S. Küchler, M. Rowlands & P. Spyer (Eds.) *Handbook of material culture*. London: Routledge, pp. 303–314.

Boyer, C. (1996) *The city of collective memory: Its historical imagery and architectural entertainments*. London: MIT Press.

Corner, J. (1999) Eidetic operations and new landscapes. In: J. Corner (Ed.) *Recovering landscapes: Essays in contemporary landscape architecture*. New York: Princetown University Press, pp. 153–169.

Corner, J. (2002) Representation and landscape (1992). In: S. Swaffield (Ed.) *Theory in landscape architecture.* Philadelphia, PA: University of Pennsylvania Press, pp. 144–165.

DeLyser, D. (1999) Authenticity on the ground: Engaging the past in a California ghost town. *Annals of the Association of American Geographers, 89* (4), pp. 602–632.

Deming, M. E. & Swaffield, S. (2011) *Landscape architecture research: Inquiry, strategy, design.* Hoboken, NJ: John Wiley & Sons Inc.

DeSilvey, C. (2006) Observed decay: Telling stories with mutable things. *Journal of Material Culture,* 11 (3), pp. 318–338.

DeSilvey, C. & Edensor, T. (2013) Reckoning with ruins. *Progress in Human Geography, 37* (4), pp. 465–485.

Edensor, T. (2005a) The ghosts of industrial ruins: Ordering and disordering memory in excessive space. *Environment and Planning D: Society and Space,* 23 (6), pp. 829–849.

Edensor, T. (2005b) *Industrial ruins.* Oxford: Berg.

Edensor, T. (2005c) Waste matter – The debris of industrial ruins and the disordering of the material world. *Journal of Material Culture,* 10 (3), pp. 311–332.

Fairclough, G. (2012) A prospect of time: Interactions between landscape architecture and archaeology In: S. Bell, I. S. Herlin & R. Stiles (Eds.) *Exploring the boundaries of landscape architecture.* London: Routledge, pp. 83–114.

Franck, K. & Stevens, Q. (2007) Tying down loose space. In: K. A. Franck & Q. Stevens (Eds.) *Loose space.* London: Routledge, pp. 1–33.

Garrett, B. (2011) Assaying history: Creating temporal junctions through urban exploration. *Environment and Planning D: Society and Space,* 29, pp. 1048–1067.

Heatherington, C. (2012) Buried narratives. In: A. Jorgensen & R. Keenan (Eds.) *Urban wildscapes.* London: Routledge, pp. 171–186.

Ingold, T. (2012) Introduction. In: M. Janowski & T. Ingold (Eds.) *Imagining landscape: Past, present and future.* Farnham: Ashgate Publishing Company, pp. 1–18.

LVRPA (2012) *Lee Valley Regional Park: Park Development Framework. Thematic Proposals for Community, Landscape and Heritage and Environment.* LVRPA.

Lynch, K. (1972) *What time is this place?* Cambridge, MA: MIT Press.

Lynch, K. (1990) *Wasting away.* San Francisco, CA: Sierra Club Books.

Massey, D. (1994) *Space, place and gender.* Oxford: Polity Press.

Massey, D. (2005) *For space.* London: Sage Publications.

Oakley, P. (2015) A permanent state of decay: Contrived dereliction at heritage mining sites. In: H. Orange (Ed.) *Reanimating industrial spaces: Conducting memory work in post-industrial societies.* Walnut Creek, CA: Left Coast Press, pp. 49–71.

Orange, H. (2015) Benders, benches and bunkers: Contestation, commemoration and myth-making in the recent past. In: H. Orange (Ed.) *Reanimating industrial spaces: Conducting memory work in post-industrial societies.* Walnut Creek, CA: Left Coast Press, pp. 191–211.

Pink, S. (2007) Walking with video. *Visual Studies,* 22 (3), pp. 240–252.

Pink, S. (2009) *Doing sensory ethnography.* London: Sage.

Potteiger, M. & Purinton, J. (1998) *Landscape narratives: Design practices for telling stories.* New York: John Wiley and Sons, Inc.

Rishbeth, C. & Powell, M. (2013) Place attachment and memory: Landscapes of belonging as experienced post-migration. *Landscape Research, 38* (2), pp. 160–178.

Roscher, R. (2011) *Personal Communication, The Hidden Gardens.* To: C. Heatherington.

Scannell, L. & Gifford, R. (2010) Defining place attachment: A tripartite organizing framework. *Journal of Environmental Psychology,* 30 (1), pp. 1–10.

Smith, L. (2006) *Uses of heritage.* London: Routledge.

The Hidden Gardens (2011) *The Hidden Gardens, Design.* Available from: www.thehiddengardens.org.uk/design-of-the-hidden-gardens.php [Accessed 3 October 2012].

Threpsiades, A., van Asseldonk, E., Iglesia, H. B., Groves, L., Perez, R., Matabuena, R., Kanchwala, R. & Li, Z. (2010) *Justice in the green: Being with nature.* London, UCL. Available from: www.justiceinthegreen.org.uk/IMG2010/BWN/ES3%20Being%20With%20Nature%20Presentation.pdf [Accessed 25 March 2013].

Tilley, C. (2006) Part 1, Theoretical perspectives. In: C. Tilley, W. Keane, S. Küchler, M. Rowlands & P. Spyer (Eds.) *Handbook of material culture.* London: Routledge, pp. 7–11.

Treib, M. (2002) Must landscapes mean? (1995) In: S. Swaffield (Ed.) *Theory in landscape architecture.* Philadelphia, PA: University of Pennsylvania Press, pp. 89–101.

Treib, M. (2011) Commentary 2: Must landscapes mean? Revisited. In: M. Treib (Ed.) *Meaning in landscape architecture and gardens: Four essays, four commentaries.* London: Routledge, pp. 126–133.

Watts, L. (2012) OrkneyLab: An archipelago experiment in futures. In: M. Janowski & T. Ingold (Eds.) *Imagining landscape: Past, present and future.* Farnham: Ashgate Publishing Company, pp. 59–76.

Temporalities at Orford Ness

The second interlude

Secret, mysterious, bleak, ominous, scary, unique, windswept, flat, isolated, these are some of the words that I had dreamt up in my imagination to describe Orford Ness[1] over the years before my visit in 2014. I knew it was a former military site, a shingle spit of land separated from Orford village in Suffolk by a short stretch of water. I knew it was full of secrets. Writing this now, I still think that all those words are appropriate but here I will try to describe the Ness in terms of its time layers, its temporalities, its pasts and futures as seen through my eyes and the words of others.

We make the short boat trip and start walking in a group, strung out, dawdling. I am full of anticipation, excited, apprehensive – what if it is not as amazing as I had hoped? I half listen to the guide talking of the military history, but I am too excited and too occupied with both camera and binoculars to fully concentrate. And then – my first awe-inspiring moment. But it's not about the past at all but an intimation of the future. I spot a spoonbill flying with huge white wingflaps above my head. (Spoonbills are a new visitor to England and in the last few years have started to breed in some sites, but not yet here (Natural England, 2010).) Then present and past merge as I photograph a rare breed sheep brought onto the Ness as a 'grazing management tool' (The National Trust, 2003: 25), with military structures, known colloquially as the pagodas, in the distance (Figure ii). We follow the designated path, cross a bridge, walk between regimented lines of concrete fence posts that must have long been bereft of their barbed wire. We are surrounded by shingle.

The shingle spit is 16 kilometres long and at its highest is only four metres above sea level. It has acquired many official protective designations over the years to reflect its importance as a special geomorphological feature and habitat (Cocroft and Alexander, 2009). But this is not a static place, the Ness changes, is built up and is destroyed again, sometimes bit by bit and sometimes dramatically. The shingle is a series of shallow ridges and valleys each one a record of time passing (The National Trust, 2003: 10). Longshore drift moves material along the shore and it is deposited in ridges. Some are broken or destroyed, rebuilt or added to, so it's not possible – contrary to what you might imagine – to work out the age of each. Time is not so easily

Figure ii The pagodas at Orford Ness

sedimented in place. Smaller pebbles are graded towards the tops of the ridges so this is where the vegetation takes a foothold – sweeps and straggles of greenish brown in the whites, greys and browns of the shingle.

Pieces of metal, machinery and concrete are dotted at random amongst the pebbles. A hare darts across and disappears behind a ridge. To our right is the former Atomic Weapons Research Establishment (AWRE) site with its iconic pagodas; to our left is Cobra Mist. The former are solid, strangely shaped masses rising from the landscape. Or perhaps the landscape rises with them – shingle and sand are mounded around their walls and roofs. The Cobra Mist building is ephemeral, gradually becoming more defined as the weather changes. It appears ghost-like in the distance. It was built in the late 1960s and closed shortly after in 1973 and is said to have been some sort of experimental radar station that never worked (The National Trust, 2003). People talk of UFO sightings there.

In front, across the shingle, is the lighthouse. Behind us is a traditional – appearingly timeless – pastoral scene: greens and blues in the foreground and Orford village with its twelfth century castle keep in the background. The temporalities of the Ness are waiting for us to find them. The lighthouse is the oldest building, built in 1792. It was sold to Nicholas Gold in 2013 and now its future is the subject of controversy (Fletcher, 2014). The National Trust point out that in 2010 when the lighthouse was decommissioned they agreed with Trinity House, the original owners, that they 'would allow natural forces to dictate the future of the building' (The National Trust, 2014). But Gold has other ideas. 'Long term I cannot stop nature. The sea will come in, I recognise that. It would cost a fortune to make it last 50 or a hundred years ... but in the short term I can slow things down' (Lampard, 2014).

The Atomic Weapons Research Establishment (AWRE) buildings, including the pagodas, are normally out of bounds although we do visit Laboratory 1, built in 1956, where tests were made on the UK's first atomic bomb (The National Trust, 2003). Davis writes of her feelings after chancing upon a defused bomb on display next to Laboratory 1. She sees it as:

> The *real* destructive force at Orford Ness: before the site had seemed under nature's power, the strange shapes you walked past the result only of the long process of decay; now the Ness pales suddenly into nuclear wasteland ... the idea of instantaneous ruin hits you hard.
>
> (2008: 148)

Every view, including from Orford quay and the marshes, seems somehow to include the pagodas. Through my binoculars I can see seagulls nesting on the sandy mounds of their concrete roofs. They were constructed as vibration test buildings during the 1960s. Each has a concrete roof covered in shingle and sand, and supported by 16 reinforced concrete columns (Cocroft and Alexander, 2009). The tests took place underground. The intention was that if the blast was too intense the columns would collapse and the concrete roof could then contain the full force of the explosion. This never happened. Both pagodas still stand – for now.

The AWRE closed in 1971 and the Ness was abandoned until the National Trust took over in 1993. They protect the sensitive and unusual habitats on the shingle by not intervening, doing little. But Grant Lohoare (Motion, 2007b), a warden on the Ness interviewed for a short film by Andrew Motion, explains that the rusted artefacts could have been part of the scientific and military experiments or they might just be bits of detritus – there is no way of knowing and so they are left undisturbed. This applies to the buildings too. Much of what happened here is unknown – kept secret.

MacFarlane (2012) describes their 'controlled ruination ... when glass shatters or tarmac cracks, it is left unfixed. Rust spreads in maps. Buildings dilapidate. The splintered, the fissile, the ruderal: these are the Ness's textures'. But for Lohoare (Motion, 2007b) the 'decay is part of the whole philosophy of what's happening here'; rather than being seen simply as material structures, the buildings now stand as symbols of the cold war era. Still the secrets of the Ness will remain hidden. Motion (2007b) reminds us that the decaying buildings are actually concealing the real story, 'they seem to imply that what they were here to experiment with is also no longer with us', but of course this cannot be true.

On the Ness I have reimagined the unknowable, secret, hidden, lost, classified, filed away, never spoken of. John Hughes-Wilson, a military historian, believes that 'it may only be our children who find out all the secrets of Orford Ness' (Motion, 2007a). I wonder if by then the secrets will be buried deeper, circular craters all that's left to mark the explosions. Evidence of experiments and bombs hidden beneath the shingle only partially revealed when a wild storm breaks through the spit. But the mysterious stories of the Ness will still be told. And the spoonbills will probably be breeding there.

Note

1   Orford Ness is a shingle spit of land on the East coast of England that was once the home of the Atomic Weapons Research Establishment and is now owned by the National Trust. It is an internationally important site for nature conservation and on certain days it is open to visitors who take a ferry from Orford quay.

References

Cocroft, W. & Alexander, M. (2009) *Atomic weapons research establishment, Orford Ness, Suffolk, Cold War research and development site survey report.* Portsmouth, English Heritage. Available from: http://services.english-heritage.org.uk/ResearchReportsPdfs/010_2009WEB.pdf [Accessed 10 August 2014].

Davis, S. (2008) Military landscapes and secret science: The case of Orford Ness. *Cultural Geographies,* 15 (1), pp. 143–149.

Fletcher, M. (2014) Slipping away: Row threatens centuries-old lighthouse. *The Telegraph,* 12/1/2014. Available from: www.telegraph.co.uk/news/10566068/Slipping-away-row-threatens-centuries-old-lighthouse.html [Accessed 18 November 2014].

Lampard, V. (2014) *The race is on to save an iconic lighthouse.* ITV, Anglia. Available from: www.itv.com/news/anglia/2014-05-21/the-race-is-on-to-save-an-iconic-lighthouse/ [Accessed 13 July 2014].

Macfarlane, R. (2012) Robert Macfarlane's untrue island: The voices of Orford Ness. *The Guardian,* 8 July 2012. Available from: www.theguardian.com/culture/2012/jul/08/untrue-island-orford-ness-macfarlane [Accessed 8 August 2014].

Motion, A. (2007a) *The island: A search for the secret history of Orford Ness conclusion.* YouTube, fender200. Available from: www.youtube.com/watch?v=qg7Ofs6OUpA [Accessed 13 July 2014].

Motion, A. (2007b) *The Island: A search for the secret history of Orford Ness Part 2.* YouTube, fender200. Available from: www.youtube.com/watch?v=oLlcLt-g4xM [Accessed 13 July 2014].

Natural England (2010) *Breeding spoonbills cause a stir.* Available from: www.rarebirdalert.co.uk/RealData/Spoonbills_breed_in_Norfolk.asp [Accessed 15 July 2014].

The National Trust (2003) *Orford Ness.* London, The National Trust, pp. 1–24.

The National Trust (2014) *National Trust's position on the Orford Ness lighthouse.* The National Trust. Available from: http://ntpressoffice.wordpress.com/2014/01/12/national-trusts-position-on-the-orford-ness-lighthouse/ [Accessed 12 July 2014].

6   Perceptions of temporal
       qualities in developed sites

One way of understanding temporality in the landscape is to imagine layers of past interactions and interventions made up of traces left to be read by the visitor. In the context of the sites I am examining, these traces might include the industrial remains, decaying artefacts, industrial infrastructure, evidence of planning and development policies, informal activities, opportunistic practices, spontaneous interaction and natural succession. There may also be evidence of layers from previous periods in the near and distant past such as the Villa Minerva at Ballast Point Park that I mention in Chapter 4. However, temporalities can be conceived of in multiple ways, not merely thought of as a set of different time frames physically present in the landscape. Hence when I talk of the temporal qualities of a derelict site that might be incorporated in the developed landscape I am referring, not only to processes of decay and succession, but also to those interrelations with material qualities that might engender awareness of different time frames. Hillier (2011) describes the changes in the composition and understanding of a place in terms of relationships which 'fold and unfold, compose and decompose' and suggests that understandings of places are fluid and dependent on interactions. It is possible to imagine space and time – the material and the temporal – as randomly folded layers on, in, between and through which we might form relationships. Because space is always in the process of becoming something new, and cannot ever be understood to be completed, it has the potential for multiple interrelations and happenings and thus opens the possibilities for new narratives and understandings (Massey, 1999).

The concept of space being composed of multiple temporalities is more than merely an understanding of how various actions occurring in different time frames leave marks on the landscape. At its simplest one can imagine the landscape as a palimpsest of past interactions that have left traces to be read by the visitor; each of the physical layers or traces are part of a particular time frame. Bender puts this another way, '*landscape is time materializing*; landscapes, like time, never stand still' (2002: S103). However, an understanding of the interlinking of space and time is more than a discussion of spatial change in different time frames. The embodied relationships we have with landscapes can include perceptions of processes, rhythms of change, continuity and discontinuity, together with cognitive and intuitive responses to the physical site, such as recollection, reflecting on the past through the present and expectations of future change. Temporality can be understood as 'the lived-experience of time ... the dense association of memory, present awareness and expectation' (Relph, 2004: 113). In Chapter 7 I discuss the way memory can transport the individual (or group) to another time frame as part of the spatial experience.

The nature of landscape is to be the setting for temporal occurrences whilst also being itself contingent on temporality. It is therefore to be expected that interviewees at all three research sites engaged in a range of temporal experiences: recollecting past visits; describing stories and memories; taking part in habitual daily and weekly events such as dog walking and playing with their children; experiencing the changes that occur with the seasons and with the maintenance of the site; planning future visits; campaigning for or against future changes; imagining new possibilities, and many more. However, the landscape is not only a place to engage in temporal experiences; it also contributes its own temporalities in the form of seasonal changes, decaying structures and successional vegetation, and these in turn affect interviewees' awareness of the passage of time.

In this chapter I look at the roles nature and the material and spatial qualities play in engendering this sense of the passage of time. I outline the ways in which interviewees perceive and value these temporal qualities and how they respond to the intertwining of the natural and the cultural worlds. I use the terms nature and natural here in the same way as my interviewees have used them. Nature describes the vegetation and wildlife in the site and natural describes a landscape or parts of a landscape that **appear** to have occurred naturally, with little human intervention. However, it is important to note that the interviewees are aware on some level that there is an element of human involvement in the development and management of these sites and thus both nature and culture affect their experience of temporality.

In the remainder of the chapter I discuss the interviewees' responses in the light of Lynch's (1972) discourse on temporal collages and look at the way juxtapositions between nature and culture can create disjunctions in these temporal layers. I examine both the sense of indeterminacy and of continuity that these juxtapositions can create within the sites, and finally I consider how the temporal qualities might have an impact on interviewees' perceptions of the future of these sites.

Temporalities of the past, present and future

Temporal collages and time layers

Lynch's (1972) concept of the temporal collage is particularly appropriate when describing brownfield sites where layers become intermingled. In

Chapter 4 I categorised such landscapes as natural and abstracted palimpsests. The term temporal collage is perhaps a more pertinent term, making clear the diverse ways in which new elements of the palimpsest can be combined with old: acknowledging visible juxtapositions and disjunctions between layers as well as a blurring at the edges. It is clear that nature plays an important part in the creation of temporal collages and time edges (the juxtaposition between different time periods) (Relph, 2004) and it features time and again in the responses of the interviewees. In the Filter Beds there are many examples of time edges between artefacts, structures, surfaces, new industrial materials and the vegetation. Interviewees made reference to the *crumbling remains* of the ruined structures describing them as having a *feeling of decay* that contributed to the atmosphere of the site. As one student in her 30s walking her dogs explained, *that's the ambiance of it isn't it you know, it's the crumbling brick.* Others commented on the juxtapositions of specific material artefacts with nature, such as the decaying walls running through the vegetation in the beds, and one young woman took photos of the *dead seedheads there and the contrast with the cement wall and then the big rusty pipe in the background.* Far from seeming discordant and out of place, the contrast and inherent tension of these time edges at the Filter Beds is appreciated by interviewees, and they serve to highlight the processes of change, adding to the complexity of the landscape. When commenting on the detailed juxtapositions between the ruined structures and the vegetation, interviewees are not describing a sense of the passage of time that encourages reflection on mortality, often mentioned in writings on the sublime and picturesque ruin (Roth, 1997a; Roth, 1997b; Woodward, 2002). Nor are they indulging in nostalgia for a lost era (Edensor, 2005; Walsh, 1992). Neither is there any evidence they are enjoying some form of ruin porn, seeing the decaying structures in terms of their aesthetics with little understanding of their social context and historical background. Rather they are enjoying the contrasts and strange juxtapositions whilst also utilising them in their frame for reading the landscape: as another way of understanding the site as it is in the present.

In contrast, at Rainham I found that time edges at the small scale between the military remains and the natural vegetation are rarely noticed. The more common response was to suggest that the structures and the materials used in the site blend in with their surroundings; their role is secondary in a landscape that is primarily a bird reserve. However, interviewees did point out the contrasts between nature inside the site and industrialisation outside; one man insisted on showing me photos he had taken over the years showing these connections – *so you've got all the barbed wire ... you've got this lovely little bird in the middle of all this industrialness, and it has its own beauty.* A second interviewee echoed these sentiments, stressing the importance of these large-scale contrasts:

Maybe if it was all cleaned up and we never saw all the industrial buildings or what's left, the warehouses, it may lose part of its glamour,

> *I don't know. Everything's about contrast. The contrast of the cows in the middle and then the local Javelin* [high speed train] *going past at the same time.*

Although I did not elicit many comments that included the military remains in the temporal collage at Rainham, one example of the time layers within the immediate surrounding landscape did stand out. The lookout tower on the edge of the marsh beside the path along the Thames no longer 'looks out'; the river wall is above the top of the tower obstructing the view of any would-be looker-outer (Figure 6.1). A regular bird watcher, who sometimes led history walks around the site, explained this apparent anomaly:

> *Well the wall in front is 1953, from the great flood ... It's got bigger and bigger, over the years. Directly in front of that is the Victorian wall, and directly in front of that is the Tudor dock. So when the tide's out you can see the ... wooden beams sticking out of the mud that was once the Tudor dock.*

Small-scale nature–culture juxtapositions can serve to highlight discontinuity or they can appear to be a natural part of the processes that make up the whole landscape, engendering a sense of continuity. In the former case it

Figure 6.1 Rainham Marshes: Top row – view to stop butts, artefacts underneath the mantlet banks; bottom row – the lookout tower, the entrance to the cordite store

is the contrast between the material qualities and elements of nature – such as vegetation, lichens, birds – that is commented on by the interviewees, whilst in the latter there is a blurring of the boundary between the natural and the cultural. However, in both cases temporality is signalled through a combination of material forms, and interviewees experience a sensual response to these interactions and processes.

More generally at Rainham many of the interviewees' responses to the temporal qualities take account of the site's context and its spatial relationships with the surroundings. This awareness of the larger scale temporalities may be due, in part, to the horizontality of the estuarine landscape and the visual permeability of the site and the surrounding area. Interviewees express their delight that a landscape such as this can exist so close to London and surrounded by industry; a retired professional man told me, *it's a borderland between the river and the industrial part.* They perceive the temporal collage over a large scale, focusing on the spatial relationship of the nature reserve with the industrialised area. A Canadian visitor summed up the appropriateness and attraction of this large-scale temporal collage, incorporating as it does the past, present and future of the landscape:

> *Well I like all the diversity, the industry, the marshlands, the former er, London rubbish dump, that's now a green hill, far away. Er, the pylons, it's a real, sort of er, it's a modern snapshot isn't it, of industry and green space.*

I referred in Chapter 4 to Cathy Dee's (2010) suggestion that different time spans can be accentuated through the design of landscape forms. In the derelict site the decaying structures and artefacts speak to the visitor of time passing, drawing attention to temporalities. Dee points out that the differences in the rates of change of these forms create tensions that can be exploited by the designer. I suggest that the small- and large-scale juxtapositions in the case study sites are also highlighting temporal change through a combination of forms. It may not have been the designer's intention to create dynamic landscapes that foreground process, however 'encounters with ambiguous temporal juxtaposition' (Dee, 2010: 28) are a pleasurable part of some interviewees' experiences. They appreciate the relationships between these decaying objects and the agencies of the natural world **in the present** perceived, both in the forms of, and contrasts between, the objects, and in the processes that are taking place between them. The pleasure derived from the action of nature on the material artefacts is much the same as that mentioned by writers describing reactions to the industrial ruin (DeSilvey, 2006; DeSilvey and Edensor, 2013; Edensor, 2005).

In Chapter 5 I discussed how the chimney at the Hidden Garden fails to function as a symbolic expression of the past history of the landscape; however, a few interviewees did make reference to the outlines of lost buildings visible on the facade of the Tramway and speculated about the history of these ghostly traces. One pointed out that on the rear wall of the Tramway *you can see there's been doorways and obviously it's been bigger but they've taken it away and I quite like that – it's stayed old, I like that sort of decay.* Their perceptions of the juxtapositions and time edges were of a reflective nature and this reflection was also noticeable in the comments of interviewees about the juxtapositions between (what are seen as) naturally occurring trees on the mound and the new landscape: in this case epitomised by the Xyloteque. One young man on his first visit commented: *it's interesting you've got the city on the outside and then the garden and then you've got sort of a structure, and then the tree. Er that's quite nice. I like that a lot* (Figure 6.2). As with the other two sites, the time edges appear to add to the complexity of the garden, and the temporal juxtaposition highlights the sense of progress and renewal that some interviewees expressed when discussing the site. The interviewees appear to perceive the garden in layers rather than as a collage; the design has grown up **around** the historic artefacts and, in this case, around the natural vegetation. A self-employed photographer expressed this relationship in symbolic terms:

> The one thing that stands out is that sort of shed thing there [the Xyloteque]. It's built around a tree. That sort of sums up what it's like building something around something ... to make it more and they've accommodated what had originally been there in the first place.

Although the responses of some interviewees demonstrate an understanding of the ways in which the old and new merge in the design of the gardens, for many the palimpsestual layering of histories does not achieve the awareness of different temporalities that might be expected or intended. The designers have attempted to juxtapose the material qualities with new interventions, however, experiences of the garden itself, as a whole, take precedence over any understanding of the historical remains. It is impossible to say with any certainty why interviewees responded in this way; it may be purely because the garden is a lovely, safe place to enjoy on its own terms. However, it could also be due to the fact that the material qualities incorporated from the derelict site are removed from their original functions, in states of arrested decay, and thus do not 'speak' of their temporal qualities; they are not the dynamic landscape forms advocated by Dee (2010).

Nature – indeterminacy and control

As I have mentioned, interviewees frequently used the words nature and natural in their discussions about all three sites, nevertheless a count of the occurrences of the words wild and wilderness in my interview transcriptions showed that these terms were used by half of the interviewees at the Filter Beds but by only one person at Rainham. It is evident that in both sites interviewees perceive nature as a driving force, however, there is a difference

Figure 6.2 The Hidden Gardens: Top row – facade with stables corridor, the chimney; bottom row – the Xyloteque, an industrial palette of materials

in the way they interpret the relationship between nature and culture. At Rainham the understanding is that the RSPB is controlling the return of the site to how it has always been, or should be, whereas in the Filter Beds it is nature itself that is apparently asserting that control. Interviewees at the Filter Beds value the indeterminacy and heterogeneity of the site, with its temporal collages and time edges, and compare this favourably with more maintained parks in the surrounding area. The weatherworn-ness and decay of the structures and artefacts is seen as attractive; one interviewee, discussing the photos he had taken, showed me the *wonderful worn quality* of the stone that had had *rain and wind and all sorts of things on it*. A retired local resident who was brought up in the area summed it up, *it's all subsided all over the place in there, falling apart like, but I mean that's part of it*. The decay that has become a natural part of the Filter Beds is brought about by the agency of the weather, the vegetation and organisms such as mosses and lichens that interact with the built materials. In some cases these create unusual patinas and attractive textures whilst also imbuing the site with a disordered and chaotic quality (DeSilvey and Edensor, 2013). Interviewees described this relationship between the natural vegetation and the ruined structures as *nature taking back* – the site was *overgrown* or being *overtaken by nature*. For the canal boater the site has *got this previous order taken over by new chaos and it can go either way, it doesn't have to go that way, it would interest me in either direction*. It is clear that interviewees valued this relationship between the industrial artefacts and nature and relished the ambiguity about who or what was in control and, although they might be proud of the achievements of their Victorian forefathers, they also enjoyed the idea of nature taking charge once again. This sense of indeterminacy is a positive one for the interviewees; this is not an 'aesthetically and behaviourally controlled and homogeneous "themed" environment ... where nothing unpredictable must occur' (Franck and Stevens, 2007: 3). However, the people interviewed were making the choice to visit the Filter Beds and could be expected to be positive in their responses. As the professional photographer put it – *if it's not really your heritage it's just a piece of wasteland*.

Although for some the concept of nature taking back appeared to imply a return to an imagined, pre-industrial past, this did not seem to be the case for most of the interviewees; the development of a natural landscape was not seen as an attempt to reinstate the countryside as it had been prior to the advent of industrialisation. Rather, visitors understood and appreciated the long industrial history that was an important part of the local area and saw the Filter Beds today as a new development in that history. The blogger and sign writer who had grown up in the area told me:

> all the boats come along here 'cos this river goes up to Hertford, Bishop's Stortford. They would come mostly from the docks, um, foreign timber would be loaded at the docks and fetched up here. They were nearly all with horse and carts but now and again you'd get a train of eight or ten

boats even, I'm not sure how many, pulled by a tug. We used to think they were terribly modern.

The perception of indeterminacy and of a loosening of control at the Filter Beds contrasts with the interviewees' perceptions at Rainham, where they are very aware that the site is being managed by the RSPB for particular purposes. Any reference made to nature was almost invariably about wildlife in general rather than about the details of juxtapositions between nature and the military remains or about the disintegration of the artefacts. Where interviewees did talk about the military structures it was in relation to the wildlife that inhabited them. A regular bird watcher pointed out the rifle targets above the stop butts – *of course they're trying to keep it as much as they can, 'cos I think the fact that they've still got the numbers up for the targets... I was reading about some particular wasp which is nesting there.* Even in the cases of the cordite store and the mantlet banks, both encountered on the circular walk around the reserve, no one commented on the juxtapositions of the natural with the material artefacts. It was only a garden design student who delighted in the disordered properties of the decaying artefacts; referring to the mantlet banks she explained, *I like the fact they haven't cleaned it up too much. They've left the kind of debris in there.*

Nevertheless, there is a perception that nature can undermine this control and interviewees understand that eventually the military artefacts will disappear, crumbling beneath the force of ever-encroaching natural agencies. Some interviewees in their comments on the wider landscape appreciated this sense of nature taking control and mentioned the reclamation of local landfill sites and told me of the West Thurrock Marshes, a nearby brownfield site that supports a mosaic of different habitats – *the power station got deactivated, decommissioned, 'n flattened so the area was left to waste. But it's very good for all sorts of insects, they call it the Amazon of the UK, it's got so many bees.*[1] One local resident and volunteer was eloquent in her defence of nature, and demonstrated her understanding of what could happen if it was allowed free rein:

> We had housing development people wanting to come down and build on all of the grass that's over the back of behind our estate, bordering along the Thames. And they were saying, what would you rather have? ... Big piles of dirt because of what's been dredged up from the Thames for the DP World[2] or houses that are going to be better to look at. And we said dirt, because that will get taken over by nature. And we'd rather have massive banks of dirt than houses.

There is a case for valuing and even introducing interstitial wilderness landscapes in urban environments, as I discussed in Chapter 2: spaces in cities that 'accommodate the spontaneous development of wild nature' (Jorgensen and Tylecote, 2007: 458). Beard (2006: 6–7) suggests the term 'slack nature' to describe 'those fragments of raw wilderness that were never planted, designed or managed', and yet manage to still exist in the urban landscape, and he calls for such spaces to be valued and incorporated into the fabric of our urban lives. Jorgensen and Tylecote (2007) suggest that these wastelands are disturbing because it is unclear whether nature or humans are in control. Our personalities may determine the types of landscape we find attractive, an anthropocentric person preferring to see the hand of humans in control whilst the ecocentric character may find a wasteland more acceptable (De Groot *et al.*, 2011; Jorgensen and Tylecote, 2007, citing De Groot and Van Den Born, 2003) .[3]

The design and maintenance of the Filter Beds and Rainham Marshes ensure that the ambiguity about who or what is in control is resolved – they are not now abandoned wastelands – and all the interviewees felt that the level of maintenance and intervention was sufficient. This was the case even at the Filter Beds where people enjoyed the perception that nature was taking over. It would seem that both sites, in aspects of their design, enable visitors to engage with the sense of indeterminacy engendered by the inter-weaving of the natural and the cultural worlds. There is a mutability and a dynamism to these landscapes that the interviewees value. At the Filter Beds this is best seen in the micro: the detail of juxtapositions of brick, concrete and vegetation. At Rainham it is more often observed on a large scale, in the way the landscape forms uneasy links with its surroundings. Saito suggests that the pleasure we gain from the aging object may be in part due our under-standing of the 'contrast between exerting control and power and letting things and natural processes be' (2007: 182). Although Saito does not directly address the question of the attraction engendered by the juxtapositions and entwinings between the natural and cultural worlds, the idea of control is an important one. The interviewees at Rainham and the Filter Beds enjoy the potential that nature has to take over, whether they are watching a kestrel perching briefly on an electricity pylon or observing the roots of a birch slowing merging into a brick wall. However, although some interviewees speak about their understanding of what happens when nature takes over, the sense of pleasure this engenders does not appear to be about a conscious weighing up of human control versus nature. Rather it is an enjoyment in the power of nature, in spite of human endeavours. This experience is much more akin to that of the visitor to a wasteland who is unsure whether nature or humans are in charge and yet enjoys that ambiguity.

A sense of continuity

The concept of the landscape appearing to have occurred naturally is an important one for the interviewees. At the Filter Beds interviewees speak of a timeless quality, of a sense that the landscape has always been there, whilst at the same time suggesting that nature is taking over, and this sense of timelessness is also evident in both the official and unofficial narratives of Rainham Marshes. I discussed earlier how some visitors, perhaps those who have heard the RSPB story, see nature as somehow reverting back to how it should be. One of the staff members explained, *I've watched this place go from ... an enormous thistle bed to a recreated medieval, lowland, wet-grazing marsh. It's um, it's 100s of years old and it's looking how it should have done.* Although the sense is that the landscape is returning to a previous centuries-old state, interviewees also see the changes as part of a continuum: an everyday part of their experience of the temporal landscape collage as it is today. There is the impression that the site has been saved from the industry around it and it is this aspect that is mentioned when interviewees discuss the military remains. In this reading of the site the MOD's occupancy is seen as something positive in that it allowed the marshland to exist. A local man in his 60s who used to work in the container industry surmised – *I suppose that's why it's here because otherwise I expect it would have been developed ... it would have been swallowed up, I would imagine. Warehouses, or houses, whatever.*

At the Hidden Gardens there is no sense of the site reverting to nature, this is after all primarily a garden. However, interviewees do have a preference for 'naturalness', a desire for things to blend in and not appear manufactured. A staff member in her 40s commented, *it's different, it's not all manufactured and ... precise, they can see it's bits of old buildings that have been used,* and the social worker when talking about this mix of old and new explained, *well I think it just makes it feel more natural not just something that's just been created.* A young, unemployed man felt that the conversion of the Tramway building contributed to the special atmosphere of the site, *it just, adds a lot more you know ... having, you know, the old building that they've done up and all this rather than just something flashy* and a young woman who was also unemployed and recently arrived in Glasgow explained, *it's just the nature that's here but you've just built you know, around it, and it makes it sort of better and more like nature-y and peaceful.* Others spoke of the ways the old and the new had merged in the designed space, *I think they've blended in really well actually with the landscaping of the garden, blended well yeah, you can see how the garden's been constructed around them.*

Across all three sites these impressions of naturalness are linked to a sense of the passage of time and seem to suggest the importance of continuity for the interviewees. Although they understand that change has taken place and that it will continue to do so, they also have an underlying sense that these changes are part of a natural process. However, the importance placed on continuity does not preclude interviewees also valuing discontinuities and time edges. The juxtapositions, and indeed the blurring, of nature–culture and old/new time edges are particularly important for the complexity they add and, for my interviewees, these relationships do not seem to be counter to the naturalness of the landscape. The visitor to Rainham, from Canada, described the sense of connection to the past that these juxtapositions engendered: *the fact that you can see powder magazines from decades or centuries ago possibly. Erm, and double-decker buses. I really like that sort of juxta-positioning of all these modern and traditional things ... because it connects you up with history too.* At the Hidden Gardens a part-time gardener in her 20s felt that the repurposing of buildings and artefacts was a particularly Glaswegian way of proceeding saying, *I really like the old and the new, I think ... that's just a big part of it and it's a big part of Glasgow.* I asked why she thought that this way of working was appreciated in Glasgow and her reply expressed her sense of a natural continuity:

> *I always just thought it was a more relaxed approach to things. You're not trying staunchly to preserve, preserve ... conserve. It's just kind of like – right, progress is happening and we've got these old buildings and we can use them.*

At the case study sites the past, in the form of the qualities, and in terms of the narratives told, does not remain static: it is unfixed, changed and changing. The past, to a certain extent, has also been chosen: but by whom? At all three sites, decisions have been made by the managers and designers about which elements of the past to save, preserve and renew, and they have also selected particular narratives to tell about the past, present and future of these landscapes. However the interviewees also make their own choices about how to understand the past through these qualities. It appears that they use their knowledge and understanding of these places, together with their experiences of other landscapes in the surrounding areas, to construct a past that flows into the present, maintaining for themselves an important sense of continuity. This ability of the interviewees to make their own narrative of continuity – in Massey's (2005) terms, to negotiate these interrelationships that contribute to place – highlights the fact that these landscapes are unfixed and unfinished and even unbounded. As Massey (1999) would say: if space is the source of multiple new stories it can never be fixed and contained.

Nevertheless, interviewees at the Filter Beds and at Rainham did talk about loss and sometimes expressed resignation about the future of these sites. The interviews at the Filter Beds took place during the construction of the nearby 2012 London Olympic site and, because many people witnessed the destruction that occurred on the marshes and around the River Lea during this process, there was a feeling that maybe the Filter Beds could be lost at some point in the future.[4] The retired lawyer explained: *London, this is an area that constantly renews itself, when things are superfluous they're levelled and built upon, um, it's slightly against the odds in a sense that a place like this survives, all the more important for that.*

Others also understood that in the modern world things might have to change. The photographer compared the site with the wider landscape:

> *this seems to be like a very isolated thing, five or six years ago there were lots of old factories, there was like an old toy factory and some old*

gas works, but they've all been turned into flats since so it'd be ... it's nice if they can keep something but you know the world turns what can you do?

However, the sense of loss was more significant for some of the interviewees at Rainham. There was a general sense that all the green spaces in the local area, and further down the Thames, were under threat of development: a justified fear as the Buglife report shows (Robins *et al.*, 2013). However, as I discuss above, this was coupled with a belief that the RSPB site has now been saved. A young woman volunteer who had grown up in the area explained:

I'm all for open spaces and if this wasn't here something else would be built on it. It would be a housing estate. They work out a way of building houses on there, as part of the Thames Gateway. And that would just be criminal. We've got so many new estates and housing developments opening up from Purfleet all the way down through up to Southend. It's pretty much if it's empty or if it's an old warehouse, they're knocking it down and building on it. So I'm so glad that we, as the RSPB, have got this and it won't be built on.

She went on to explain her feelings about the reserve now and how she imagined her place in the future of the landscape:

I feel like it's mine. I do feel like it's mine. I go out, if I can, I get out there as much as I can. And I work out there as well. I've got a strimmer's licence to actually work out there and do some cutting down the grass so I feel like I'm putting something back.

However, there were two exceptions to this general perception of the RSPB's role: the interviewees from the Purfleet Heritage Centre who had known the site both when it was occupied and when it was derelict. Their interest was in military history, and over the years they had often scavenged spent ammunition and other artefacts and remnants for the museum. They perceived only discontinuity in the destruction of the military remains when the RSPB took over. This discontinuity informs their stories about the site and they feel so strongly about the changes that took place that they no longer visit; in effect they refuse to re-negotiate their relationship with the changing site. They too wished for a natural continuity that allowed nature to take a hold, whilst still preserving the buildings and infrastructure, however they did not appear to take account of the responsibilities that the RSPB would face in terms of maintenance and safety if such a course of action were taken.

The sense of natural continuity is different for each interviewee and in some cases the derelict stage in the timeline for the site is seen as a disjunction or discontinuity. For the bird watchers at Rainham, the activities of others on the derelict site made bird watching unpleasant and sometimes dangerous, and the interviewees at the Hidden Garden had no knowledge of the derelict site behind the Tramway. In fact many saw the period in which the site was transformed from the Transport Museum to the Arts Centre as a discontinuity; they did not feel that the Tramway catered for their interests and it was only with the opening of the garden that they began to visit again. However for these interviewees the period of dereliction and/or development is expressed as a short detour off the timeline. For others, however, the derelict period is a part of the continuum; many bird watchers still went to Rainham Marshes and local people used the site as their playground.

At all three case study sites some interviewees fear their perceived sense of continuity will be broken in the future, others understand that changes will occur and the material structures and artefacts may become unrecognisable, and yet this progression is accepted as part of the natural continuity. This sense of natural continuity is also expressed through the interviewees' understanding and desire for young people to engage with the site as it is now, sometimes learning from it or taking their own memories from it. It is perhaps the perceived element of naturalness in the processes that created these landscapes that makes the element of indeterminacy an acceptable factor in the ways in which visitors choose to make their own pasts in the present; nature is permitted, or even expected, to be uncertain and unpredictable. Jorgensen and Tylecote (2007: 458) call for a re-evaluation of wastelands as places where we might 're-connect our natural-cultural selves' in an urban environment. Although the sites examined here are no longer wastelands, the responses of the interviewees demonstrate an awareness and understanding of the interconnections and interrelationships between nature and culture in the city. The narratives they create around the continuities and discontinuities of these relationships seem to indicate that these landscapes do indeed allow for a re-connection and a merging of our natural and cultural selves. The fact that interviewees accommodate this unpredictability of natural processes is a practical example of Massey's (2005) assertion that we re-negotiate our relationships with places as they, and we, change.

Notes

1   The Buglife report (Robins. J. *et al.*, 2013) mentioned in Chapter 2 discusses in detail the case of West Thurrock Marshes and the numerous species, including Red Data Book species, and habitats that were lost when a warehouse development was approved. Despite legal challenges the planning system failed to protect this significant landscape.
2   DP World London Gateway is a new deep-water container port and logistics park on the north bank of the Thames about 12 miles east of Purfleet.
3   As one of my interviewees pointed out, the 'wildness' of the Filter Beds will not be appreciated by everyone and context is also important: *if this was growing at the side of the road someone would chop it down and put it on the bonfire.* The interviewees at all three sites were largely self-selecting – they were already visiting so it is probably safe to assume that they like these types of landscape.

4   During the build up to the 2012 Olympics a significant loss of community green spaces, allotments and wildlife habitats was documented (Antebi, T., 2011). The legacy of the Games promised to make good these losses, but during my research people were very aware of the destruction that was taking place on their doorstep and were also afraid of the disruption that would occur during the Games themselves.

References

Antebi, T. (2011) *London 2012 Olympics: What's the hidden cost to green spaces and wildlife habitats? The Ecologist.* Available from: www.theecologist.org/investigations/society/812270/london_2012_olympics_whats_the_hidden_cost_to_green_spaces_and_wildlife_habitats.html [Accessed 30 November 2016].

Beard, P. (2006) *East London Green Grid: Slack nature and the working wild.* London, Greater London Authority, pp. 6–7.

Bender, B. (2002) Time and landscape. *Current Anthropology*, 43 (SUPPL. 4), pp. S103–S112.

De Groot, M., Drenthen, M. & De Groot, W. T. (2011) Public visions of the human/nature relationship and their implications for environmental ethics. *Environmental Ethics*, 33 (1), pp. 25–44.

De Groot, W. T. & Van Den Born, R. J. G. (2003) Visions of nature and landscape type preferences: An exploration in The Netherlands. *Landscape and Urban Planning*, 63 (3), pp. 127–138.

Dee, C. (2010) Form, utility, and the aesthetics of thrift in design education. *Landscape Journal*, 29 (1), pp. 21–35.

DeSilvey, C. (2006) Observed decay: Telling stories with mutable things. *Journal of Material Culture*, 11 (3), pp. 318–338.

DeSilvey, C. & Edensor, T. (2013) Reckoning with ruins. *Progress in Human Geography*, 37 (4), 465–485.

Edensor, T. (2005) Waste matter – The debris of industrial ruins and the disordering of the material world. *Journal of Material Culture*, 10 (3), pp. 311–332.

Franck, K. & Stevens, Q. (2007) Tying down loose space. In: K. A. Franck & Q. Stevens (Eds.) *Loose space*. London: Routledge, pp. 1–33.

Hillier, J. (2011) Encountering Gilles Deleuze in another place. *European Planning Studies*, 19(5), pp. 861–885.

Jorgensen, A. & Tylecote, M. (2007) Ambivalent landscapes – Wilderness in the urban interstices. *Landscape Research*, 32 (4), pp. 443–462.

Lynch, K. (1972) *What time is this place?* Cambridge, MA: MIT Press.

Massey, D. (1999) Philosophy and politics of spatiality: Some considerations. The Hettner-Lecture in human geography. *Geographische Zeitschrift*, 87. Jahrg., H. 1 pp. 1–12.

Massey, D. (2005) *For space*. London: Sage Publications.

Relph, E. (2004) Temporality and the rhythms of sustainable landscapes. In: T. Mels (Ed.) *Reanimating places: A geography of rhythms*. Aldershot: Ashgate Publishing Limited, pp. 111–122.

Robins, J., Hensall, S. & Farr, A. (2013) *The state of brownfields in the Thames Gateway.* Buglife. Available from: https://www.buglife.org.uk/sites/default/files/The%20State%20of%20Brownfields%20in%20the%20Thames%20Gateway_0_0.pdf [Accessed 30 November 2016].

Roth, M. S. (1997a) Irresistible decay: Ruins reclaimed. In: M. S. Roth, C. Lyons & C. Merewether (Eds.) *Irresistible decay.* Los Angeles, CA: The Getty Research Institute Publications and Exhibitions Programme, pp. 1–23.

Roth, M. S. (1997b) Preface. In: M. S. Roth, C. Lyons & C. Merewether (Eds.) *Irresistible decay.* Los Angeles, CA: The Getty Research Institute Publications and Exhibitions Programme, pp. xi–xii.

Saito, Y. (2007) *Everyday aesthetics.* Oxford: Oxford University Press.

Walsh, K. (1992) *The representation of the past: Museums and heritage in the post-modern world.* London: Routledge.

Woodward, C. (2002) *In ruins.* London: Vintage.

My memories at Bentwaters

The third interlude

Bentwaters is a former US military base that opened during World War II on heathland near Woodbridge in Suffolk. I was taken on a tour of the decommissioned base with a group of about 30 people, organised as part of the Place – Occupation weekend at Snape Maltings in January 2014. When I visited the site I had no intention of writing this interlude, however shortly after, I decided to record my memories of the visit. I include this as the third interlude to demonstrate examples of my spontaneous memories that were part of my experience of the landscape. It is not possible when interviewing people to catch this element of spontaneity but in this interlude, by writing about my own memories, I am able to examine the different ways in which they relate to the materiality of a landscape previously unknown to me.

My mind wanders as the tour leader recites all the makes of aircraft that were stationed at the site from 1944, when it opened, until its closure in 1993; I imagine the group is divided into those who perhaps could be described as fighter plane enthusiasts and those who are interested in abandoned places. We climb the staircase to the watchtower that overlooks the runway; there are bird droppings and masses of dead flies festooning the cheap laminated tables. The view is not that interesting, but as we are all crammed in the tower I find myself beside a highly varnished wooden table with a glass top beneath which is a circular arrangement of shiny golden bullets. It reminds me of the armouries I saw as a child, where guns, swords, daggers and knives are arranged on the walls in huge circles; I remember being fascinated at the beauty and yet unsettled, knowing that perhaps I should not be feeling like this. I wanted a sword. I wanted to take one home with me. The thought crossed my mind that perhaps I could take a bullet – of course I didn't, but surely the table had been left behind, forgotten in the dead-fly room because it was unwanted.

From the window I watched a group of men and boys flying large model aeroplanes where once fighter planes took off on their missions.

The coach dropped us further into the site and the security gates opened to let us through into the area where the nuclear warheads were once stored. There was a double gate with a control room and a no-man's land in between. Surrounding the area were three layers of barbed wire fences and apparently the telegraph poles that criss-crossed the site had originally had wires strung across them to prevent helicopter attacks from above. I remind myself to stop photographing and to experience the place; as the first security gate closes and we all wait in the no-man's land, I feel a frisson of excitement – perhaps this is what is was like when you were protecting nuclear warheads.

The bunkers contained the detonators and warheads for the planes that were sited at Greenham Common.[1] How ironic that when, in the early 1980s, I was joining hands in protest around the airbase at Greenham, the nuclear warheads were stored just 20 miles down the road from where I was born and brought up. I remember the day we went to Greenham, men and woman holding hands round the perimeter fence, the feeling that surely together we could make a difference to the world. Now I'm taking photos from inside a similar former US base, of barbed wire fences contrasting with the vertical trunks of pine trees.

Two teenage boys in the group are bored; the cold war probably means little to them. They run up the grassy bank that protects one of the bunkers, but immediately someone in charge shouts for them to come down. I take a photo looking up at the base of the watchtower; the corroded metal plates remind me of the Piazza Metallica at Duisburg Nord. Was there a link between that steelworks and the military or am I imagining this?

Walking along the line of bunkers there are traces of history to be read, but what do they mean? The bunker itself could be a Rachael Whiteread artwork, a concrete box in a concrete bunker. Several others are also taking photos of these traces, of decay, of contrasts; perhaps we are the *ruin porn* group. When I look at the photo I have taken of a mysterious sign saying Nato 399, I see three black-clad figures in the background; they could almost be guards, they are just lacking the rifles.

We wander through the pines and across the endless tarmac and concrete routes that traverse the site. Again I stop to photograph some concrete blocks and again I have no idea what they were; they have become pleasing forms against a larger landscape of pines and grass (Figure iii). How is it that the grass is so short? Is it mowed or grazed? Surely the rabbits that we spot can't keep it at this length.

A man who works on the site tells us that he doesn't think about the past history of the place; that's not what it's about for him. He thinks about the future, about the many films and stunt routines that have been shot here. Someone says they keep expecting to see Private Pike emerging from the trees. Wasn't *Dad's Army* shot in Norfolk? I seem to remember my father telling me that.[2]

The hanger for testing engines is pitch black when we enter. We stand in the control room, peering through the glass, imagining what it could have been like. There is still an instrument panel there that helps in our imaginings, but no planes, engines or airmen. In the dark we creep around the empty

Figure iii Concrete remnants at Bentwaters

space listening for whispers of the past until, dramatically, the vast hanger doors are slid open and light floods in, bringing us instantly back to the present.

Outside the view across the site is mundane – flat grass punctuated by the mounds of hangers and tall stacks of crates that are used by a vegetable distribution company. Local farmers bring their potatoes and onions here. We are told that the original owner of the land, before the airfield came here, now owns it again.

Outside the perimeter fence is a Norman church. It stands alone in a ploughed field. The landowner we meet tells us that people are unsure why a church was built there although some think that once it was on the course of a river that has long since diverted south. The memory of the landscape is perhaps written in the worn flints of the church. Apparently only two cottages had to be demolished when the airfield was built. They were right next to the runway.

Notes

1   In the 1980s Greenham Common airbase in Berkshire, UK, became the focus of protests against nuclear weapons. A permanent peace camp was established outside the gates and in 1982 protesters joined hands around the perimeter fence to demonstrate against the decision to site American cruise missiles on the site.

2   *Dad's Army* was a BBC television sitcom that ran from the late 1960s and through the 1970s, and is still repeated today. It followed the mishaps of a group of Home Guard volunteers based in a fictional town of Walmington-on-Sea. Private Pike was the youngest of the volunteers and perhaps the most hapless. Many of the outdoor scenes were shot on an army training ground in Norfolk.

7 Perceptions of the qualities and their impact on memories

The entanglement of history, memory and place

The question of whether buildings, landscapes and artefacts can have memories embedded in them – almost as if the memories are lying dormant, waiting to be reactivated by the user – is contentious. People often speak of the importance of preserving historical artefacts so that we can remember, however, the remembering is not usually in these cases a personal memory about our own life history, but rather an awareness of a past that we might already know about or might choose to find out about in more detail. Thus, the boundary between what is defined as history and what is spoken of as memory can sometimes become blurred. The term heritage also serves to complicate these understandings. As I discussed in Chapter 2, at one extreme there is the heritage site specifically created to display a particular aspect of cultural history; stories are presented at a defined point in the site's history in order to support a certain cultural identity, whilst ignoring other pasts and other stories (Tilley, 2006). However, the term heritage is also used to describe the everyday history and memories of small localised communities. This latter understanding stresses the importance of community but in doing so assumes that all members of the community agree, that there are no differences and no one is excluded; however, this is not always the case (Waterton and Smith, 2010). Waterton and Smith point out the inequalities in the accepted discourse around traditional heritage practice where 'communities of expertise have been placed in a position that regulates and assesses the relative *worth* of other communities of interest' (Waterton and Smith, 2010: 13). In the light of these understandings, derelict sites are often held up as examples of landscapes where engagement with the abandoned physical objects can give rise to diverse involuntary memories rather than the fixed meanings espoused by the traditional heritage site (Swanton, 2012).

Hand-in-hand with this interest in heritage, towards the end of the twentieth century, attention has focused on the historical artefact. This is a reaction, suggests Huyssen (1995), to the sense of constant change, the celebration of the new and the rejection of the obsolete that characterises the modern world. The result has been an awakening of interest in preserving local ways of life and conserving objects that might previously have been seen as worthless (Huyssen, 1995). The expectation that everyday objects might tell the story of people's lives long after they are gone (discussed by Küchler (2006)) is not, however, a recent development, as evidenced by our museums overflowing with artefacts and remains from past cultures. However, Huyssen rightly points out that recently there has been an increased interest in our own local histories and the personal and quotidian objects that tell these stories. Till (2005) and Lowenthal (1985) suggest that this interest is driven by the need to confirm that the past existed and to validate our sense of self through our memories; there is a desire to preserve objects, 'reaffirming memory and history in tangible format' (Lowenthal, 1985: 191).

The urban historian Christine Boyer's (1996) discourse on memory and the city is also relevant to the ways in which landscape and memory are inter-twined. She comprehensively examines and attempts to untangle the links between the city, history and memory and describes how in the nineteenth and early twentieth centuries there was the expectation that 'place and monuments [would] transfer meaning and knowledge across generations' (Boyer, 1996: 17), and that these buildings and artefacts would be direct sources of memories. From the industrial revolution onwards, the writing of history has been a linear process that describes a progression whereby the future is always seen as an improvement on the past (Boyer, 1996; Sharr, 2010; Till, 2004).[1] Boyer (1996) posits an alternative 'City of Collective Memory' that is composed of layers of history that may remind us of forgotten memories or, because we no longer know or understand the original purpose of the artefacts we encounter, may allow us to 'substitute invented traditions or imaginary narrations' (Boyer, 1996: 19).[2] This conceptualisation of the city is much like Schama's description of how a greater understanding of landscape might be gained by 'digging down through layers of memories and representations toward the primary bedrock' (1995: 16–17). Similarly in his paper on the industrial landscape of the Ruhr in Germany, Swanton (2012: 267) suggests that a 'montage of fragmentary encounters' with the wastelands and derelict landscapes left behind after the regeneration process can contribute to multiple and diverse memories, allowing space for stories about the lives of the people who worked there.

However, Boyer's city is one where history and memory are opposed; memory is as de Certeau suggests 'a sort of anti-museum; it is not localizable' (1984: 108), 'it moves things about' (de Certeau, 1984: 87), whereas history is concerned with fixing things and processes 'within newly erected frame-works' (Boyer, 1996: 133). For Boyer, as for de Certeau, memory cannot be localised and as such the city that she is envisaging is one where memory can be activated through the creative connecting of disconnected events that might come about as a result of 'randomness, disturbances, dispersions and accidents' (Boyer, 1996: 68). The reimagining of memories through place becomes an embodied experience as we move through the city: 'memory is worked again and again, differently, and embodied thereby, grasped and wound up in body-performance and interaction with place' (Crouch and Parker, 2003: 396).

Embodied and emplaced memories

Boyer's creative and indeterminate ways of remembering contrast with the philosopher Edward Casey's (2000) ideas of how memory is in some way emplaced in the landscape, ready for us to remember as we, as embodied beings, move through a specific place. Tilley also suggests that 'places and landscapes anchor memories because we do not remember in a disembodied placeless manner' (2006: 25). This results, says Casey, in a place that is bounded and specific and can thus become a way of holding memories that we can then connect with through our bodies as we re-experience the place. Place is conceived of as an enclosure for our memories, and it is in the things we encounter within place that we can emplace past memories (Casey, 2000).

There are two problems with this conceptualisation of memory and place. The first is political; if place – and the material objects therein – becomes a way of containing the past, then problems can arise when the memories associated with this place are contested and appropriated for particular purposes (Till, 2005). I also have difficulty with the importance Casey puts on the specificity of both place and memory; we have all experienced how a particular sensory experience can lead to a memory that might be unrelated to the place we are in. This is most evident in the case of the sense of smell; for me it is a particular combination of fresh coffee and hot porridge that can transport me to my grandparents' breakfast table as a child. This is an example of what Connerton (1989) would call a personal memory, one in which I reflect on my life history; this form of memory requires a context or centres on a particular experience. In my case the context is the breakfast table, but the sensory perception that brings the memory to mind is a chance experience that may occur in a very different context from the original.

Casey (2000), like many of the academics who write about memory, quotes Proust to support his argument:

> As soon as I had recognised the taste of the piece of madeleine soaked in her decoction of lime-blossom which my aunt used to give me … immediately the old grey house upon the street, where her room was, rose up like a stage set to attach itself to the little pavilion opening on to the garden … house … town … errands … country roads … flowers … sprang into being, town and gardens alike, from my cup of tea.
>
> (Proust, 1981: 51)

However, this quote makes clear that although the memory is emplaced in the madeleine, it opens the mind to a wealth of different experiences and places; the memories run from one to another like relay racers passing the baton between them. As Küchler explains, the madeleine 'does not stand in for, and thus assist in the recollection of forgotten events, but effects a synesthetic experience of remembering' (1999: 54). Proust, although interested in the ways in which a thing might spark a memory, stresses that this process is haphazard and cannot be predicted or depended upon.

The idea that objects can retain memories also informed the work of the architect Aldo Rossi (1981) who believed that it was possible to design using universal forms – such as columns, the lighthouse and the coffee pot – that people would be able to understand and relate to. There is the expectation that people will recognise these forms and gain a sense of continuity from the feelings and memories that they engender. Crinson (2005: xii) suggests using the phrase 'urban memory' to describe the ways in which objects in a city can conjure up memories of the past. This is similar to Lynch's (1972: 198) concept of the 'psychological anchors'. However, some see the idea that buildings can 'provide a complete and satisfactory analogue for the mental world of memory' (Forty, 1999: 13–14) as problematic, especially in today's global world where people come from different upbringings and educational backgrounds.

Nevertheless, it would appear that both sides of this argument have some merit. Küchler (1993: 86) does not totally reject the idea of a connection between landscapes and memories, but attempts to distinguish between two types of memory landscapes; 'landscapes of memory', created for the purpose of remembering, and 'landscapes as memory', lived in and constantly changing. Bender summarises these respectively as: 'landscape as inscribed surface from which social and cultural relations can be read' and 'landscape as process' (1993: 11). Küchler is an anthropologist and is concerned with the social memories of non-Western societies, however, the concepts of landscape as inscribed surface and landscape as process can equally well be applied to landscape architectural discourse.[3] The difference between the two landscapes in terms of the emplacing of memories appears to be to do with intention and change. The landscape of memory is contrived to create a permanent historical record, whilst the landscape as memory is a place in which experiences and memories can take place and can be remade and re-remembered over time.

The idea of memory landscapes is also examined from an environmental psychological perspective by Lynne Manzo (2005), who suggests that there are two ways of looking at the interrelation of memory and place. In one the memories allow places to emerge as significant, whereas in the other the contrary is true and place enables memory to emerge. She sees both of these aspects of landscape as 'bridges to the past' (Manzo, 2005: 74) and ways of maintaining continuity, implying that there is fluidity between the past and the present and that the flow can go in both directions. This is not quite the same as thinking of landscape as an aide memoire, but rather it acknowledges the interrelation of memory and place and of past and present: place in the process of becoming.

Perhaps the best description of how memory and place are interrelated is given by Till (2005) who also draws on the idea of place as process; memory is a process of reflection that is informed by the materiality and temporality of place, within the context of the knowledge and past experience of the individual. It is not an unchanging artefact that stimulates remembering but the process that draws the object into new contexts (Crinson, 2005) stimulating a train of associations that extends beyond any apparent physical boundary (da Costa Meyer, 2009).

The question arising from the ideas discussed above is not only whether places can be designed to engender memories but also, if they can, what is it that 'should be brought to mind' (Lyndon, 2009: 63). Lyndon believes that places become memorable through a combination of events and experiences that take place within and around specific formalised structures. In a similar fashion to Rossi, he suggests forms of the dome, pyramid and colonnade as examples of such structures and describes the dialogue that is set up in architecture between the stabilising form – the encompassing formal structure – and the sensory experience of moving around and thus experiencing different visual effects (Lyndon, 2009). Lyndon is suggesting that places can be created that both allow for individual experiences and retain elements that speak to a common understanding; 'we need places where we can lodge hooks that can be used to secure common ground' (2009: 83). His hope is that certain forms can be universally read and understood, however, the possibility of these being comprehended in a collective fashion diminishes as our cities and urban environments become more and more socially diverse in their makeup. The people using these spaces are not only from different cultures but also from different educational backgrounds and the intended meaning may be indecipherable or misunderstood.

There are also metaphorical ways in which architecture can make reference to past histories and create space for recollection whilst remaining open to new possibilities and new memories. Sharr (2010) describes how this has been achieved at the Chapel of Reconciliation, designed by Peter Sassenroth and Rudolf Reitermann, and built on a former border strip between East and West Berlin to replace a church destroyed in 1985 by East German border guards. New materials invite comparison with archeological sedimentations of past buildings and landscapes; the aggregate for a rammed earth wall consists of fragments of rubble and stone taken from the site. Sharr (2010: 509) describes how 'millions of small deposits of the detonated church are cast into the mud', some are visible but there are many more hidden inside the walls. 'The rammed earth literally sediments together countless deposits of memory in built form' (Sharr, 2010: 509). For Sharr it is the material elements of the Chapel, both new and old, that embody memories and the ways in which historical materials are incorporated within the design both conceal and reveal their meanings, drawing attention to the tensions between absence and presence.

Lyndon and Sharr, both with an architectural background, focus on the role significant and important buildings can play in remembering and recollection. However, when discussing former brownfield sites it is the everyday landscape that is perhaps the most relevant. Mah (2010, 2012) considers these places in her discussion of memory with relation to the changes caused by the closure of the Swan Hunter shipbuilding industry in Walker,

Newcastle-upon-Tyne. She uses the term 'living memory' to describe the memories of the people who are experiencing the process of destruction of their industry, jobs and livelihood, and are facing the regeneration of their local area. Mah (2010) suggests that living memory is experiential – a part of the process of industrial decline – and it takes different forms for different people. The shipyard workers spoke of the politics that was the background to the closure of their industry, and their memories were of loss and sadness, combined with resignation. However, Mah also details accounts of community life played out against a background of the industrial history. Many wanted to protect the memory of their industrial and communal past from the forces of regeneration, understanding that, in some way, this was a threat to their memories. Mah (2010) concludes that when finally all trace of the industrial past is erased, living memory will also end. She also adds a note of caution for the future, questioning whether 'official memory' (similar to the concept of an official narrative) 'will mesh with local memory in Walker, and whether it can offer any kind of "closure" or gateway to a future, particularly one without jobs' (Mah, 2012: 95–96).

Memory and forgetting

There is a tension that can arise between absence and presence in architecture (Sharr, 2010), and it is clear that the concepts of absence, loss and forgetting are relevant to a discussion of memory in relation to derelict sites. The ruin has traditionally been seen as a symbol of loss and a reminder that all things will eventually decay and return to nature; it is a physical embodiment of the passage of time (Merewether, 1997; Roth, 1997). A ruin is also an aide memoire, a way to ward off forgetting. However Treib questions whether the industrial ruin, when incorporated into a developed site, can be understood by people who did not know the site when it was operational. He comments that 'buildings are ... stubbornly inarticulate and the stories they have to tell are latent rather than overt' (Treib, 2009: 209–210). Those interested in the discourse around industrial ruins would disagree however, and point to the experiential qualities of the ruin that can conjure up forgotten memories, the traces of workers lives that stimulate the imagination and the embodied memories that are experienced when moving through the derelict site (DeSilvey and Edensor, 2013; Edensor, 2005a; Edensor, 2005b; Garrett, 2011).

The decaying ruin, although a source of memory and recollection, is very different from a monument designed specifically to engender memories. However, monuments are often in danger of becoming a part of everyday life – something to walk past and ignore (Crinson, 2005). It is only by re-remembering, for example at an anniversary, that monuments can retain their mnemonic power, however, as DeSilvey (2010) points out, research into the memories engendered by preserved and displayed historical artefacts shows that such memories cannot be controlled. It was this understanding that led to a move in the late twentieth century to find ways of bringing the temporal into the creation of monuments – thus the counter-monument was conceived.[4] These alternative monuments draw attention to the ways in which temporality and memory interact in the hope that their changing, temporary and ephemeral aspect can help memories endure (Stevens *et al.*, 2012).[5]

The idea of the disappearing monument can inform thinking about the derelict and the ruined. Is it possible that the absence, rather than the presence, of an object or structure can provoke memories? The artist Sophie Calle visited the former East Germany and singled out empty plinths where monuments to the leaders of the communist regime had once stood. She asked passers-by to describe the objects that had once occupied the plinths and 'photographed their absence and replaced the missing monument with their memories' (Kaernbach, not known). Calle found that the memories of the residents were not only contradictory, but it appeared as if the monument 'had been detached from people's memories', and yet the memories were very emotional, demonstrating the enduring links between residents and their history (Kaernbach, not known). Nevertheless, such memories sparked by absences must eventually fade as the people who had once known the monument die or move away; then the plinth may become the source of new memories unrelated to its political history.

The role of the qualities – memories and materiality

How then do the material elements in the case study landscapes evoke memories? Interviewees speak of memories that are emplaced as part of their experience of the landscape, evoked either by the site as a whole or through individual material elements. They remember by recollecting, re-enacting or re-telling events, and such memories encourage the musing on, questioning and referencing of experiences or knowledge in the present. Memory is 'a potential for creative collaboration between present consciousness and the experience or expression of the past' (Boyarin, 1994: 22), and therefore is something that is lived in the present. It is possible to understand these collaborations in the light of Massey's (2005) writings; the memories evoked by the material qualities are a part of the multiplicity of stories that make up space and, in forming linkages between these stories, place can be experienced as something specific and special. Massey might question whether memories can be emplaced in material objects to evoke pre-ordained memories, however, I suggest that the concept of emplacing memories does not necessarily run counter to her theories. Such memories form one strand in the multiple relationships of space, however, as Massey would contend, and as my interviews confirm, these memories cannot be controlled and the visitor remains free to make their own connections and tell their own stories.

Emplaced memories

I use the term 'emplaced memories' here to describe those memories, recollections and reminiscences that can arise whilst directly experiencing or remembering the landscape as a whole or the material objects within it. The implication of the word 'emplace' is that something is put in place or in position, and this implies intention. However, here I use the term to also apply to memories that might occur by chance through the experience of the physical object. I describe these memories in this way to distinguish them from the embodied memories that I discuss in the next section.

Several interviewees at the Filter Beds described material qualities that could be considered to be sources of memories about the site's history (Figure 5.2): the incised grinding lines in one of the surfaces; the rusty holes in the Hackney Henge; the crumbling footprints of the buildings; clasps on the sides of the beds; small sections of lettering and swirls of metallic coloured paint staining the ground. The qualities that appeared to have the potential for conjuring up memories were often those that bore evidence of some form of process having taken place. The process itself was not understood and the memories were lost; they were someone else's memories and yet they were worthy of comment. The landscape architecture student pointed to a surface where *something has been dragged along it and so it bears sort of echoes of that*. Similarly at the Hidden Gardens a few interviewees commented on the facade of the Tramway and the weathering of the bricks on the chimney (Figure 6.2). As we were walking a musician reflected:

> *strange, isn't it the way the brick changes... It looks older above. It looks newer down below ... Oh maybe there was a building against it ... I wonder if that's what it is. So it was, you know it was exposed to the elements above that point.*

These lost memories emplaced in the fabric of the site have become puzzles to be solved and sources of new imaginings.

At Rainham Marshes the local people interviewed at the Heritage Centre also described how memories were emplaced in the material structures and artefacts; however, for these interviewees the memories were relived in the stories they told me. This differs from imagined memories that were evoked through perceiving processes at work on the material qualities. One told the story of a disturbed World War II soldier who started driving a gun carrier in circles until it collided with the wall of one of the military buildings and *just gouged it all away and knocked some of the brickwork out and all the marks were all still there*. The interviewee spoke of his sadness that the physical memory of this event was lost when the building was demolished. Another described how the tanks used to be unloaded at Purfleet Station and how *you can go round there even today and look at the granite kerbstones and you can see lumps knocked out of them where the tanks knocked them*. He also told me of a bomb that had fallen on the marshes and sunk into the ground leaving a depression as evidence of its presence – *where it's gone down it's drawn the earth down with it*. Interviewees also spoke of personal memories of visits to the site when it was in use by the military and when it was abandoned. Sometimes these memories related to structures such as the lookout tower where one bird watcher recollected ringing swallows, the firing range where there was a *little owl … I think between numbers 5 and 6* and the cordite store where one family picnicked. However, it was more often the landscape as a whole, together with the River Thames, the railway and the roads that brought back memories of the noise of gunfire, the military presence and of adventures on the site itself including: bird watching; racing motorbikes; jumping ditches; fishing; cadging chocolate and chewing gum from the US soldiers; picking up ammunition and the view from the train on the way to work.

The two interviewees who had been brought up near the Filter Beds when they were operational, spoke in a similar way to those at Rainham of their memories of the site and its surroundings. The River Lea, the Navigation, the power station (on the opposite bank of the Navigation) and the wall of the Filter Beds, beside the towpath, were all sources of personal memories. A blogger and retired signwriter vividly described how when he was a boy the boundary wall had been the site for illegal gambling games – *the Spiel was here just behind that corner. I used to sit up on this wall here and get 2 bob a day or a shilling a day to keep a look out for the police.* At the Hidden Gardens it was the Tramway rather than the gardens themselves that was a source of personal memories about the site's past; interviewees spoke of visits they had made to the Transport Museum, of the smell and hanger-like industrial quality of the building that contributed to these memories. A few also had memories of the Tramway as a theatre that acknowledged the derelict site. A musician remembered playing in an opera, *it must have been in the winter because I remember the snow coming through a hole in the roof.* An artist, who has a sculpture in the gardens, described the building in the early days of its incarnation as a theatre and artspace – *you used to be able to just go in there, there're empty, empty spaces … and … a friend of mine put on a large installation performance in one of the end rooms and it was literally an empty, huge, empty space, with kind of weeds growing in it.* Although it was almost always the building as a whole that inspired these memories there was one part that had become a source of collective rather than personal memory: the shallow ramp that leads to the upper storey. I was told by many interviewees that this ramp was used to take horses up to the stables on the first floor above the industrial workshops. The corridor that ran alongside the stables still exists (Figure 6.2). The Coplawhill Works opened in 1899, and in 1901 the trams were converted from horse-drawn to electric (Scotland's Places, Not known) and yet it is the story of the horses that is remembered by many people. One worker at the Hidden Gardens spoke of visitors to the site, saying: *they remember the horses, they remember when there were horse drawn trams and they used to run under the horses,* and yet this cannot possibly be true. A retired man who was interested in the history of the site explained, *my father was ... born in 1916, 1913 something like that. So he remembered when he was a boy because, obviously he was a Glaswegian and he stayed round about here most of the time. You know, so he used to tell us about the horses.*

Interviewees, when asked about the chimney at the Hidden Gardens, spoke of it as a landmark, *just to remember*, and one young unemployed man explained *I'd imagine there were a lot more at one point, probably, so it's nice to have...one.* However, as I discussed in Chapter 5, it is not clear that people know the original purpose of the chimney and, if anything, it stands as a general reminder of an industrial age. It is this that the volunteer coordinator I interviewed spoke of when she told me of a young man with learning difficulties who looked at the chimney:

> *he started talking about Govan Hill and he doesn't live there now but he had all these memories so from looking over and by looking at the chimney he could remember things from his childhood and he was telling me all about this area.*

In addition to the specific memories that were evoked by the sites and their material qualities, interviewees spoke more generally about the patterns and symbols within the landscape that reminded them of other places. In the case of the Filter Beds it was the temporal processes of decay and ruination that evoked memories of ruined churches and abbeys as well as other abandoned industrial and military sites. The seemingly natural and wild look of the landscape also brought memories of the countryside. More specifically the material artefacts reminded interviewees of other places and times: the Hackney Henge was reminiscent of ancient standing stones; the riveted pipe conjured up ideas of the medieval; the structure and colours of one of the industrial artefacts reminded an interviewee of a Japanese cemetery and the contrast between order and disorder seen in the bricks evoked pebbles on a beach. This contrasts with the interviewees at Rainham Marshes who spoke more generally about how the landscape reminded them of the local area; of other marshes along the Thames Estuary, of landfill and other neighbouring industrial sites.

In a few cases interviewees spoke to me of significant memories that they had emplaced in the site. Obviously there were many memories of past visits and also hopes of good and lasting memories into the future, but in a few instances at the Filter Beds they were of a more ceremonial nature and were specific to the site. In one instance a father spoke of a place overlooking the river where he had a naming ceremony for his son, and in another a retired man described the 'beating the bounds' event that he initiated.[6] He and a friend, who I also interviewed, had erected and inscribed a post, made of oak that was more than 450 years old, near the boundary of the London Boroughs of Hackney and Waltham Forest, which runs along the River Lea.

The event took place for many years and the oak post had become so important to him that he wanted his ashes scattered there.

Embodying memories

In Chapter 2 I discussed how someone might experience embodied memories through spatial relationships such as when crossing a threshold or remembering and imagining the experiences of others through the ways in which they move around a landscape (Vergunst, 2012). Similarly, the ghosts of workers might be imagined through bodily interactions in derelict industrial sites (Edensor, 2005a). None of my interviewees spoke about their memories in this way, however they did have recollections of their own movements in and through the landscape: diving into the Filter Beds; swimming in the river; sliding down outlet pipes; climbing on the vehicles at the Transport Museum and jumping the ditches at Rainham. An elderly woman at the Filter Beds narrated a childhood memory of her husband's – *it used to be filled with water and him and all his friends used to dive in there and swim.* The elderly blogger also reminisced about the Navigation and the power station and how in his youth:

> all the coal barges would come along here and there would be a crane, a big grab lifting them up, and one of the tricks we used to get up to when we were kids, we used to jump off these bridges here and swim, go onto the coal barges, roll in the soot, come out looking like a devil and dive in the water and come out clean as a whistle.

His walk with me was the first time he had actually been into the Filter Beds although he knew the area so well. He made a point of showing me the pipe across the Lea – *we used to get across the pipe, walk across the pipe and in the middle there was a cap or a stop cock or whatever it was ... you could balance easily, that bit was the daring bit.*

The most distinct memory for many of those I spoke to at Rainham was of how they had accessed the site when it was owned by the MOD. These memories were not evoked by existing material qualities or by a particular section of the site, although they were sometimes emplaced in the memory of the red flag that was raised by the MOD to warn people whenever firing was taking place. Rather they were expressed as embodied memories of danger and excitement, and were evoked as soon as I asked about the site prior to the RSPB's ownership – *the red flag went up and the people were down here and they were firing every weekend. And erm, if you were standing in the middle sometimes you got one that whizzed past your head.* As well as the danger of straying into the path of the bullets and the thrill of trespassing, there was frustration at not being able to start bird watching as the flags were still up. *There was one time I did venture over the lagoons when the flag was up and you could hear the odd bullet whistling ... i didn't stay too long ... Even for me I felt quite nervous.* Others spoke of the physical and sensual experience of getting into the site, of how they *used to have to clamber over and creep along the bottom* to avoid being seen and how they

> *were belly-crawling out through the reeds because you didn't want to stand up in case the red flags were flying. There are some big metal pipes that stick up down there from the early dredging things over there and you'd hear the overshoots pinging off of the metal pipes.*

Landscape of memory – landscape as memory

For the interviewees it would seem, therefore, that the case study sites are functioning as landscapes **as** memory rather than landscapes **of** memory (Küchler, 1993: 86); memories are created over time as part of the lived experience of the landscape. In this respect my research appears to contradict Millman's (2011) statement that there is only a small window of time when a place might be seen as open to diverse memories before the recognised and agreed story of these memories is written; in fact interviewees' memories seem to be varied and multiple rather than static and singular.

There are several properties of the material qualities that evoke memories. In the case of the Filter Beds it is often processes or actions evidenced in the textures and patinas of the structures and artefacts that suggest forgotten memories and stimulate new imaginings. The interviewees do not have specific recollections about these particular material qualities and yet the mystery that surrounds them gives the impression that there are stories waiting to be told; I recount my own experiences of this type of memory emplacement in the third interlude. At Rainham emplaced memories also evoked memories and inspired the re-telling of stories. Here it was often the topography of the Rainham Marshes site as a whole that evoked memories of embodied sensory experiences of past visits – of bodily moving through the landscape. In particular, embodied memories often featured in stories that interviewees told of their childhood or of trespassing on the site when it was operational or derelict. One local woman, talking of her childhood, told me:

> *there was so many of us used to come over here. We used to camp out over there ... Further out over the back more. We used to go over there ... Then as a teenager we used to go there ... A lot of my youth was actually spent out there ... Even now the kids that live locally, they all still come over there. They all still get in the ditches. They all still climb on the concrete buildings ... All bolshie bouncing along.*

In addition, the recognisable patterns and symbols that interviewees perceived in the material qualities and the landscapes as a whole – such as decaying ruins, industrial materials and natural vegetation – served as reminders of other places and other times. This confirms the findings of Rishbeth and Powell (2013) who suggest that people create layers of memories in landscapes, reminding them of other places they have known.

These different ways of emplacing and embodying memories in the material and spatial qualities of the site could be seen to confirm Casey's (2000) theories of place and memory; memories are waiting in places to be re-remembered. However, this conceptualisation of place is problematic, partly because of the implied specificity of such memories and the intentionality of their emplacement. Boyer's (1996) concept of memory in the city as being unlocalisable, random and left to chance is more apt. The creative act of remembering can be likened to a process of reflection on past memories that are brought into the present, re-remembered and re-told in new ways and new contexts (Boyarin, 1994; Boyer, 1996; Crinson, 2005; Till, 2005). I suggest that the memories interviewees experienced through the material qualities of the site are in some cases akin to this creative process of remembering. Sometimes interviewees told me stories that they had told many times before; the tales of the interviewees at the Purfleet Heritage Centre are examples of this, as is the story of the horses at the Hidden Gardens. However, there are other instances when the stories developed as we talked, with interviewees remembering more details and reflecting on their remembering, and thus re-making the past in the present. As Tilley asserts 'whatever we remember ... we get a different past, a different sense of place, and a different landscape every time' (2006: 29).

These diverse memories and the multiple ways in which the interviewees experience them would suggest that these sites fall into the category of landscape as memory (Küchler, 1993). However, the Hidden Gardens also aims to be a landscape of memory, where designers have utilised the idea of the palimpsest or sedimentary landscape in their inclusion of the material qualities and also to make reference to previous uses of the site in more abstract ways. The spatial arrangement of the rows of trees on the western boundary relates to the nursery, which occupied the site prior to the development of the Tramcar works, although this historical reference was not mentioned by any of my interviewees. The layering of the material structures into the landscape appears to have been only marginally successful in signalling the history of the site; the interviewees see the material qualities as important reminders or landmarks. Nevertheless, it was often necessary for me to specifically ask about the chimney and the other artefacts; they were so familiar, they did not require comment. Memories that do arise do not appear to be connected with the material qualities of the gardens, but rather with the Tramway itself and the memories of interviewees' past experiences and sensations within the building. I suggest therefore that the creation of the Hidden Gardens as a landscape of memory (Küchler, 1993) has been only partially successful and this draws into question the purpose of a design approach that attempts to create strata or layers that make visible the signs of past histories (Lynch, 1972). The idea of the site as landscape as memory is perhaps more appropriate; for the people who knew the site and had visited when it was a Transport Museum, there was a sense of continuity that was engendered through remembering.

Boyer describes the difference between history and memory thus; 'history always stands against memory, the one as a constructed or recomposed artifice, the other a lived and moving expression' (1996: 69). This is evident in the ways in which interviewees discussed new memories connected with the experience of being and playing in the garden as a whole rather than through specific engagement with the qualities of the site. The cleaner who had brought her sons to the transport museum as children explained,

> *my boys still when they meet up, this is where they come for coffees ...*
> *I think you need landmarks, just to remember, I mean, when I go,*
> *my sons are not going to remember the chimney, they're just going*
> *to remember the play area and the nice times, the coffee house, as they*
> *get older.*

However the mother of a young child did feel that the chimney might feature in her son's memories – *he's going to remember the place fondly, and the features that he would remember might be things that he didn't necessarily notice or speak about but, he might say, oh do you remember there was a big chimney in there?* Although the inclusion of historical layers in the Hidden Gardens to create a landscape of memory has, to a certain extent, worked against the remembering of the past, instead the landscape is full of changing recollections, unpredictable and contradictory, and yet part of the encounter and the relationship between person and place (Boyer, 1996).

There is, however, one element of the history of the Tramway that has become part of a collective memory for many of my interviewees and this is the story of the horses. I mention above how the official history acknowledges the horses as a small part of the overall story of the Tramway. However, in the memories of my interviewees they have taken on a greater significance than their historical role would warrant and the interviewees' understanding of the part the horses played in the history of Glasgow's trams is perhaps overstated and at times incorrect. These inaccuracies emphasise the difficulties of intentionally emplacing predetermined memories. Nevertheless it is clear that memory of the horses is emplaced in the ramp and, to a lesser extent, the former stable corridor, and that these material structures form an important element when reimagining and retelling the story.

Experiences of absence and forgetting

Many interviewees spoke of the importance of remembering, of being reminded, and of how material qualities such as the chimney at the Hidden Gardens and the mantlet bank and stop butts at Rainham had a role in this process of remembering. However, I discussed in Chapter 5 how such arte-facts often go unremarked upon and it is not clear to people exactly what they should be remembering. I have also observed the sense of loss that some of the interviewees at Rainham Marshes felt when the buildings were demolished and the emplaced memories erased, and these interviewees celebrated the artefacts that they had scrounged, scavenged and saved for the Purfleet Heritage Centre. Overall, the feeling of the interviewees was that it is necessary to remember the past, as it is a part of our history. An interviewee at Rainham summed this sentiment up:

> *I think it's nice as well for future generations to know about it. This is where their parents might have grown up, or grandparents. It's just part of British history I suppose. Whether you're from here or not. It's nice to see. When you see somewhere you have far more belief in it, you know ... You relate to it and things like that, you know.*

Interviewees also remembered the sites as a whole when they were waste-lands. In the case of the Filter Beds and Rainham Marshes, I spoke to several interviewees about the DUN sites, and at the Hidden Gardens inter-viewees remembered other derelict sites when they reflected on the trans-formation of the garden. I discussed interviewees' responses to the abandoned sites in some detail in Chapter 5 with reference to creating frames for reading. The few who remembered the Filter Beds described vandalism and destruction and many of the interviewees' memories of Rainham Marshes during this period were of dereliction, danger, fly-tipping and trespassing. It was these memories that were re-told when interviewees described the transformation of the sites; the memories of the clean-up operations were emplaced in absent material qualities. These qualities were often seen as polluting: things such as tyres, burnt out motorbikes and spent ammunition. However, there were also memories of overgrown vegetation and of the wildlife. The sense was usually of a wasted and problematic landscape, but one that was full of presences rather than absences; interviewees did not speak in terms of forgetting and loss when describing the site in its derelict phase, viewing this period as another stage in its history.

However, in the sites as they are experienced in the present there were several structures and artefacts that were remembered in their absence; the memories were emplaced in a particular part of the site even though the physical object was no longer there. This was most noticeable in the comments about the empty plinth at the Filter Beds. This large slab of concrete had been the base for a pylon and the memory of the pylon was still writ large in several of the interviewees' minds. A woman walking her dog commented, there *was even outcry at the pylons going because that's also part of industrial heritage, people said aah, leave the pylons, but they didn't, they took 'em* (Figure 7.1). Other absences were also noted at the Filter Beds; the canal boater, when talking about a photo he had taken, spoke of the way the *hints*

Figure 7.1 The plinth at Middlesex Filter Beds

of the missing structure, the structure continues in your mind somehow. The local blogger who played on the river as a child was animated when describing a missing statue of a woman pouring water from an ewer that used to stand on the side of the Navigation marking the beginning of the Filter Beds:

> *She was on that point … let's have a little look … Of course she was a local landmark, and … she was beautiful. A bit diaphanous, as far as I can remember and it was the nearest thing to classical art that we would see around here … I suppose it was Greek art or whatever they call it … not an expert at these things. But it was always lovely, we always thought it was nice because the water was coming out … that's where she was on that corner there.*

I have endeavoured to find pictures or references to this classical woman and have not succeeded although I have found a sculpture of a river god complete with urn that was displayed on top of the Turbine House at the Middlesex Filter Beds (Lea Bridge Heritage, 2012). This statue, commissioned in 1809, was relocated to the Coppermill Lane Waterworks in 1971 (Public Monuments and Sculpture Association, Not known). I also located a painting by Cyril Mann from 1967 (BBC in partnership with Public Catalogues Foundation, 2014) that depicts an empty plinth at the spot indicated by my interviewee and appears to show a sculpture that could well be the reclining river god on the roof of a nearby building.

At Rainham Marshes and the Hidden Gardens it was the absence of rail and tram tracks that were commented on. A woman employed as a cleaner at the Hidden Gardens was disappointed that the tramtracks and the cobbles had disappeared in the garden when it was still possible to see them in areas outside the ballet school, and a man I interviewed on a walking for health morning at Rainham described in detail how the topography of the site reminded him of the railway – *I'll show where the railway line used to come off the Tilbury line … up further there was a branch which took the munition trucks into the garrison and there's still some of the concrete abutments left.* Another interviewee described walking round the site with an old friend who had been in the Territorial Army and had been on the site when it was operational:

> *I think you'll find if you look down on the right hand side* [of the boardwalk] *… I mean it's not a railway station, you can see a bit of a platform. 'Cos they used to bring in the ammunition by rail, and that's where it used to come in to.*

I later found more evidence of the branch line that once served the rifle range; opposite the mantlet banks on a brick building is painted a graffiti-like image of a signal box[7]. On the side of the building itself is affixed an old railway sign saying 'Purfleet Riflerange Halt'. This station is shown on old maps of the area but was in fact several hundred metres across the site next to the existing railway. The memory of the station at Purfleet Riflerange Halt is now emplaced in the simple brick building, but is absent and almost forgotten in its original setting.

However, it is not only absent qualities that become lost or invisible. The chimney at the Hidden Gardens acts in a similar way to a historic monument: it is very present and yet relatively unnoticed. In contrast, the Filter Beds, with its decaying structures, surfaces and artefacts, more closely resembles the changing ruin and can be compared with the temporal counter-monument: a place where interviewees engage with multiple and diverse personal memories (Stevens *et al.*, 2012). Through perceiving the decaying object we can reflect on its history and also imagine possible futures, as the object continues to decay and eventually vanishes (DeSilvey, 2006).

It is clear therefore that specific absences produce memories and in some cases material structures and the physical attributes of the landscape can 'emplace' an absence. This was evident in the comments interviewees at the Filter Beds made about the empty plinth and the missing pylon, and the patch of land where once the lost river god or goddess was sited, whereas at Rainham it was the topography of the landscape that reminded one interviewee of the absent railway lines. The memories remain emplaced in the landscape even though the physical objects are long gone. However, these memories are ephemeral and will be lost completely when the people who remember are gone and new memories will take their place; the plinth without the pylon has already become a place to sit and chat. I have also shown how memories prompted by absences might change and take on new forms; the river goddess is just one example and the story of the horses at the Hidden Gardens demonstrates how collective memories emplaced in the ramp, can embrace inaccuracies that serve to make the story more attractive. I wonder how the story of the Purfleet Riflerange Station might be told in the future? Memories change as they are re-remembered through the lens of past experiences, knowledge and imagination; they become fluid and adaptable, most particularly when they are evoked by absences.

Ghosts and presences

Although the discourses about derelict industrial landscapes speak of how embodied experiences of visitors might include an awareness of the ghosts of past workers inhabiting the site, it was mainly in the Hidden Gardens that interviewees reflected on people who might have made their living in these places. Interviewees at the Filter Beds speak of the decaying material qualities as sources of memories about the past, however, they appear distanced from these memories; they can only imagine and conjecture about the uses of the artefacts and only occasionally do they think of the people who worked there. These interviewees did not have access to the site when it was working or when abandoned, with the result that the memories of absences are more romanticised than those of the interviewees at the other case study sites. Lowenthal (1985, 1996a) suggests that we are distanced from the past; it is necessarily 'other' from our present day experiences and knowledge and that it is this sense of difference that marks our understanding of history. The alternative to this sense of the past as 'other', is an approach that asserts that the only way we can understand people from the past is through the knowledge and understanding of others and ourselves in the present (Feeley-Harnik, 1996). The past is conceived of as 'the very ground on which, in which, with which we stand, move and otherwise interact; out of which we continually regenerate ourselves in relations with others' (Feeley-Harnik, 1996: 216). The danger of this approach, however, is that it leads to the assumption that the past is just like the present, viewed through the lens of our present knowledge, beliefs and prejudices with the result that certain individuals and groups of people can be forgotten or excluded (Lowenthal, 1996b). 'It is important to recognise that many pasts *must not be known* by others if they are to retain their power and significance for ourselves' (Lowenthal, 1996b: 242).

There is a sense that for some of the interviewees at the Filter Beds, the past is as Lowenthal suggests, something separate and other, but they see in the decaying material qualities, multiple ways of reimagining this past for themselves in the present. In contrast at the Hidden Gardens and, to a lesser extent, at Rainham Marshes the interviewees are reflective about the people who have worked on the sites and also about the materiality of the derelict landscapes. These absences were, for some, very present in the everyday places that surrounded them and they were eager to talk of their memories. At the Hidden Gardens one elderly woman in particular looked back on those times with reference to her life, imagining what it might have been like for people working in these industries:

> *It reminds you that people worked here and they probably had hard times. You know I always think compared to the people who worked here I have such an affluent life. I can volunteer, volunteering to them would have been unheard of! They'd have thought I was crazy to volunteer. I mean they'd be working from eight to eight, sort of. Um ... long hours. My father worked on the railway in the 40s, 50s and he was working like ten hour days ... workers then would be paid peanuts and now people coming in and having coffee. I think it's very good to look back ... and look at the lives people had. It makes you more appreciative of what you've got.*

A professional woman in her 40s also reflected on the links between the industrial history of the Tramway site and the history of immigration in the surrounding area:

> *I mean you just think of Glasgow and the shipbuilding and the heavy industries, which are no longer existing and I think it's a really poignant reminder of all of those things. Erm, and you know there's a huge garage just across the way which is a bus depot ... Glasgow had about half a dozen massive bus depots that were all linked and the whole kind of transport system and the transport museum being here, and the traffic levels and, so something about all of that actually I think resonates with this place ... And there was a high immigrant population where people were enticed to come and drive buses in Scotland, erm, back in the 50s ... it was all heavy industry and none of the men would drive buses. So there was a massive piece of work went on for encouraging people, erm, particularly from Pakistan, to come over and drive buses, so a lot of them settled in these areas and surrounding areas.*

I discussed in Chapter 5 how at Rainham Marshes one of the interviewees imagined what life might have been like for the women working in the ammunition and cordite stores and other interviewees also reflected on the memories that certain structures and artefacts could evoke. The garden design student, after photographing the mantlet bank reflected – *you just think about the people who've been there and used it and hidden under there* and another interviewee described feeling sad when he recollected that many of the soldiers who trained at Rainham did not return from the war. At the Filter Beds the photographer told me that he was *quite proud of my Victorian forefathers, they made a lot of changes, so it's nice to have some respect, or to feel a little bit part of that or to see something they made.*

However, I usually had to ask the interviewees specifically if they thought about the people who had worked there and responses often focused on what the workers would feel if they saw the Filter Beds today: a sense of pride in their achievements or sadness that the industry was now gone and the place abandoned.

The role of memories in perceptions of continuity

In the naming ceremony and the beating the bounds event at the Filter Beds we can see how people create and emplace personal memories in landscapes ready for them to be re-remembered in the future. These are Manzo's (2005: 74) 'bridges to the past': the concept that there is a continuity between past, present and future that is expressed through the landscape. This sense of continuity is evident in the ways interviewees reflect on the past through their understanding of the present, and make connections between their memories, the stories told about the past, and their knowledge of life today. It is particularly noticeable in the interviewees' responses to the Hidden Gardens and the Tramway, and may be due to the fact that many of my interviewees were local residents and remembered the site when it was the Transport Museum. In some cases their parents had worked in similar transport industries so they had an indirect connection with the history of the site. These interviewees attempt to understand the past through their knowledge of themselves and others in the present, however, they also see the past as different and separate from themselves and they reflect on these differences. The past is not a foreign country (Lowenthal, 1996a), completely distanced from their present lives, but it is something different that they then attempt to accommodate in the here and now. In Chapter 5 I discussed how Massey (2005) incorporates continuity into her conceptualisation of space and place as the continuing accumulation of experiences as one returns to a place over and over again. For my interviewees, the memories that are told and re-told, recalled and reimagined, contribute to this sense of continuity. The differences they perceive between themselves and people from the past histories of the site are another aspect of their experience: their negotiation between the different relationships and linkages that go to make up place (Massey, 2005). The sense of continuity achieved through memories, is part of a landscape as memory. Remembering is one way in which we rewrite our narratives of the past but 'remembering has its own history' too (Küchler 1996: 228): an iteration of recollections.

Some designers (Lyndon, 2009) assert that certain universal stabilising forms and structures can serve as centring elements in people's understandings of the landscape. I suggest that my case studies show that rather than a formal structure being the stabilising element to the design, the centring element and the sense of continuity is in the mind of the visitor; it is created through their knowledge, experience and memories. I observed this on a personal level in my third interlude. In effect my interviewees' memories (and my own) become one factor in the frame for reading the site, an aspect I discussed in detail in Chapter 5. If we are able to create this sense of continuity for ourselves then is it possible that designed landscapes can present new and exciting aspects that challenge this understanding, creating opportunities for experiencing unpredictable and chance memories? I will discuss this in the next chapter.

Notes

1   Sharr (2010) suggests that negative discourse critiquing the Modernist approach to a linear and progression-oriented method of history writing has become too pervasive and calls for this approach to have its place in the discussion of memory. In this I agree; although much of the writing on memory stresses the unpredictability and sense of randomness that is a part of recollection it might be useful to consider how we use a framework for reflecting on our memories. It is clear that this framework is constructed of our experiences and knowledge, one element of which is the sense we have of a linear progression between past, present and future.

2   Although Boyer (1996) speaks of collective memory with relation to the city, the unpredictable memories she is describing here are experienced by individuals and I think she is using the term collective to speak of the collective memories and histories that form the layers of this conceptual city. These are then experienced randomly and by chance by the individual as they engage with the city.

3   Küchler (1993) is discussing the ways that the history and memory of land-use and ownership are embodied in the landscape. She introduces the term memory-work to describe the process of emplacing memory in landscape. Although her focus is non-Western cultures, this way of looking at landscape as process is now fundamental to an understanding of landscape within the landscape design discipline; individual memories are one part of the process of landscape.

4   An example of a counter-monument given by Young (1993) is the 12 metre tall, lead-covered column, the Harburg Monument against fascism that opened in 1986 and was designed by Jochen Gerz and Esther Shalev-Gerz. Visitors to the column were encouraged to write on its lead surface and as each accessible section was filled with messages and graffiti the column was lowered into the ground until in 1993 it disappeared completely.

5   Stevens *et al* (2012) suggest that although counter-monuments can be successful in the ways they engage with personal memory they face the same problems as traditional monuments when the memory of a group or nation is considered. I do not propose to examine this aspect of the monument in detail. In this book I focus on individual rather than collective memory. However, Stevens *et al* (2012) suggest that there is an ever-increasing range of groups of people who make 'conflicting claims on memory and history' and it is therefore important to consider how the design of the counter-monument can speak to different people and interest groups (2012: 968).

6   Beating the bounds is an ancient custom of walking the boundaries of a parish whilst beating the boundary with branches of willow or birch, or apparently even beating and bumping the heads of little boys in order for them to remember the route. The River Lea forms the boundary between Middlesex and Essex, hence the names of the two sets of Filter Beds. The Filter Beds also lie in the London Borough of Hackney and across the river is the borough of Waltham Forest and it this boundary that was the focus of the event described to me.

7   Several murals, by John Chandler, depicting military life on the marshes have been commissioned by the RSPB. The signal box is painted on a small brick building opposite the mantlet banks and other images showing soldiers in action hang from the roof of the mantlet banks themselves.

References

BBC in partnership with Public Catalogues Foundation (2014) *Your paintings.* Available from: www.bbc.co.uk/arts/yourpaintings/paintings/metropolitan-water-board-works-lea-bridge-road-walthamsto135408 [Accessed 3 November 2014].

Bender, B. (1993) Introduction: Landscape-meaning and action. In: B. Bender (Ed.) *Landscape politics and perspectives.* Oxford: Berg, pp. 1–18.

Boyarin, J. (1994) Space, time and the politics of memory. In: J. Boyarin (Ed.) *Remapping memory: The politics of timespace.* Minneapolis, MN: University of Minnesota Press, pp. 1–38.

Boyer, C. (1996) *The city of collective memory: Its historical imagery and architectural entertainments.* London: MIT Press.

Casey, E. (2000) *Remembering. A phenomenological study.* Bloomington, IN: Indiana University Press.

Connerton, P. (1989) *How societies remember.* Cambridge: Cambridge University Press.

Crinson, M. (2005) Urban memory: An introduction. In: M. Crinson (Ed.) *Urban memory: History and amnesia in the modern city.* London: Routledge, pp. xi–xxiii.

Crouch, D. & Parker, G. (2003) 'Digging-up' Utopia? Space, practice and land use heritage. *Geoforum*, 34 (3), pp. 395–408.

da Costa Meyer, E. (2009) The place of place in memory. In: M. Treib (Ed.) *Spatial recall: Memory in architecture and landscape.* London: Routledge, pp. 176–193.

de Certeau, M. (1984) *The practice of everyday life.* Berkeley, CA: University of California Press.

DeSilvey, C. (2006) Observed decay: Telling stories with mutable things. *Journal of Material Culture*, 11 (3), pp. 318–338.

DeSilvey, C. (2010) Memory in motion: Soundings from Milltown, Montana. *Social and Cultural Geography*, 11 (5), pp. 491–510.

DeSilvey, C. & Edensor, T. (2013) Reckoning with ruins. *Progress in Human Geography*, 37 (4), 465–485.

Edensor, T. (2005a) The ghosts of industrial ruins: Ordering and disordering memory in excessive space. *Environment and Planning D: Society and Space*, 23 (6), pp. 829–849.

Edensor, T. (2005b) *Industrial ruins.* Oxford: Berg.

Feeley-Harnik, G. (1996) 1992 debate, the past is a foreign country. In: T. Ingold (Ed.) *Key debates in anthropology (Management of innovation and change).* London: Routledge, pp. 212–218.

Forty, A. (1999) Introduction. In: A. Forty & S. Küchler (Eds.) *The art of forgetting.* Oxford: Berg, pp. 1–18.

Garrett, B. (2011) Assaying history: Creating temporal junctions through urban exploration. *Environment and Planning D: Society and Space*, 29, pp. 1048–1067.

Huyssen, A. (1995) *Twilight memories: Marking time in a culture of amnesia.* London: Routledge.

Kaernbach, A. (not known) *Art at the German Bundestag: Sophie Calle*. Berlin, German Bundestag, pp. 1–2.

Küchler, S. (1993) Landscape as memory: The mapping of process and its representation in a Melanesian society. In: B. Bender (Ed.) *Landscape politics and perspectives*. Oxford: Berg, pp. 85–106.

Küchler , S. (1996) 1992 debate, the past is a foreign country. In: T. Ingold (Ed.) *Key debates in anthropology (management of innovation and change)*. London: Routledge, pp. 224–228.

Küchler , S. (1999) The place of memory. In: A. Forty & S. Küchler (Eds.) *The art of forgetting*. Oxford: Berg, pp. 53–72.

Küchler, S. (2006) Part IV process and transformation: Introduction. In: C. Tilley, W. Keane, S. Küchler, M. Rowlands & P. Spyer (Eds.) *Handbook of material culture*. London: Routledge, pp. 325–328.

Lea Bridge Heritage (2012) *The view from the bridge: Large turbine house*. Available from: http://leabridge.org.uk/gazetteer/archaeology/large-turbine-house. html [Accessed 13 June 2014].

Lowenthal, D. (1985) *The past is a foreign country*. Cambridge: Cambridge University Press.

Lowenthal, D. (1996a) 1992 debate, the past is a foreign country. In: T. Ingold (Ed.) *Key debates in anthropology (management of innovation and change)*. London: Routledge, pp. 206–212.

Lowenthal, D. (1996b) The debate: The past is a foreign country. In: T. Ingold (Ed.) *Key debates in anthropology (management of innovation and change)*. London: Routledge, pp. 229–248.

Lynch, K. (1972) *What time is this place?* Cambridge: MIT Press.

Lyndon, D. (2009) The place of memory. In: M. Treib (Ed.) *Spatial recall: Memory in architecture and landscape*. London: Routledge, pp. 62–85.

Mah, A. (2010) Memory, uncertainty and industrial ruination: Walker Riverside, Newcastle upon Tyne. *International Journal of Urban and Regional Research*, 34 (2), pp. 398–413.

Mah, A. (2012) *Industrial ruination, community, and place: Landscapes and legacies of urban decline*. Toronto: University of Toronto Press.

Manzo, L. C. (2005) For better or worse: Exploring multiple dimensions of place meaning. *Journal of Environmental Psychology*, 25 (1), pp. 67–86.

Massey, D. (2005) *For space*. London: Sage Publications.

Merewether, C. (1997) Traces of loss. In: M. S. Roth, C. Lyons & C. Merewether (Eds.) *Irresistible decay*. Los Angeles, CA: The Getty Research Institute Publications and Exhibitions Programme, pp. 25–40.

Millman, Z. (2011) *Landscape narratives and the construction of meaning in the contemporary urban canal-scape*. Unpublished PhD thesis, Birmingham City University.

Proust, M. (1981) *Swann's way: Book one of the remembrance of things past*. Middlesex: Penguin Books.

Public Monuments and Sculpture Association (Not known) *National recording project: River God*. Available from: www.pmsa.org.uk/pmsa-database/2891/ [Accessed 3 November 2014].

Rishbeth, C. & Powell, M. (2013) Place attachment and memory: Landscapes of belonging as experienced post-migration. *Landscape Research*, 38 (2), pp. 160–178.

Rossi, A. (1981) *A scientific autobiography*. Cambridge, MA: MIT Press.

Roth, M. S. (1997) Irresistible decay: Ruins reclaimed. In: M. S. Roth, C. Lyons & C. Merewether (Eds.) *Irresistible decay.* Los Angeles, CA: The Getty Research Institute Publications and Exhibitions Programme, pp. 1–23.

Schama, S. (1995) *Landscape and memory.* New York: Vintage Books.

Scotland's Places (Not known) *Glasgow, 522 Pollokshaws Road, Coplaw Horse-tram Depot.* Available from: www.scotlandsplaces.gov.uk/record/rcahms/150610/glasgow-522-pollokshaws-road-coplaw-horse-tram-depot/rcahms?item=1027168#carousel [Accessed 14 June 2014].

Sharr, A. (2010) The sedimentation of memory. *The Journal of Architecture,* 15 (4), pp. 499–515.

Stevens, Q., Franck, K. A. & Fazakerley, R. (2012) Counter-monuments: The anti-monumental and the dialogic. *Journal of Architecture,* 17 (6), pp. 951–972.

Swanton, D. (2012) Afterimages of steel: Dortmund. *Space and Culture,* 15 (4), pp. 264–282.

Till, K. (2004) Emplacing memory through the city. The New Berlin, lecture delivered at the "Spatial Turn in History" Symposium. *German Historical Institute Bulletin,* 35, pp. 74–83.

Till, K. (2005) *The new Berlin. Memory, politics, place.* Minneapolis, MN: University of Minnesota Press.

Tilley, C. (2006) Introduction: Identity, place, landscape and heritage. *Journal of Material Culture,* 11 (7), pp. 7–32.

Treib, M. (2009) Remembering ruins, ruins remembering. In: M. Treib (Ed.) *Spatial recall: Memory in architecture and landscape.* London: Routledge, pp. 194–217.

Vergunst, J. (2012) Seeing ruins: Imagined and visible landscapes in North-East Scotland. In: M. Janowski & T. Ingold (Eds.) *Imagining landscapes: Past, present and future.* Farnham: Ashgate Publishing Company, pp. 19–38.

Waterton, E. & Smith, L. (2010) The recognition and misrecognition of community heritage. *International Journal of Heritage Studies,* 16 (1–2), pp. 4–15.

Young, J. (1993) *The texture of memory: Holocaust memorials and meaning.* New Haven, CT and London: Yale University Press.

8   Implications for practice

In Chapter 2 I explained how government planning policies affected DUN sites and suggested that when implementing these policies the significance of these sites for local people may be underestimated. Often sites are described as a blight on the area and regeneration – sometimes accompanied by the erasure of historical elements in the derelict landscape – is advocated as the solution. My research shows that the assumption within this policy, namely that DUN landscapes are of no value (unless they can be shown to be of 'high environmental value' (Department for Communities and Local Government, 2012: 26)) is far from the case. Although I am not examining participants' responses to the derelict sites themselves, in this book I have demonstrated the importance people give to the elements of pastness that are found in these landscapes and incorporated into the developed site. Below I discuss in detail the diverse ways participants responded to these historical elements and it is clear, I suggest, that there is a case for considering as part of the planning process both the historic and the environmental value the DUN landscape might have for local people. Such a move would be in line with the principles of the European Landscape Convention (Council of Europe, 2000) that stress how everyday landscapes can form part of the local heritage and contribute to people's sense of identity.

In the preceding chapters, through references to the writings of social scientists, anthropologists, philosophers, planners, geographers, environmental aestheticists and landscape archaeologists, I have explored the multidisciplinary nature of this research and drawn links between these disciplines and theory in landscape architecture. In this penultimate chapter I bring together the multiple areas of discussion that have run through this book and examine the implications of these findings for those tasked with designing and developing DUN landscapes. Massey's (2005) theories of place, space and time provide a valuable conceptual framework for landscape architectural discourse in this field. Her assertion that place is a random selection of stories thrown together, and involves experiences (negotiations) between the human and the non-human, is borne out in my research findings. However, this sets a challenge for landscape architects. How are they to create places that are open to different understandings, unfixed and unfinished? Often a designer's brief requires the opposite: defined control, order and containment. There may also be a requirement to fix meaning within place through design with the intention of creating an official narrative that leads to the exclusion of some groups of people and the shutting down of imagination. However, I have shown how the official narrative is sometimes only one strand of an interviewee's understanding as they seek to make sense of the landscape in the light of their present perceptions and their prior knowledge and experiences. As Treib (2002, 2011) points out there can be no assumption that the landscape will be read in the same way by everyone; what may be perceived as everyday and matter-of-fact by one may be seen as unique and marvellous by another.

If Massey defines space as the possibility of stories or the 'simultaneity of stories-so-far' (2005: 130) and place as one collection of these stories, then the question must arise; are designers creating spaces or places? I suggest that during the design process, in undertaking their own negotiation with layers and linkages both locally and in the wider landscape, designers are creating their own understanding of a place. However, in doing so they are also adding to the multiplicity of stories that comprise space and it is from these that individuals can, and do, negotiate their own places (Massey, 2005). Thus the resulting landscape design contributes to the multiplicity of narratives and becomes part of a new specificity. The very fact that individuals are capable of a range of responses can be seen as an invitation to the designer to create places that are open to these multiple understandings as an alternative to designing easily understood and homogeneous landscapes. Rather than creating landscapes that smooth over or deny difference they can create openings for imagination and memory. In creating or permitting the possibility of change, of chance encounters and interactions, the designer is leaving the way open for the individual to engage with their own collection of stories.

Landscape designers might, in practice, wish for the places they create to be unique and special and yet any understanding of these former DUN landscapes is necessarily contextual and contingent; experiences can change as the relationships change or as other and different relationships become part of the story. I found evidence of these relations at small and large scales, within and beyond the site and between the natural and the cultural, the human and the non-human. Is it possible therefore to consider these places as having a specific character or as being in some way special? Sources of specificity are to be found in the distinct mixture of wider and local social relations reacting with the history of a place – a history that can be understood as layers of linkages both with the local area and the wider world (Massey, 1993). It is this form of understanding that the interviewees demonstrated in the ways in which they created frames for reading and a sense of continuity.

However, the challenge is to envisage how material places might actually be designed and yet always be changing and never completed. Designers talk of process and event and yet it is not always clear what this means to the individual experiencing the landscape. In this book I highlighted how the connections between Massey's writings and Dee's (2010) call for an approach to design that considers the **material** forms in ways that make evident the **temporalities** of the landscape, and I have shown how valid this approach can be for visitors to these sites.[1] In examining the responses to the material and spatial qualities of the DUN sites, I have demonstrated the significance of these forms to the understanding of temporalities and shown the importance of context in these interrelations. Although it is often the case that meaning develops over time as Corner (2002) and Treib (2002) assert, I have found that this is not necessarily a linear development. Individuals create narratives that make sense of the passage of time in the landscape and relate this to their own experiences. However, the fact that frames for reading are composed of complex interrelations of understanding suggests that meanings are contingent and changing, and may be part of a one-off event as well as the accretion of many layers of experience.

Using materials as symbols of past use

It is evident that if a designer is aiming to make reference to the past history of the site through the incorporation of material symbols they should be aware that the effectiveness of this approach is limited. The use of an industrial palette of materials, the recycling of materials into new features and the incorporation of artefacts as symbols do not on their own necessarily signal the pastness of the site to the visitor.[2] It appears that these symbols merge into, and become an accepted part of, the new site rather than presenting as a contrasting time layer. It was also noticeable that symbols such as the chimney at the Hidden Gardens failed to give any idea of the scale of the industrial landscape prior to its dereliction. This was in contrast with comments from interviewees about the boundary wall at the Filter Beds and the Tramway building itself, both of which signalled that something important had once happened here. However, there are significant exceptions; as might be expected, the interviewees' prior knowledge affected their responses to these symbolic references and those with an art and design background had more appreciation of the meaning behind the inclusion of the materials. Responses to the Hackney Henge were also more varied; perhaps in this case it was the physical interaction between the materials and the visitors that encouraged a questioning and imaginative response.

Creating palimpsest landscapes through processes and retained material and spatial qualities

In the case study sites designers integrate the material, spatial and temporal qualities of the DUN site as time layers within the new landscape where they function as aides memoires rather than as symbols of the past history of the site. They are to be seen for themselves and for what they are now, and how they relate to other layers within the landscape, rather than as a stand-in for something more that is no longer present. This is not to say that these time layers are not reminders of the site's past, but it is their very incompleteness that leaves the way open for many possible interpretations. In this way the sites differ from the traditional heritage landscape where artefacts are on display in ways designed to convey a particular aspect of history. Woodward (2012) suggests that juxtapositions between time layers are necessary for the visitor to have an aesthetic appreciation of decay and dereliction. Designers working with these landscapes to create natural or abstracted palimpsests can emphasise and exploit these juxtapositions to enhance the aesthetic appearance and to create tensions, contrasts and disjunctions. However, the palimpsest landscapes that I discuss in this book are also landscapes where choices have been made about what to keep and what to destroy and therefore there is an element of control in the display of pastness. Contamination, health and safety and financial issues all play a part in these decisions, however, it is also important to be aware that the layers within the palimpsest can be utilised by different interest groups to foreground differing understandings of a site's history and to close down others. In Chapter 4 I pointed out layers of meaning in the history of Duisburg Nord – the use of Jewish labour during the war – that are buried and remain unmentioned in most discussions about the site.

One way in which designers draw attention to the histories of the landscape is through the inventive incorporation of the existing material forms and the spatial layouts of the DUN site. Designers at sites such as Ballast Point Park and Duisburg Nord create abstracted palimpsests that subvert the material qualities of the DUN site to create new interventions and temporalities, and time edges between the old, the new and the invented are made explicit. The relationship approach, discussed below, attempts to make the visitor aware of these disjunctions. Abstracted palimpsests differ from the light touch interventions evident in the natural palimpsests at the Filter Beds and Rainham Marshes, where the material qualities of the site remain as a time layer within the new design and may eventually become engulfed with vegetation and fall into partial dereliction. There are differences between the ways in which these natural palimpsests are perceived which may be due to: the demographics of the interviewees; the size and visual permeability of the site; the purpose for which the site is intended or the familiarity visitors have with the landscape. However, I would suggest that the ways in which visitors can engage with the artefacts is a factor in their differing responses. At the Filter Beds there is the opportunity for embodied engagement. Visitors can walk, run and play on the artefacts and they can experience them sensually with little interference or control. The range of responses to this form of engagement was considerably more varied and diverse than at Rainham Marshes where the artefacts are, in the main, separated from the public.

However, this does not mean that the interviewees did not engage with the palimpsest landscape at Rainham in other ways. Beard (2011) makes a deliberate decision to leave the derelict artefacts to 'get on with what they do' whilst making subtle interventions, or 'gestures', in other parts of the site. The outcome of this light touch approach is that the juxtapositions of new interventions, ruined structures and the surrounding landscape appear unplanned and arbitrary – sometimes even serendipitous as, for example, when a bird alights momentarily on a section of metal handrail. In much the same way as the design of the Filter Beds has left traces and artefacts to be stumbled upon, at Rainham these juxtapositions are also encountered by chance and will change with each visit.

Interviewees showed an awareness of the passage of time and this was noticeably manifested in terms of their concept of renewal. At the Filter Beds this is evident in the perception and understanding of the processes of 'nature taking back'. At the Hidden Gardens and Rainham Marshes the concept of renewal arises from an understanding that the sites have been, in some ways, saved from their derelict state and become something new. This belief is informed by the interviewees' prior knowledge and experiences of specific and generic wastelands. The complex personal time layers formed by these processes – or temporal qualities – combined with the prior knowledge, memories and experiences of the interviewees contribute to the ways in which they make sense of the new landscape.

Finally, there is the emplacing of memories within the time layers of the palimpsest landscape. It is clear that memories are specific to an individual and cannot be contained or predicted and, for these reasons, designers face challenges if they intentionally attempt to create landscapes of memory. The Hidden Gardens is such a landscape and yet the memories that I discussed with the interviewees only rarely related to the garden as a whole, or to the elements of the garden that might be expected. However, there is evidence that some memories do become emplaced in material qualities and can become part of a narrative that is told by many visitors to the site. I am thinking here of the story of the horses and the very visible ramp and stable corridor that remain as part of the Tramway building; whatever the original intention of leaving these emplaced memories in the building, the resulting story of the horses appears has taken on life of its own.

However, more often memories come about as a result of chance inter-actions and experiences. They are sometimes emplaced in particular material qualities, sometimes in absences and they are more often engendered in discussions of the site as a whole or in the embodied experience of being in the landscape. Therefore it is questionable whether designers should seek to create time layers with the intention of conjuring up predetermined memories. If landscapes can be designed to remain open for visitors to encounter memories by chance, to create imaginary pasts or to emplace their own memories to be re-remembered on another visit, then the possibility is there for these sites to become landscapes 'as memory' rather than 'of memory' (Küchler, 1993: 86). Whatever the intention of designers and developers, memory opens up possibilities for creative interactions between the past (in its varied forms) and embodied experiences in the present. This understanding seems to me to be the most useful way of thinking about landscape and memory. The designer, by making the past accessible through time layers and by ensuring there is the possibility of engaging with these landscape elements – in effect making chance possible – can leave the way open for a 'creative collaboration' (Boyarin, 1994: 22) that might result in multiple, unpredictable memories.

Taking the extended relationship approach

In Chapter 4 I discussed how some designers have taken a relationship approach (Raxworthy, 2008) to the design of DUN sites and I suggested that this approach is a useful one when considering the design of the Filter Beds and Rainham Marshes. At the Filter Beds the spatial layout and mate-rial forms of the site allow visitors access whilst maintaining some separation between them and the sensitive habitats in the beds. The enclosed nature of the site and the fact that it cannot be viewed as a whole but has to be walked around to be fully experienced engenders a sense of mystery and discovery, and allows the visitor to stumble upon things and question their purpose. Time layers and time edges are also encountered in this way, not fully visible from the start but exposed whilst exploring. There are small-scale juxtapo-sitions between vegetation and artefacts and larger scale contrasts between the site and its surroundings. The wider landscape becomes more important as the leaves fall from the trees and boundaries become more visually per-meable with the result that the river, former power station and the industrial site on the far bank of the Lea can be seen. However, these juxtapositions are never completely forgotten whatever the season; the sounds are always present as a reminder.

The design of Rainham Marshes also brings the visitor alongside the time layers in the landscape but prevents much direct engagement with the arte-facts. This landscape is very different from the Filter Beds; it is a horizontal marshland and most of it can be seen as one panoramic vista from the visitor centre and from the A13 and the Channel Tunnel Rail Link (CTRL). However, this very horizontality helps the low buildings and structures to merge with their environment. At times the visitor can be completely unaware of the military remains amongst the reeds or covered with vegetation. It is perhaps because of this that visitors talk of the materials blending in with their surroundings. Even Beard's seemingly dramatic intervention of using three rusting shipping containers as an education centre does not perturb the watery, blending-blurring nature of this landscape. My findings suggest that it is not sufficient to merely put the visitor into a visual relationship with the landscape, something more is needed if they are to fully experience the layers of change. At Rainham, Beard has not focused on pointing out the obvious time layers in this landscape; his paths and boardwalks are not designed to guide the eye to military artefacts as focal points. Instead the relationship approach draws attention to the small and large-scale juxtapositions and connections both inside and outside the site. There is no attempt to hide the industrial buildings, landfill site and transport infrastructure. The directional emphasis of the boardwalks running through the reed beds allows the visitor both to get up close to the immediate landscape and to be constantly aware of the wider environment beyond the site with all its own merging time layers. Visitors talk not only of the small-scale juxtapositions between new and old, industrial and military but also of connections and interrelations between this site and others, with the immediate wider landscape and with other landscapes in Essex and London. To my mind Beard also points to a future – one long boardwalk takes the eye outside the site to the wind turbines on the horizon (Figure 8.1).

Taking a relationship approach (Raxworthy, 2008) to design is a useful tool for drawing attention to the pastness of the landscape and is especially effective when considered in combination with the creation of natural and abstracted palimpsests. Massey's (2005) theories also have relevance when understanding and employing this approach. She stresses the importance of linkages on a local and global scale and challenges the individual to negotiate their relationships with others and with the non-human. The relationship

Figure 8.1 The stop butts and view to wider landscape with wind turbines at Rainham Marshes, mantlet banks concealed beneath vegetation in foreground

approach, in drawing attention to change and to the pastness of place assists or encourages negotiation in the present between the individual and their perceptions, memories and understanding of the past.

Raxworthy (2008) describes how the designers of the BP Park (this is not the same park as Ballast Point) on the Sydney Harbour attempt to make clear the history of the occupation of the harbour through the relationships made between the visitor and the site, and suggests that the view of the harbour contributes to this. This extended relationship approach gives insights into interrelations between the site and the wider surroundings. The ways in which designers might signal these relationships is dependent on the site itself; the flat landscape of Rainham calls for a very different treatment from the enclosed Filter Beds. Designers also need to consider the different scales at which this approach functions. It can bring visitors into relationships with anything from small-scale, intimate juxtapositions through to the large-scale of the surrounding landscape.

It is interesting to consider what impact such an approach would have on the responses of interviewees at the Hidden Gardens. Although the chimney is the largest feature of the site it does not form a conventional focal point – the eye is not drawn to it as the main aspect of a vista from a particular viewpoint, it is just there, always visible. The same applies to the other artefacts; they form part of the new design but the visitor's attention is not drawn to them or to the juxtapositions between the old and the new. The exception is the facade of the Tramway with its ghostly traces of doors and windows that is partially visible, framed at the end of an avenue of trees. However, access to this vista is not easy and the area next to the Tramway is used as a temporary store and is often cordoned off. Here again taking a relationship approach to the spatial layout of the whole site might have been more successful in drawing attention to the contrasting time layers.

Understanding landscape continuity and change

Landscapes are often described as timeless, as if they have been there forever, and it is this concept of place as static and unchanging that Massey challenges in her writing on place, space and time. In my research it at first appeared that the interviewees subscribed to these views of landscape and indeed they used phrases that seemed to support this when describing the case study sites. They were also apprehensive about possible changes in the landscape around them, expressing horror at what the 2012 Olympics would do to the marshes and concern at the way in which the green spaces in their area were threatened with development for housing. They wondered what would happen to their local area and the site in particular if certain plots of industrial land were sold off to developers and questioned why old buildings were so often demolished to make way for new. And yet they also showed resignation about these things happening; this is the way the world goes.

However, when I looked further into what they were saying about their experiences of the landscape the picture became more complex. Figure 8.2

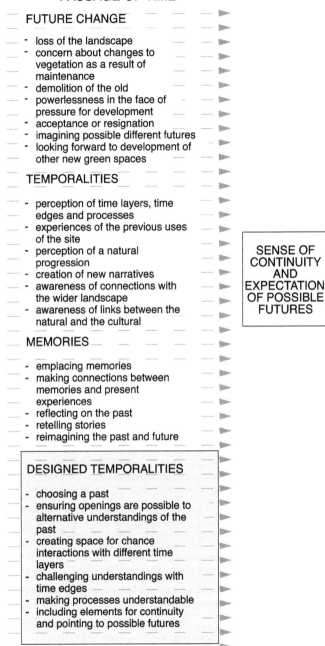

EXPERIENCING THE PASSAGE OF TIME

FUTURE CHANGE

- loss of the landscape
- concern about changes to vegetation as a result of maintenance
- demolition of the old
- powerlessness in the face of pressure for development
- acceptance or resignation
- imagining possible different futures
- looking forward to development of other new green spaces

TEMPORALITIES

- perception of time layers, time edges and processes
- experiences of the previous uses of the site
- perception of a natural progression
- creation of new narratives
- awareness of connections with the wider landscape
- awareness of links between the natural and the cultural

MEMORIES

- emplacing memories
- making connections between memories and present experiences
- reflecting on the past
- retelling stories
- reimagining the past and future

DESIGNED TEMPORALITIES

- choosing a past
- ensuring openings are possible to alternative understandings of the past
- creating space for chance interactions with different time layers
- challenging understandings with time edges
- making processes understandable
- including elements for continuity and pointing to possible futures

THE EMBODIED AND QUESTIONING INDIVIDUAL

SENSE OF CONTINUITY AND EXPECTATION OF POSSIBLE FUTURES

Figure 8.2 Understanding landscape continuity and change

outlines the ways in which an individual's sense of the passage of time draws on a complex set of factors, and how understandings of a place might be constantly renewed. Some interviewees were aware of the processes at work within the case study sites, in particular at Rainham Marshes and the Filter Beds, and they also had an appreciation of the temporality of the sites as they evolved from industrial or military use, through a wasteland and dereliction stage, to the present and further to possible futures. There is a sense that the sites are subject to a natural progression and individuals create their own narrative of natural continuity filtered through their experiences, memories and prior knowledge. Often they are able to seamlessly merge what might appear to be discontinuities such as change of use, dereliction and destruction into this natural continuity, although I have pointed out in Chapter 7 that there are those who feel the disjunctions cannot be ignored. This is continuity expressed through rhythms and a sense of the passage of time (de Solà-Morales Rubió, 1995) rather than one offered by an official and planned narrative. The possibilities these landscapes afford for visitors to experience the passage of time range from looking back at the multiple histories, through experiencing the pastness of the site in the present, to pointing towards different futures.

In Chapter 7 I referred to Manzo's discussion of continuity and its relationship with place meaning. Manzo asserts that places become significant when they are seen as 'bridges to the past' (2005: 74); there is a connection between people's memories and places that they find significant. She refers to Gustafson (2001) who suggests that places are meaningful when they form part of a person's life story or because they are reminders of past histories. Manzo also discusses continuity and place with reference to Twigger-Ross and Uzzell's (1996) concept of place as a means of creating self-identity. My research appears to support these ideas of connections between the place, memory and history, and continuity. However, I also show how the sense of continuity is manifested in an awareness of the passage of time and an ability to reflect on this – and to make connections – as an embodied person in the present. The physical landscape, through juxtapositions and relationships, becomes one aspect of the dialogue between person and place.

Massey's (2005) understanding of the concept of places changing requires us to be open to constant re-negotiation of our relationship with them. This appears to be somewhat exhausting and in practice when experiencing everyday landscapes we often are unaware of any such responsibility. Instead we walk through places and return to places day after day, sometimes not noticing changes, small or large. Massey suggests when we move between places we find those that are relevant to us and reinsert ourselves into them by 'weav[ing] together different stories which make this "here" and "now"' (2005: 130). In the preceding chapters I have shown how, in a changing environment, individuals negotiate a sense of continuity in place, both through their external perceptions and their internal memories, knowledge and emotions. In applying Massey's theories at a practical level it is necessary to not only address possibilities for change but also to be aware of the accumulation of individual memories and prior knowledge that each person brings with them to any understanding of place.

At the end of Chapter 7 I suggested that an awareness of how individuals create their own sense of continuity through memories gives designers an opportunity to design landscapes that challenge this, creating spaces for chance interactions with time layers that give rise to different understandings of the passage of time. It is not necessary to invoke a specific heritage to create continuity between past, present and future (Bangstad, 2014). Interviewees create their own centring devices to suggest continuity through their own memories and stories, rather than needing to rely on universal forms supplied by the designer as stabilising structures. This understanding could also be applied to those engagements with the landscape that form that sense of natural continuity I describe above. If the visitor is able to understand and relate to elements of the landscape in a way that can provide the security of a natural continuity, it may be that disjunctions and time edges can present opportunities rather than threats. Designers Langer, at Südgelände, and Yu, at Zhongshan, both agreed that a sense of the passage of time was an important factor for visitors to these landscapes. The cold war and the division of Berlin is a significant part of Südgelände's history and might challenge the concept of continuity, nevertheless Langer felt that 'although it's part of a dark chapter of history – I don't have the feeling people want to fade out bad historical periods' (2017). Yu suggests that:

> People need historical (and geographical) references to get the meanings of the site … at the same time people need surprises and get refreshed and stimulated. These two aspects are two sides of one coin of landscape perception and landscape aesthetics. I will say continuity is the main stream of a river flow, while a break is the rock or waterfall on this river, together they make the experience drifting down the river amazing.
>
> (Yu, 2017)

Of the case studies it is perhaps Ballast Point Park that best utilises time layers and time edges to create surprises and excitement within a framework of continuity. Designer Philip Coxall recounts a visit to the site:

> I find that people do slowly pick up on the historic references and they start to understand what the site used to be and in a real way I think it adds to their experience and gives the park a place in time. On one occasion I was there a past worker of the site, when it was owned by Caltex, was visiting and he noticed one of the tools he used to use in the wall and he was with his family and he nearly broke down in tears explaining it to them, I was a silent observer visiting the park separately at the time.
>
> (Coxall, 2017)

Coxall agrees that the relationship approach allows the visitor to engage with the materiality of the site – 'the very tactile nature of the design, the juxtaposition of the old and the new and the layers and texture contained within the walls' – whilst they are also aware of the wider landscape that 'locates the site as a part of its surroundings and anchors it as part of its place' (Coxall, 2017) (Figure 8.3). Yet, as I have discussed in Chapter 4, this is a controversial landscape and the inclusion of time layers that highlight the industrial past in such a gritty and hard-edged manner has been criticised. The designers of this landscape are not afraid of challenging the visitor but they also create time layers that suggest both continuity and hope. The museum-like vitrine with the remnants of the Villa Menevia, the gardenesque lawns in the footprints of the oil tanks, the native planting palette, the artefacts made safe and contained in the gabion walls, the skin of the oil tank that now supports wind turbines, all take the past history and memories of the site and point towards possible futures. This is a much more extensive approach to the inclusion of time layers than the use of symbols or references to the past and therefore allows many opportunities for different engagements and multiple and diverse responses.

Creating frames for reading

The idea of whether landscapes can or should mean something, or if they can be made to mean something, has run through this book. This is partly

Figure 8.3 The relationships at Ballast Point Park: Cut walls, polished concrete, view to the Sydney Harbour

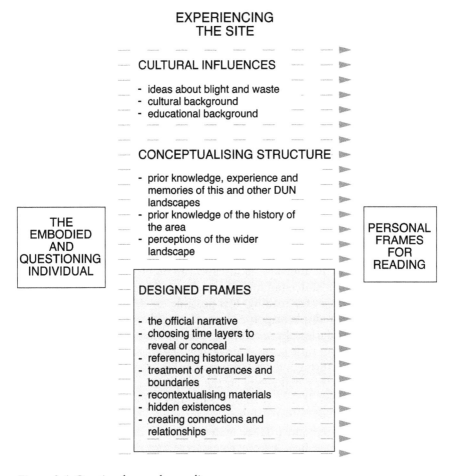

Figure 8.4 Creating frames for reading

due to the questions I asked the interviewees, calling on them to reflect on their experiences of the landscape and to try to make sense of it. To do this many interviewees drew on not only what they were seeing or experiencing, but also on what they already knew or had experienced and thus there is an interplay of these factors in their replies (Figure 8.4).

Visitors try to make sense of these landscapes using their personal frames for reading that they construct from the connections they perceive between the material and temporal layers within the site and between the site and its surroundings. They also make links between experiences of the landscape in the present and past experiences and memories of this or other DUN sites. Prior knowledge, including that of the history of the area, and cultural bias, such as preconceived ideas about the value of wastelands, are also factors in the construction of a personal frame for reading. Although official narratives about the site play a part in these personal frames, visitors' reflexive experiences may run counter to these traditional narratives; not only do different individuals construct different frames for reading the landscape, but also there is the possibility that these frames can change.

These practical findings can again be seen with reference to Massey's theoretical writings demonstrating how space is a 'simultaneity of stories-so-far' (2005: 130), however, I have also shown that the official narrative can sometimes take precedence over other narratives and relationships and this might be one reason for the difference in responses found at Rainham Marshes and at the Filter Beds. In choosing particular artefacts and structures, certain stories about the history of a site can be emphasised and others hidden; there is always the question of who is controlling the relationships between people and place. Designers and developers sometimes wish to imbue the landscape with a particular meaning, or hope it will become part of a predetermined narrative, but my research suggests that although this narrative may form one part of a frame for reading, it is not the only contributory factor. However, the ways in which designers use the qualities of the DUN sites in the new landscape can influence the interviewees' responses and their understanding of the site, and therefore can contribute to the possible frames for reading. It is possible for designers to close down opportunities for multiple responses by enclosing the site and restricting the porosity of boundaries, by excluding certain time layers and drawing attention away from time edges. Conversely designers can choose to signal possible meanings through the relationship approach and decide how much and in what ways they make explicit the links between the site, its history and its surroundings. If they wish to create sites with the potential to open up the imagination to rich and diverse understandings there are many ways in which they can recontextualise materials and incorporate the qualities into the new design whilst acknowledging the fact that these qualities are not necessarily knowable and are not perceived as having obvious predetermined meanings. This allows visitors space to bring their own experiences and knowledge to add to the frame for reading.

Doing very little

It might appear from the above discussion that I am suggesting that designers create complex time layers and time edges with old and new materials and signal a range of processes in the new landscape – do a lot in other words. However, my research also demonstrated the usefulness of doing – or at least appearing to do – very little. This supports Jorgensen and Lička's call for an approach to the urban wild that recognises the value in 'doing as little as possible' (2012: 234) enabling characteristics such as mutability, multiplicity and dynamism to flourish (Jorgensen and Lička, 2012: 233).

I pointed out in Chapter 6 how an individual's perception of continuity is partly reinforced by the impression that the site has developed naturally;

change is seen as a constituent element of what interviewees perceive as natural processes. Ingold's (2012) quotidian mode of imagining, where the past merges seamlessly with the present, is a useful way of describing interviewees' perceptions of this sense of natural continuity and their matter-of-fact responses. However, this is not to say that the interviewees' responses to doing little are always of a quotidian nature. At the Filter Beds the use of the existing topography, material forms and spatial layout has allowed the LVRPA to do very little and yet ensure that the time layers are not only visible but also there to be experienced and engaged with in multiple ways. Even the empty pylon plinth can be seen as an example of the benefits of doing very little; the pylon has been removed but the plinth is left on the edge of the path and has thus become a noticeable reminder of change. Beard's subtle interventions at Rainham also give the appearance of doing little and yet create small and large-scale juxtapositions and time edges that contribute to frames for reading, the sense of the passage of time and expectations of future change. The concept of doing little is also of significance in decisions about the management of change in these landscapes. I discuss this in more detail in the next chapter.

Notes

1 Roe and Taylor in their recent book suggest something very similar to the findings that I discuss here, namely that cultural landscapes are valued precisely for the ways in which 'change is revealed in the materiality of landscape features' (2014: 17).
2 Raxworthy (2008) states that the idea of using an industrial palette of materials to signal past use has become clichéd. He points out that the inclusion of some materials, such as corten, is now ubiquitous. My research shows it is probable that many people never recognised these materials as symbols of past use. However it is also difficult to imagine what other materials could be used in many of the sites I discuss. The blending in of materials at Rainham is seen as important by my interviewees and the more gritty industrial palette achieves this where a gardenesque palette would not.

References

© Department for Communities and Local Government
All resources licensed under the Open Government Licence v3.0 except where otherwise stated. To view this licence, visit www.nationalarchives.gov.uk/doc/open-governmentlicence/ version/3.

Bangstad, T. R. (2014) Industrial heritage and the ideal of presence. In: B. Olsen & Þ. Pétursdóttir (Eds.) *Ruin memories: Materialities, aesthetics and the archaeology of the recent past.* London: Routledge, pp. 92–105.
Beard, P. (2011) *Personal communication – Rainham Marshes.* To: C. Heatherington.
Boyarin, J. (1994) Space, time and the politics of memory. In: J. Boyarin (Ed.) *Remapping memory: The politics of timespace.* Minneapolis, MN: University of Minnesota Press, pp. 1–38.

Corner, J. (2002) Representation and landscape (1992). In: S. Swaffield (Ed.) *Theory in landscape architecture*. Philadelphia, PA: University of Pennsylvania Press, pp. 144–165.

Council of Europe (2000) *European Landscape Convention*. Available from: www.coe.int/t/dg4/cultureheritage/heritage/landscape/ [Accessed 2 August 2014].

Coxall, P. (2017) *Personal communication, Ballast Point Park*. To: C. Heatherington.

de Solà-Morales Rubió, I. (1995) Terrain vague. In: C. Davidson (Ed.) *Anyplace*. Cambridge, MA: MIT Press, pp. 118–123.

Dee, C. (2010) Form, utility, and the aesthetics of thrift in design education. *Landscape Journal*, 29 (1), pp. 21–35.

Department for Communities and Local Government (2012) *National Planning Policy Framework*. London: Department for Communities and Local Government.

Gustafson, P. (2001) Meanings of place: Everyday experience and theoretical conceptualizations. *Journal of Environmental Psychology*, 21 (1), pp. 5–16.

Ingold, T. (2012) Introduction. In: M. Janowski & T. Ingold (Eds.) *Imagining landscape: Past, present and future*. Farnham: Ashgate Publishing Company, pp. 1–18.

Jorgensen, A. & Lička, L. (2012) Anti-planning, anti-design: Exploring alternative ways of making future urban landscapes. In: A. Jorgensen & R. Keenan (Eds.) *Urban wildscapes*. London: Routledge, pp. 221–236.

Küchler, S. (1993) Landscape as memory: The mapping of process and its representation in a Melanesian society. In: B. Bender (Ed.) *Landscape politics and perspectives*. Oxford: Berg, pp. 85–106.

Langer, A. (2017) *Personal communication, Südgelände*. To: C. Heatherington.

Manzo, L. C. (2005) For better or worse: Exploring multiple dimensions of place meaning. *Journal of Environmental Psychology*, 25 (1), pp. 67–86.

Massey, D. (1993) Power geometry and a progressive sense of place. In: J. Bird, B. Curtis, T. Putman, G. Robertson & L. Tickner (Eds.) *Mapping the futures local cultures, global change*. London: Routledge, pp. 59–69.

Massey, D. (2005) *For space*. London: Sage Publications.

Raxworthy, J. (2008) Sandstone and rust: Designing the qualities of Sydney Harbour. *Journal of Landscape Architecture*, 3 (2), pp. 68–83.

Roe, M. & Taylor, K. (2014) New cultural landscapes: Emerging issues, context and themes. In: M. Roe & K. Taylor (Eds.) *New cultural landscapes*. London: Routledge, pp. 1–23.

Treib, M. (2002) Must landscapes mean? (1995). In: S. Swaffield (Ed.) *Theory in landscape architecture*. Philadelphia, PA: University of Pennsylvania Press, pp. 89–101.

Treib, M. (2011) Commentary 2: Must landscapes mean? Revisited. In: M. Treib (Ed.) *Meaning in landscape architecture and gardens: Four essays, four commentaries*. London: Routledge, pp. 126–133.

Twigger-Ross, C. L. & Uzzell, D. L. (1996) Place and identity processes. *Journal of Environmental Psychology*, 16 (3), pp. 205–220.

Woodward, C. (2012) Learning from Detroit or 'the wrong kind of ruins'. In: A. Jorgensen & R. Keenan (Eds.) *Urban wildscapes*. London: Routledge, pp. 17–32.

Yu, K. (2017) *Personal communication, Zhongshan*. To: C. Heatherington.

9 Managing change

The management of the material and spatial qualities

It is not unusual for designers and developers to create heritage landscapes as visitor attractions in which buildings and machinery are restored and remain *in situ*, preserved at a certain point in their history and telling a particular narrative. This approach to the pastness of landscapes is very different from that of many of the case studies discussed in this book, where artefacts, structures and surfaces, rather than being preserved and conserved, are subject to changes wrought by external agencies or by encroaching vegetation. Peter Latz's philosophy when working with an abandoned site is to signal it as something more than simply derelict whilst simultaneously maintaining its wildness:

> Destruction has to be protected so that it isn't destroyed again by re-cultivation. New places have to be invented, new places at the fault lines between what was destroyed and what remained.
>
> (Beard, 1996: 35)

How can destruction be protected? This would appear a contradiction in terms, and yet it is important to signal that these sites were once cultural landscapes. Interviewees were clear that, although they liked the impression of nature taking back control, they felt that something would be lost if the traces of pastness in the landscape disappeared completely. This then raises the question of how the derelict structures, artefacts and surfaces that are evidence of these cultural landscapes should be maintained into the future. In the preceding chapters I have described the ways in which material and spatial qualities are treated ranging from elimination, through preservation, to allowing them to crumble, rust and decay. Figure 9.1 schematically describes this gradient of management regimes. At one end is the *tabula rasa* approach whereby all evidence of the past use of the site is erased prior to development. This is followed by stasis, a state describing those material artefacts, structures and buildings that have been restored and subsequently preserved, as far as possible. The difference between stasis and arrested decay

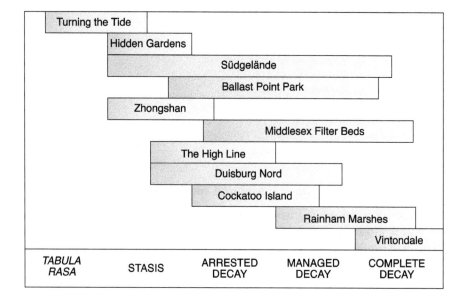

| TABULA RASA | STASIS | ARRESTED DECAY | MANAGED DECAY | COMPLETE DECAY |

Tabula rasa: starting from a blank canvas
Stasis: elements of the landscape are restored and subsequently
                      preserved at that point in time
Arrested decay: the decay and ruination of the landscape is halted at a certain point
Managed decay: the decay is an ongoing process but is managed to ensure it does
                      not become complete decay
Complete decay: decay and ruination are allowed to proceed and eventually the
                      material and spatial qualities disappear

Figure 9.1 The management of change

is more subtle; positions on the gradient slip back and forth. Arrested decay can be understood as an approach to management whereby the decay and ruination proceed to a certain point and are allowed to go no further (DeLyser, 1999; DeSilvey, 2005). Both stasis and arrested decay are in evidence at the case study sites, although sometimes it is unclear to the casual visitor to what extent restoration has taken place. At Südgelände the painted steam engine appears to have been restored, as does the chimney at the Hidden Gardens. The display case at Ballast Point Park containing the historical fragments of pottery from the pre-industrial landscape of the Villa Menevia is an alternative type of stasis: one where the remnants are not restored but preserved as if in a museum.

Although the Turning the Tide project necessarily started with erasure of what had gone before, stasis is also evident in the inclusion of the pit cage artwork at Easington Colliery. Here the artist has repurposed a section of restored machinery and sited it in an open space on the clifftop (Durham County Council, 2002); however, what was once a moveable cage for transporting miners deep underground has now been shorn of all moving parts and stands as a static memorial. Preserving an industrial structure in stasis affects the stories told about the site and this is particularly noticeable in this artwork at Easington where, not only is the pitcage divorced from its original context, but also less tangible elements, such as dirt, contamination and danger, have been removed leaving little more than a sanitised version of the history of the area.[1] However, preserving an artefact in a state of stasis can also be innovative; at Zhongshan the water tower encased in solar glass is undoubtedly in stasis – it is trapped like an insect in amber (Saunders, 2012) – and yet it points both to the past and the future (Figure 9.2).

Falling somewhere between stasis and arrested decay are the sluices and hoppers at the Middlesex Filter Beds; broken sections of these structures make it clear that they have not been restored, however, the intention was to preserve them so that they might remain unchanged into the future. The rail tracks on the High Line also hover around this section of the gradient. Contamination of the infrastructure necessitated major remedial work; each rail track was dismantled, logged, removed and repaired before it could form a part of the new landscape (Martin, 2009). This differs from the structures, infrastructure and artefacts at Duisburg Nord, Ballast Point Park and Cockatoo Island that appear to be in a state of arrested decay and yet, if you look closely, it is evident that in places these material qualities sometimes edge towards the managed decay section of the gradient. This term is used by DeSilvey (2006) to indicate how interventions are made in the on-going processes of decay to ensure that material structures and artefacts do not ultimately fall into complete decay. The aim for the designers at Cockatoo Island was to ensure minimal intervention in the existing industrial fabric whilst still allowing the public access (JMDD, 2011); by keeping visitors safe on the new walkways, structures are permitted to remain in a state of arrested or managed decay. At Duisburg the designers have signalled areas that are safe to enter in other ways. Latz (Weilacher, 2008) describes how repurposed sections of steps and bridges were painted, encouraging the visitor to explore. These 'new' steps then contrasted with the 'rusty sections with "keep out" on them' (Weilacher, 2008: 120).[2] At Ballast Point Park structures mostly remain in a state of arrested decay, however, in small corners of the park it is possible to find tree roots working their way into crumbling walls, indicating that in places there is a managed decay approach to maintenance. For the designer, Philip Coxall, this is the way such places should evolve; 'the designer's hand cannot, and possibly should not, control past the point of construction … the maintenance crew will shape it in their own image' (Coxall, 2017).

The intended management of the military remains at Rainham Marshes is more obviously towards the managed decay area of the gradient, although it is evident that the boundary between managed and complete decay is tenuous; remaining sections of the shooting range are in danger of falling into irreversible decay (Beard, 2011). Both the Middlesex Filter Beds and

Figure 9.2 Zhongshan Shipyard Park water towers

Source: photo by Yu Kongjian

Südgelände are designed around the existing material forms and spatial layout of the industrial site – the filter beds themselves and the railway tracks respectively. At the Filter Beds the LVRPA wanted to ensure that there was as little formal design as possible, leaving the beds much as they were when they were functioning. However, in order to preserve the structural walls they stressed the importance of removing any trees that threatened to undermine the brickwork (LVRPA, 1988). At Südgelände there was a requirement for a flexible approach to maintenance to ensure that natural succession was balanced with other objectives for the site (Langer, 2012). This balance between maintenance and wilderness is always going to be controversial and although Langer believes that the original maintenance concept works well, he admits that there are a few critical voices 'complaining about the loss of the wild character of the site' (Langer, 2017). Noel Kingsbury (2017) also suggests that recently the successional flora has been allowed too great a prominence, detracting from the cultural elements; in places the rail tracks are becoming completely subsumed by vegetation thus approaching the complete decay end of the spectrum. He points out that, even with intervention, successional vegetation in the form of trees or a dense shrub understorey will always be an issue. Langer, however, when asked whether he could envisage a time when the tracks and artefacts disappear completely replied, 'I never thought about the possibility of complete decay … I have the feeling that they are quite persistent', adding that he had 'never heard visitors speculating about a complete disappearance of the remnants' (Langer, 2017).

The decision of where to situate qualities on the management gradient is necessarily contingent on safety requirements, finances, the workforce available, and social and political constraints and therefore it is subject to change. Designers may envisage that material artefacts will be treated in a certain way but this does not preclude decisions being taken in the future to allow some structures to decay completely or, conversely, a change of plan or policy might necessitate a more conservationist approach (DeSilvey, 2012; Morris, 2013). Although visitors enjoy the juxtapositions of nature and culture, both conceptually and aesthetically, incorporating qualities at the managed decay and complete decay end of the gradient is difficult for the designer and even more difficult for those who must maintain the site into the future. Is such an approach possible or even desirable? After all, many industrial buildings were presumably never intended to be permanent. I will return to this later in this chapter.

The relationship between management of the qualities and planting approach

Landscape designers make choices about how to exploit the combination of materials and plants in gardens and parks in order to create interesting and dynamic juxtapositions. In the DUN site these combinations usually occur spontaneously, giving rise to juxtapositions that emphasise the landscape's temporal qualities. At its simplest this is illustrated by opportunist buddleia growing through the cracks in concrete and on the rooftops of derelict buildings, or the patchworks of mosses and lichens invading crumbling walls. When developing these sites decisions must be taken about what forms of intervention to make into the patterns of the existing vegetation. Peter Beard, talking about the Rainham Marshes site, explains his design ethos and how he works with both the vegetation and the existing cultural landscape to:

> Identify different characters according to different locations within the site so that at some point you might choose to make very deliberate interventions that are outside the derelict landscape, the landscape as found, and then there are other areas where you may recognise dynamics that are in place within those landscapes, for instance certain qualities of vegetation such as reed growth, and what you do is that you do things that point up or manage that natural feature of the site.
>
> (Beard, 2011)

The second gradient in Figure 9.3 examines the different planting regimes in operation at the case study sites. At one end of the spectrum are traditional horticultural methods where design decisions are made about the forms and colours of plant combinations; such schemes require an intensive maintenance regime that treats each plant individually. This is followed by extensively maintained naturalistic planting designs that focus mainly on perennials and grasses planted in large drifts or blocks in order to give the impression that they have occurred naturally. The second half of the gradient includes meadows and native vegetation – often designed to create particular habitats for wildlife – and finally natural succession. As with the gradient in Figure 9.1 the boundaries between the approaches are blurred. In some cases the vegetation management has been gradually modified over time and the need to maintain particular habitats, particularly towards the natural succession end of the spectrum, has sometimes necessitated difficult judgements about the extent to which the vegetation can be left to its own devices.

Examining the case studies in more detail reveals the ways in which both the incorporation of existing vegetation and the introduction of new planting can have implications for the management and maintenance of the material and spatial qualities. It might appear obvious that sites adopting a position of managed decay favour the habitat and natural succession approach to planting and vegetation management. However, it is not always the case that the more traditional planting techniques are only introduced in landscapes that start from a *tabula rasa* or use a stasis and arrested decay approach. As might be expected, sites such as the Middlesex Filter Beds, Südgelände and Rainham Marshes, that allow natural succession to proceed to an extent and are managed for habitat creation, incorporate qualities towards the end of the decay spectrum. At Ballast Point Park designers used

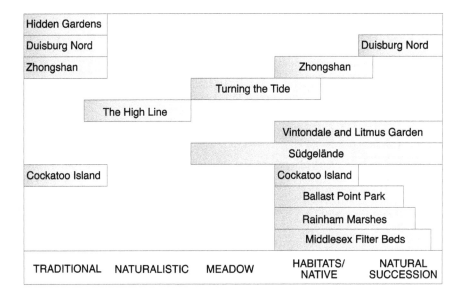

			HABITATS/	NATURAL
TRADITIONAL	NATURALISTIC	MEADOW	NATIVE	SUCCESSION

Traditional combinations:	design decisions made about forms and colour of plants
Naturalistic:	perennials and grasses give the impression that they have occurred naturally
Meadows and native vegetation:	often chosen to create particular habitats for wildlife
Natural succession:	successional vegetation proceeds without intervention

Figure 9.3 The management of the planting and vegetation

native plants from local genetic stock (Hawken, 2009) and some self-seeding is permitted – this is clearly not a traditional planting scheme – and here there is a corresponding range of approaches to the management of the material and spatial qualities. However, there are a few sites that confound expectations about vegetation management and decaying qualities. Duisburg Nord is known for the silver birches self-seeded high up on the blast furnaces and on the waste substrates of the former coke plant (Kirkwood, 2001), creating juxtapositions reminiscent of the DUN site, but also entailing careful maintenance to ensure that any structures do not approach the complete decay end of the spectrum. Grids of ornamental trees are planted in the now open space outside the blast furnaces, signalling a disruption or discontinuity in the process of change. This area was once a sintering plant that had to be demolished due to contamination. Any resulting rubble that was clean enough, was ground up and reused to create the surface and substrate for the trees (Kirkwood, 2001). At Zhongshan, Kongjian Yu also attempts to create these unusual juxtapositions with the use of native plants, particularly in the waterside areas of the site. There is no irrigation or fertilising – such as would be found in more traditionally planted parks – and Yu (2017) describes how the 'industrial structures are integrated with the "messy" native vegetation', something that would be 'unseen in other urban parks'. However, a more traditional planting design is evident in the precisely clipped hedges and the grids of trees that contrast with the self-seeded grasses growing through the old railway tracks.

In contrast, on a site such as the High Line none of the original vegetation on the DUN site remains and the planting, whilst making reference to the wild vegetation that once colonised the derelict rail tracks, requires high levels of maintenance in order to keep it attractive for visitors. Nevertheless the temporal processes of growth, decay, death and renewal are manifested in this planting and Robert Hammond of Friends of the High Line, is quoted as saying, 'one of the special things about the High Line is that it is constantly changing. And that [change] is really about the planting' (Ulam *et al.*, 2009: 101).

These designers are using juxtapositions (of planting, vegetation, material and spatial qualities) to draw attention to temporalities in the landscape and to highlight the processes of succession and decay. The different juxtapositions are used to blur the boundaries between the natural and the cultural or to make explicit the time edges or disjunctions between the past landscape and the present or even, as Latz suggests, between 'what was destroyed and what remained' (Beard, 1996: 35). However, designers' intentions can be confounded by future events and it is not only management decisions about maintenance that have an impact on understandings of the new landscape. At Zhongshan a dam has been built on the river beyond the park with the result that the tidal terraces no longer flood twice a day, changing the temporal connections between the water, the native planting and the new walkways (Yu, 2017).

Blurring the boundaries between nature and culture – designing for change

In the DUN site nature and culture combine and merge through the processes of decay and rejuvenation to form hybrid artefacts – forms that become gradually more and more indeterminate and consequently less understandable. Is it possible to highlight these processes of change in such a way that they might become part of the frame for reading and point the way to possible futures: anticipating the future in the stories they tell (DeSilvey, 2012). The blurring of boundaries between vegetation and built structures contributes to the sense of flux that DUN sites evoke; the path between nature and culture is slippery. This is reminiscent of Treib's (2005) discussion of landscapes of inflection (see Chapter 2) that sit at a point along a nature–culture continuum where the ordering of materials and forms still reflects the existing environment but just edges towards being new and different. Rather than being on a continuum between nature and culture, former DUN sites can be thought of as on three interconnecting gradients: nature and DUN culture; nature and new culture; new culture and DUN culture.

Thus, these concepts of inflection and hybridity that slip and slide along continua can inform designers' practice when faced with a DUN landscape. As Jorgensen and Lička point out 'places need not be ... *either* regulated *or* wild' [my italics] (2012: 221). Material and spatial qualities kept in a state of stasis remain towards the DUN culture end of the gradient whereas those allowed to decay – the 'do little' approach – pass through the hybrid stage before eventually appearing to merge with nature completely. Similarly those sites where little of the derelict site remains, sit beyond the point of inflection towards the new culture end of the spectrum whilst there are others that merge qualities of the DUN site with new interventions. In Figure 9.4 I suggest where the case study sites sit on these fluid gradients. It is possible to retain the material and spatial qualities in states of decay, forming hybrid

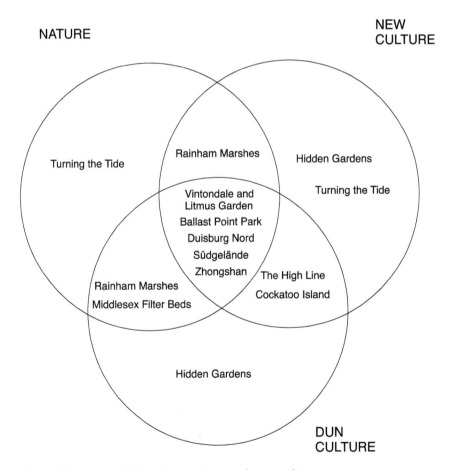

Figure 9.4 Nature, DUN culture and new culture gradients

nature–culture entities, whilst also creating new interventions in DUN landscapes. In some cases hybrid objects are left to form naturally; examples include the vegetation engulfing the mantlet banks at Rainham and the silver birches colonising abandoned machinery at Duisburg. However, there are other examples where the merging of old and new, of natural and built is intentional. Many of these sites are using the forms of the DUN site, be they natural vegetation or cultural artefacts, and from them creating new forms that reveal past processes and point towards future change (Dee, 2010). Just a few of the many examples that demonstrate the effectiveness of bringing together qualities of the DUN site, natural succession and new interventions include: the water systems at Duisburg; the walkway with views of the tracks amongst grasses and birch trees at Südgelände; the cut opening in the wall at Ballast Point with its (now hidden) view of the oil tank and the (no longer) tidal terraces at Zhongshan.

It was the problem of dealing with the high levels of contamination that influenced the way the former cooling pools at Duisburg have become unlikely wildlife ponds, and gulleys and pipes that form part of the infrastructure of the industrial site are now reutilised as dripping water features (Figure 9.5). At Südgelände the old train tracks are visible from the symbolic track/walkway as they run ghost-like between the grasses and birches (Figure 9.6). The management of the vegetation and the managed decay of the tracks work together to allow for chance glimpses – occasional juxtapositions of the time layers – with, of course, the understanding that the visitor is walking along the new time layer, represented by the raised walkway, thus becoming part of this palimpsest of interrelations. The simple slicing through of the bund wall at Ballast Point has created a time edge that draws attention to the past and the future (Figure 4.2). Looking one way the footprints of the oil tanks are visible, planted with grass, whilst in the other direction across the harbour, a still functioning tank brings the past into the present. Yet these design interventions are not as clear-cut as would first appear; trees have been allowed to grow uncontained and now the cylinder is no longer visible through the foliage. In a similar way the tidal terraces at Zhongshan (Figure 4.3) that linked the past and the future through the medium of the changing water levels now no longer flood twice a day (Yu, 2017).

The decay and disorder that signal the blurring of the natural and cultural worlds, the interventions that bring the past into the present and the changes that occur outside of the designer's control are all examples of the 'chance of space' (Massey, 2005: 151). In allowing an element of indeterminacy into the relationship between the natural and the cultural, past and present cultures and the human and the non-human, the designer can highlight the challenge of negotiation in the present and signal the possibility of future change. Designers working with DUN sites might intentionally position their landscapes on the management gradients (Figures 9.1 and 9.3) to maintain an element of the urban wild whilst ensuring such landscapes do not appear to be forgotten and derelict. There is also the potential to create interventions in

Figure 9.5 Water features at Duisburg Nord

Figure 9.6 Ghostly tracks at Südgelände

these sites that result in challenging juxtapositions. For example, designers when taking a more traditional approach to the planting design might consider introducing surprising, and perhaps challenging, temporalities by suggesting a management practice of arrested or managed decay for any material and spatial qualities. Or alternatively if the site is required to be managed for native habitats or the development of successional vegetation they can attempt to keep the qualities in a state of stasis/arrested decay. Similarly, new interventions in the landscape can be designed to call attention to the juxtapositions of time layers and, in particular, to make clear the time edges or tensions between new and abstracted elements, artefacts in states of managed decay, and wilder vegetation managed for succession. In this way designers can create inflected and hybrid landscapes that foreground the juxtapositions between time layers and allow elements of temporality into their management regime, to ensure that chance plays a part in the perceptions and interactions visitors can experience. Julie Bargmann, when writing about designing the park and Litmus Garden at Vintondale, explains the varied temporalities that operate in any landscape; 'there are different clocks on the site, and some are going to be shorter and operate like a sweeping second hand and others are going to be very slow, like geological time' (Kirkwood, 2004: 68). As Philip Coxall, designer of Ballast Point Park, points out 'the beauty of our profession is that the ultimate design is always in the future' (Coxall, 2017).

Figures 9.1, 9.3 and 9.4 also demonstrate how slippery the gradients are; it is possible that sites will move back and forth. In Chapter 8 I described how juxtapositions between the natural and the cultural contribute to an individual's sense of the passage of time in the landscape. However, if these gradients are understood to be in a state of flux and material forms are used to reveal processes, there is an inescapable question; how should these sites approach the possibility of complete decay of the material and spatial qualities? Achieving a balance between managed and complete decay is obviously a challenge; there are difficulties in the light touch maintenance approach and often safety and finance dictate the amount and type of intervention. Leaving the decaying artefacts on display, but safely inaccessible, does not give rise to the same range of responses as do those artefacts with which visitors can interact. Nevertheless, interviewees overwhelmingly felt that the artefacts were important reminders of the past and served an educational purpose. This implies that they would prefer it if the artefacts did not disappear completely: indeed many expressed this wish.

Perhaps something can be learnt from my experience of Orford Ness. DeSilvey (2017) has also visited and writes of the way the Ness is at a precarious tipping point between some form of preservation and complete destruction:

> The site is held in an implausible tension, but it remains to be seen whether the policy of continued ruination can countenance the complete loss of structural integrity, the logical end to the course now being followed.
>
> (Desilvey, 2014: 86)

Although Orford Ness remains a DUN landscape rather than a designed redeveloped site – the ultimate example of a 'do little' approach – I suggest that an awareness of the centuries of landscape change that are inherent in the natural creation of the shingle spit might lead to an acceptance of other forms of natural change, even if they result in the eventual loss of the buildings and structures in this landscape. I have shown that individuals attempt to create their own narratives around change and strive for a sense of continuity. Designing for landscape change could incorporate explicit references to the possibilities of change, much as in the design of the Litmus Garden at Vintondale that uses material forms to make reference to processes that point to the future.

At Orford Ness it is the policy of the National Trust to allow the site to gradually decay. There may be instances in other sites where changes in the economic climate or in funding mean that levels of maintenance cannot be assured and complete decay becomes the only option for the future of the site. The material qualities of the site will eventually become hidden beneath vegetation or decompose into undifferentiated matter. At Rainham Marshes this is already happening; the narrative expounded by the RSPB is one in which the site is returning to medieval grazing marsh and the material qualities are gradually decaying. I have shown, for example, that visitors do

Figure 9.7 Shingle, structures and remnants at Orford Ness

not often perceive the pastness of the cordite store but do understand the habitats that it now supports. Many of the local people I spoke to, who recounted their memories of playing on the marshes when it was under MOD control, did not need the individual material qualities to remember – the whole site and the surroundings were a part of their everyday life and they remembered the military presence, the noise of gunfire, the unexploded bombs and the red flag in the same way that they also remembered jumping ditches and spotting rare birds.

Managed decay can also be seen as a way of blurring the time edges in a landscape. As the material artefacts gradually become invisible the time edge becomes less of a disjunction until it is gone and only the memory remains. However, as I have shown with the empty plinth at the Filter Beds and as I suggest almost certainly will happen at Orford Ness, absence does not necessarily mean that something is forgotten. New stories can grow up around the absence, reimaginings, new mysteries and memories. Designers who choose to design for complete decay can exploit this by retaining an element of the material artefact, such as the plinth or the footprint of a building, whilst allowing other parts to gradually disappear. Or they may create a new time layer that points to what was there before, perhaps abstracting the form of the plinth or reinterpreting the footprint of a building. Nevertheless, the pasts and futures that individuals engage with in these new landscapes will be contingent on their own experiences and prior knowledge and designers, by creating opportunities and possibilities for understanding and interpreting landscape change, or by doing very little, can make their own contributions to the ways we reimagine these places.

Notes

1 I discuss this in detail in my unpublished MA from Middlesex University (Heatherington, 2006) and suggest that the inclusion of such an artwork when all other evidence of the industrial history of the area has been removed does little to create a meaningful narrative about the pastness of the landscape.
2 Erdem and Nassauer discuss in detail the concept of deceit in former brownfield sites questioning how designers can signal that landscapes may still be dangerous due to contamination; visitors to Duisburg are 'cued' to keep to certain sections of the park (Erdem and Nassauer, 2013: 289). However, relying on cues to direct visitors could potentially lead to problems. As I have shown, cultural background, prior knowledge and past experiences all contribute to how a visitor might understand a site.

References

Beard, P. (1996) Life in the ruins. *Blueprint,* 130, pp. 32–35.

Beard, P. (2011) *Personal communication – Rainham Marshes.* To: C. Heatherington.

Coxall, P. (2017) *Personal communication, Ballast Point Park.* To: C. Heatherington.

Dee, C. (2010) Form, utility, and the aesthetics of thrift in design education. *Landscape Journal,* 29 (1), pp. 21–35.

DeLyser, D. (1999) Authenticity on the ground: Engaging the past in a California ghost town. *Annals of the Association of American Geographers,* 89 (4), pp. 602–632.

DeSilvey, C. (2005) *Rot in peace: Putting old buildings and settlements to rest.* Available from: www.slate.com/articles/health_and_science/science/2005/12/rot_in_peace.html [Accessed 24 May 2013].

DeSilvey, C. (2006) Observed decay: Telling stories with mutable things. *Journal of Material Culture,* 11 (3), pp. 318–338.

DeSilvey, C. (2012) Making sense of transience: An anticipatory history. *Cultural Geographies,* 19 (1), pp. 31–54.

DeSilvey, C. (2014) Palliative curation: Art and entropy on Orford Ness. In: B. Olsen & Þ. Pétursdóttir (Eds.) *Ruin memories: Materialities, aesthetics and the archaeology of the recent past.* London: Routledge, pp. 79–91.

DeSilvey, C. (2017) *Curated decay: Heritage beyond saving.* Minneapolis, MN: University of Minnesota Press.

Durham County Council (2002) *The Durham Coastal Footpath.* Available from: www.durhamheritagecoast.org/dhc/usp.nsf/Lookup/Coastal%20Footpath%20V1/$file/Coastal+Footpath+V1.pdf [Accessed 3 October 2012].

Erdem, M. & Nassauer, J. I. (2013) Design of brownfield landscapes under different contaminant remediation policies in Europe and the United States. *Landscape Journal,* 32 (2), pp. 277–292.

Hawken, S. (2009) Ballast Point Park in Sydney. *Topos,* 69, pp. 46–51.

Heatherington, C. (2006) *The negotiation of place.* MA (Dist.) unpublished MA thesis, Middlesex University.

JMDD (2011) *Personal communciation, Ballast Point Park*. To: C. Heatherington.

Jorgensen, A. & Lička, L. (2012) Anti-planning, anti-design: Exploring alternative ways of making future urban landscapes. In: A. Jorgensen & R. Keenan (Eds.) *Urban wildscapes*. London: Routledge, pp. 221–236.

Kingsbury, N. (2017) *Personal communication, Südgelände*. To: C. Heatherington.

Kirkwood, N. (2001) *Manufactured sites: Rethinking the post-industrial landscape*. London: Spon Press.

Kirkwood, N. (2004) *Weathering and durability in landscape architecture: Fundamentals, practices and case studies*. Hoboken, NJ: John Wiley & Sons.

Langer, A. (2012) Pure urban nature: The Südgelände Nature Park, Berlin. In: A. Jorgensen & R. Keenan (Eds.) *Urban wildscapes*. London: Routledge, pp. 152–159.

Langer, A. (2017) *Personal communication, Südgelände*. To: C. Heatherington.

LVRPA (1988) *A Management Plan for the Middlesex Filter Beds, Lee Valley Regional Park Authority, Countryside Service*. LVRPA.

Martin, G. (2009) New York's hanging gardens. *The Observer*, Sunday 8 November 2009. Available from: www.theguardian.com/world/2009/nov/08/highline-new-york-garden-martin [Accessed 22 November 2014].

Massey, D. (2005) *For space*. London: Sage Publications.

Morris, B. (2013) In defence of oblivion: The case of Dunwich, Suffolk. *International Journal of Heritage Studies*. pp. 1–21. Available from: www.tandfonline.com/doi/abs/10.1080/13527258.2012.746718#.UaMnNZVhdUQ [Accessed 14 March 2013].

Saunders, W. (Ed.) (2012) *Designed ecologies, the landscape architecture of Kongjian Yu*. Basel: Birkhäuser.

Treib, M. (2005) Inflected landscapes (1984). In: M. Treib (Ed.) *Settings and stray paths: Writings on landscapes and gardens*. London: Routledge, pp. 52–73.

Ulam, A., Cantor, S. L. & Martin, F. E. (2009) Back on track: Bold design moves transform a defunct railroad into a 21st century park. *Landscape Architecture*, 99 (10), pp. 90–109.

Weilacher, U. (2008) *Syntax of landscape: The landscape architecture of Peter Latz and Partners*. Basel: Birkhäuser.

Yu, K. (2017) *Personal communication, Zhongshan*. To: C. Heatherington.

Appendix
List of participants

Table i gives some brief demographic details of the interviewees across the three sites. The strategy for selecting participants resulted in differences in the cohorts; rather than attempting to select people from a range of demographic groups I chose to focus, in part, on people who were visiting the site in their everyday life. This, together with the recruitment of volunteers, resulted in the large number of retired participants. In order to address my research questions it was also important for me to interview people who had known the site prior to development and this too contributed to the number of interviewees in the older age groups. At the Hidden Gardens a large proportion of the interviewees were local people, some of whom had known the Tramway when it was the Transport Museum. A second group were younger parents with small children who had started coming to the garden when their children were born. At Rainham Marshes there was also a large group of local people who had known the site when it was occupied by the military and many of these people had used the site during this period and after the military left. In contrast, at the Filter Beds I only interviewed a small number of people who had been brought up in the area and, because secure boundary walls protected the site, no one had visited the site when it was in operation, and few remembered it when it was abandoned.

Table i List of interviewees

			Interviewees' Details		
ID	M/F	Identifies as living locally Y/N	Knew the site before development	Previous visits	Professional background
Middlesex Filter Beds					
FB01	F	Y	N	Regularly	Artist
FB02	F	N	N	First visit	Retired
FB03	F	Y	N	Regularly	Teacher
FB04	F	Y	Y	Regularly	Psychotherapist

(continued)

Table i List of interviewees *(continued)*

			Interviewees' Details		
ID	M/F	Identifies as living locally Y/N	Knew the site before development	Previous visits	Professional background
FB05	M	N	N	Regularly	Director/photographer
FB06	F	N	N	First visit	Retired
FB07	F	Y	N	Regularly	Lawyer
FB08	F	Y	N	Regularly	Student
FB09	F	Y	N	Regularly	Retired
FB10	M	Y	N	Regularly	Architectural designer
FB11	F	Y	N	2–3 times	Children's services manager
FB12	M	Y	N	3–10 times	Performer/canal boater
FB13	M	Y	Y	Regularly	Retired social worker
FB14	F	N	N	3–10 times	Playworker
FB15	M	Y	Y	Regularly	Retired
FB16	M	N	Y	Regularly	Retired
FB17	M	N	N	First visit	Lecturer
FB18	M	Y	N	Regularly	LVRPA ranger
FB19	F	Y	N	Regularly	Retired/volunteer
FB20	M	N	N	Regularly	Retired/volunteer
FB21	M	Y	Y	First visit	Performer, retired sign writer and blogger
RSPB Rainham Marshes					
RM01	M	Y	Y	Regularly	Volunteer
RM02	M	Y	Y	Regularly	Retired
RM03	F	Y	Y	Regularly	Retired
RM04	F	Y	Y	Regularly	Retired
RM05	M	Y	Y	Regularly (but only before RSPB)	Volunteer, Purfleet Heritage Centre
RM06	M	Y	Y	Regularly (but only before RSPB)	Volunteer, Purfleet Heritage Centre
RM07	M	Y	Y	Regularly	Ornithological consultant
RM08	M	N	N	Regularly	Volunteer
RM09	M	N	Y	Regularly	RSPB staff

			Interviewees' Details		
ID	M/F	Identifies as living locally Y/N	Knew the site before development	Previous visits	Professional background
RM10	M	Y	Y	Regularly	Retired analytical chemist
RM11	M	N	N	Regularly	RSPB staff
RM12	M	Y	Y	Regularly	Retired paper merchant
RM13	F	Y	Y	Regularly	Volunteer
RM14	F	N	N	First visit	Librarian
RM15	M	Y	Y	Regularly	Retired
RM16	F	N	N	First visit	Garden design student
RM17	M	Y	Y	Regularly	Retired
RM18	F	Y	N	Regularly	Conservation scientist
RM19	M	Y	N	Regularly	Retired civil servant
RM20	F	Y	N	Regularly	Retired NHS worker
RM21	M	N	Y	3–10 times	Retired
RM22	M	N	N	2–3 times	Local government officer
The Hidden Gardens					
HG01	F	Y	Y	Regularly	Cleaner
HG02	F	Y	Y	Regularly	Volunteer manager
HG03	F	Y	N	Regularly	Unemployed
HG04	F	Y	Y	Regularly	Retired/volunteer
HG05	F	N	N	Regularly	Retired/volunteer
HG06	M	Y	Y	Regularly	Clarinettist
HG07	F	Y	Y	Regularly	Social worker
HG08	F	Y	N	Regularly	Cleaner
HG09	M	Y	Y	Regularly	Unemployed/volunteer
HG10	F	N	N	Regularly	Volunteer/landscape architect
HG11	M	Y	Y	Regularly	Retired
HG12	F	N	Y	Regularly	Consultant
HG13	M	Y	N	Regularly	Metal sales
HG14	F	Y	N	Regularly	Accountant
HG15	F	Y	N	Regularly	PhD graduate
HG16	F	Y	N	Regularly	Artist
HG17	F	Y	N	Regularly	Librarian
HG18	F	Y	N	2–3 times	Garden designer
HG19	F	N	N	Regularly	Gardener

(continued)

Table i List of interviewees *(continued)*

ID	M/F	Identifies as living locally Y/N	Knew the site before development	Previous visits	Professional background
			Interviewees' Details		
HG20	M	N	N	First visit	Unemployed
HG21	M	N	N	First visit	Photographer
HG22	F	N	N	First visit	Unemployed
HG23	F	Y	N	Regularly	Quantity surveyor
HG24	M	N	Y	Regularly	Artist

Note: In the case of the Filter Beds the column 'knew the site before development' indicates that the interviewee knew the area around the site and/or the derelict site and in the case of the Hidden Gardens it indicates the interviewee had visited the Tramway building, usually when it was the Transport Museum.

Index